Christmas 2003

To our Son,

This looks like
a story you
might
really
enjoy.

Love always,
Mom & Dad

D1109950

# Where The
# Earth Ends

*By the same author*

A Shorter Primer in Vice

# Where The
# Earth Ends

## JOHN HARRISON

JOHN MURRAY
*Albemarle Street, London*

The extract from *The Waste Land*, from *Collected Poems, 1909–1962* by
T. S. Eliot, is reproduced by permission of Faber & Faber Ltd

© John Harrison 2000

First published in 2000
by John Murray (Publishers) Ltd,
50 Albermarle Street, London W1X 4BD

The moral right of the author has been asserted

All rights reserved. No part of this publication may be reproduced in any
material form (including photocopying or storing it in any medium by
electronic means and whether or not transiently or incidentally to some other
use of this publication) without the written permission of the copyright
owner, except in accordance with the provisions of the Copyright, Designs
and Patents Act 1988 or under the terms of a licence issued by the Copyright
Licensing Agency, 90 Tottenham Court Road, London W1P 9HE.
Applications for the copyright owner's written permission to reproduced any
part of this publication should be addressed to the publisher.

A catalogue record for this book is available from the British Library

ISBN 0-7195-6151 5

Typeset in 12/13.5 Monotype Bembo by Servis Filmsetting Ltd
Printed and bound in Great Britain by The University Press, Cambridge

*To Elaine,*
*for believing*

# Contents

# Contents

# Illustrations

All the photographs were taken by the author except Plate 6, from the Anthropos-Museum und Institut, Germany, and Plate 8, taken by R. E. Brennan.

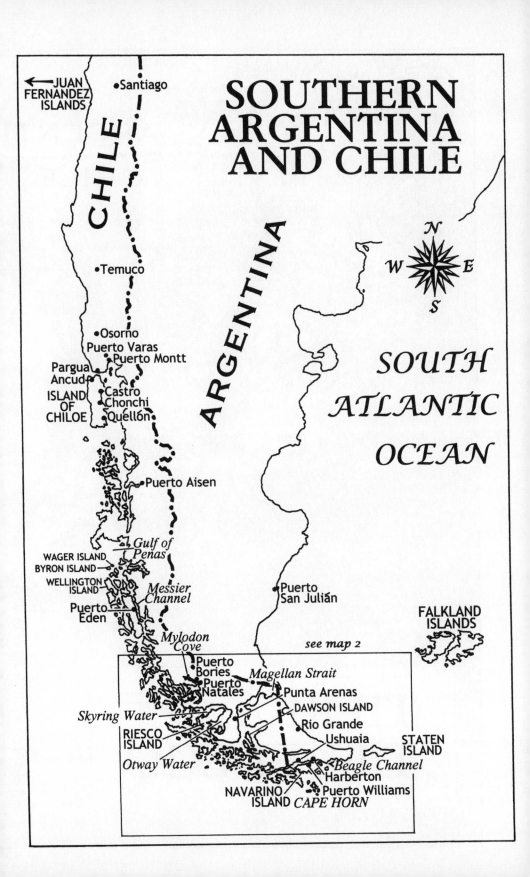

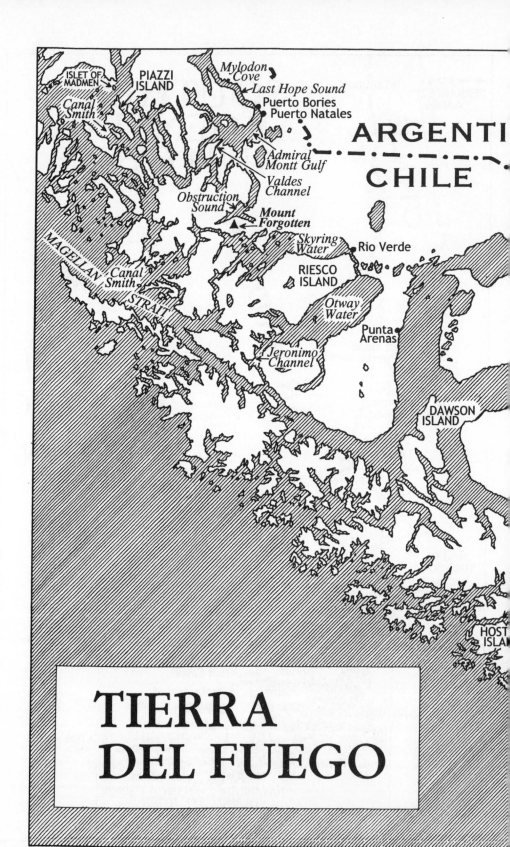

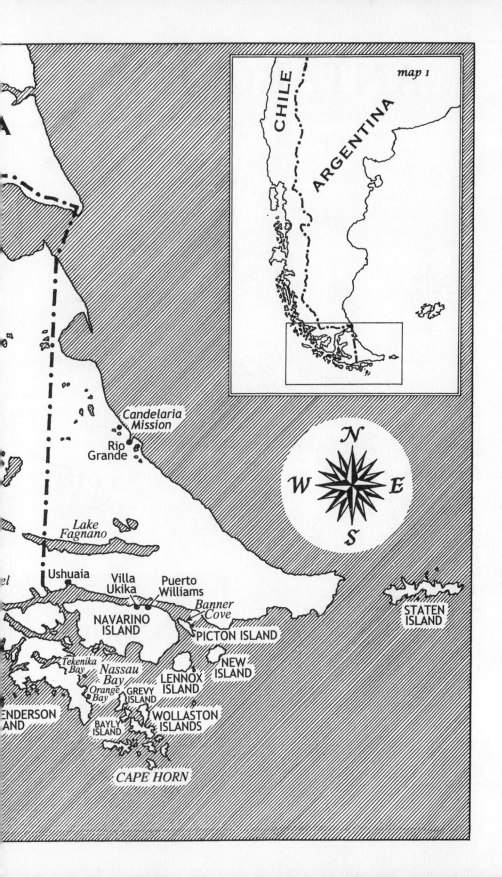

map 1

CHILE

ARGENTINA

Candelaria Mission

Rio Grande

Lake Fagnano

Ushuaia

Villa Ukika

Puerto Williams

Banner Cove

NAVARINO ISLAND

PICTON ISLAND

STATEN ISLAND

Tekenika Bay

Nassau Bay

Orange Bay

GREVY ISLAND

LENNOX ISLAND

NEW ISLAND

ENDERSON AND

BAYLY ISLAND

WOLLASTON ISLANDS

CAPE HORN

N
W
E
S

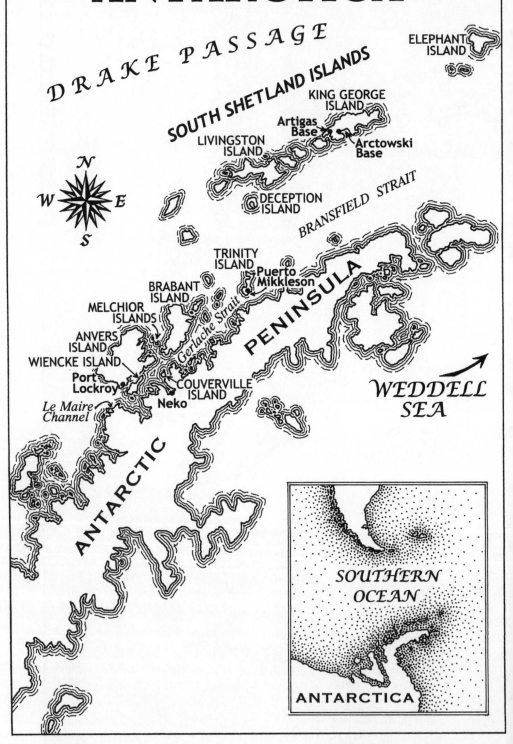

# ANTARCTICA

DRAKE PASSAGE

ELEPHANT ISLAND

SOUTH SHETLAND ISLANDS

KING GEORGE ISLAND

Artigas Base

Arctowski Base

LIVINGSTON ISLAND

N
W E
S

DECEPTION ISLAND

BRANSFIELD STRAIT

TRINITY ISLAND

Puerto Mikkleson

BRABANT ISLAND

Gerlache Strait

PENINSULA

MELCHIOR ISLANDS

ANVERS ISLAND

WIENCKE ISLAND

Port Lockroy

COUVERVILLE ISLAND

Neko

Le Maire Channel

ANTARCTIC

WEDDELL SEA

SOUTHERN OCEAN

ANTARCTICA

Chile is an Aymara Indian word meaning
WHERE THE EARTH ENDS

'Imagination, not invention, is the supreme
master of art, as of life. An imaginative and
exact rendering of authentic memories.'

Joseph Conrad, *A Personal Record*

# I

# *Patagonia*

## A Landing

December. Three in the morning. The plane shuddered down through the turbulence in the low cumulus and banked. The most southerly town on Argentina's mainland came up out of the black: Rio Gallegos. The plane abruptly fell another three hundred feet and I could see down the narrow aisle and over the pilot's shoulder, and watch the earth saucer back and forth, trying to dodge our outstretched wheels. In all the earth this was the last continental land which mankind reached. In Central Africa tool-making early humans roamed the plains 2.5 million years ago but there is no evidence of people here on the tip of South America until twelve thousand years ago.

Studying the street maps in the guide it was easy to forget which town I was looking at, each bright gridiron named after the standard set of generals. In Argentina they are San Martín, Roca, Belgrano; in Chile, O'Higgins, Prat, Montt. The orange-lit lines of dead heroes tilted and came to meet us.

I asked the taxi driver to find a mid-price hotel. He said, 'No problem.' The Punta Arenas, no vacancies. Further down the street, the Liporace sounded and looked like a skin complaint. The taxi driver pounded the locked door. Red light was making weak rents in the eastern sky, four mongrels besieged a cat in a small tree. A man appeared and talked to the driver, shaking his head. The driver came back, 'The town is full. The hotel is full.'

When a hotel named after a skin disease has no empty beds, I can believe the town is full.

The pavements were broken and sheets of water lay in the road. We did the rounds. Sleepy faces came to doors, tired bodies leaned on the jamb. They shook their heads and cut their hands horizontally across each other. At the Laguna, a stooped thin man with a ten-month-old haircut and a pensioner's cardigan declaimed 'No room' as if there was surely a Second Coming and anyone with a stable should clean out the manger.

'I know another place!' the driver exclaimed.

The Colonial was pink low concrete. It had two doors; no one answered either. The driver said, 'I am sorry, this never happened before. I'll stop the meter.' The street was nearly light.

'If I find somewhere now, will they charge me for tonight?'

'They charge eight to eight, if you book in at five to eight you pay for the night's sleep you just missed.'

'Take me to a café, the one we passed at the crossroads in the centre.'

The Monaco was at the intersection of two heavyweight generals, Roca and San Martín. It was glass-walled and brightly lit, open twenty-four hours. A third of the tables were taken, many by couples winding up the evening, talking quietly. I drank large milk coffees. 'Nothing to eat, sir?'

I had been awake forty-eight hours and three time zones. So tired I no longer knew if I was hungry.

'Nothing to eat.'

The dawn began to fix the street in place, like a photograph being developed. People drifted away, the rest were drunk, quietly and gently drunk. A tired waiter broke a glass and smiled ruefully at the applause. Everyone took turns at looking at me, the only sober customer, the only non-smoker, the only person alone. Butch Cassidy and the Sundance Kid once held up the bank here. When the shops opened, I would buy a Colt 45 and free up some hotel beds.

Sometime after six I walked to the estuary, past the building designated an historic monument to record the visit of the first president to come to Rio Gallegos: Julio Roca. He spoke from a balcony and urged immigrants to populate the south and exploit the wealth of the Magellan Straits. The historic monument is a wooden balcony hanging cock-eyed from a big shed. I am sorry, but it is. The shore was a concrete esplanade, grey and perspectiveless as childhood. A red balustrade. The sea wall dropped ten feet to shingle, which shelved to sharp-smelling mud that glued down flimsy supermarket bags. Pigeons and gulls pecked a path across the mud. The water of the mile-wide estuary lay polished, ceramic. I was looking north; low flat-topped hills on the farther shore hinted at the majestic monotony of the plains which went north, horizon after horizon. This was the last country man found, this strand, this hill, the sky shining like wet paint; the dust already sticking to the fresh wax on my boots was made from flecks of legend. This was Patagonia.

Patagonia! The origin of the word, still a byword for being off the beaten track, has been much argued over. The *Oxford English Dictionary*, which has time to ruminate on these things, is content that there is a Spanish word *patagon* meaning a large clumsy foot, and that it derives from large clumsy shoes worn by natives. Spanish regional dialects still use *patacones* for big-pawed dogs, and the depth of the footprints the dancing natives made in the sand was remarked on by the first visitor, Magellan.

A second theory involves the Incas, who explored the Andes a long way south of the territory they formally conquered. Their empire was not ancient. In 1532, when Pizarro rode his horse through its golden halls, the realm was little more than a hundred years old. In the Incan language, Quechua, the south was called Patac-Hunia, or mountain regions, and as Spanish does not pronounce 'h' the sound is very close to Patagonia. But why would men from an empire of the high Andes describe the lesser peaks of the south as mountain regions?

Bruce Chatwin was tipped off by Professor González Díaz that Tehuelche Indians wore dog-faced masks, and Magellan might have nicknamed them after a character in a novel called *Primalon of Greece* which features a dog-eared monster called Patagon. It is an anonymous romance published in Spain in 1512 and translated into English by Anthony Mundy in 1596. As an aside, Mundy was a friend of Shakespeare, who would soon after have Trinculo say of Caliban, in *The Tempest*, 'I shall laugh myself to death at this puppy-headed monster.'

Three flaws are apparent in the theory. Firstly, who names lands after novels? Secondly, it seems incredible that rough and ready adventurers would pause in their journeys on the edge of the unknown to make literary allusions; and thirdly, there isn't a shred of evidence that Magellan knew of the book.

But California is named after an island in a novel. Hernando Cortés sailed up the Gulf of California believing the land on his left was an island, not a peninsula, and named it after an island called California in the tale *The Adventures of Esplandián*, written by Garcí Ordóñez de Montalvo in 1510.

Secondly, as Bernal Díaz records, when his men walked a causeway into Mexico City in 1520, they 'said that it seemed like one of those enchanted things which are told about in the book of Amadís'. The chivalric fantasy *Amadís of Gaul* was one of the real books which Cervantes slipped into the library of Don Quixote; literate soldiers carried them round in the same way that GIs carry comics.

Finally, Magellan could perhaps have known about *Primalon of Greece*. It was published seven years before Magellan sailed, and he spent a lot of time at court where such books were read by the chattering classes of the day. There are many odd theories about the origin of the name of the strange land of Patagonia; perhaps the oddest one is true.

In the dead of early morning the town was dreadful. Although a lot of money was made here in the livestock industries, it did not stay. The moneyed families built their *belle époque* mansions to the south, around Plaza Muñoz Gamero in Punta Arenas, importing everything from Europe, from the art to the architect. Here in Rio Gallegos, the post office and one restaurant excepted, there was no building in the whole centre worth a minute's pause. All the taw-driness of a dead-end town with none of the excuses. Desperate for sleep, and groggy with lack of food, I bought cakes and savouries at a baker's and walked past the pink Colonial Hotel once again. A young backpacker came out of it and climbed into a taxi. A bed.

The landlady asked me to wait ten minutes while she changed the sheets. When she had finished, I sat on the bed and took out a cheese and ham croissant. Under the cling film it had looked quite brave. Naked, the ingredients looked like naïve patriotic things which, in a flush of enthusiasm, had signed up as food but, on reflection, had realised their utter unsuitability for the task ahead. Tasted as seen.

The room was the size of a prison cell but without the amenities. No wardrobe no chest of drawers no table no toilet no basin no water no glass no carpet no rug no curtains no view. No matter, it had a bed, and a little gap down one side of it to get in and out. I walked to the bathroom in bare feet, looked inside, and went back for my boots.

What was I doing here?

## Rainy Childhood Days

Voyages begin in books. Mine started with rainy childhood days and a house with one coal fire in the front room of our council house, near the Liverpool FC training ground. Wooden window frames with cold panes and tiny petals of orange mould in the corners. Knot resin weeping, pushing paint into blisters. A finger on the glass made two beads run together and zigzag down the glass collecting others, like chequers. My breath fogged the game.

We were three boys, I was in the middle. The first adult novel I read was *Robinson Crusoe*, when I was still small enough to curl up entirely inside the wooden arms of my mother's tiny armchair. At that time the only sea I knew was the brown of the Mersey and the racing tides of the Wirral's flat, estuarine resorts. I pored silently over the watercolour illustrations of palms and blue horizons, then took a red spade to dig my own fort in the back garden.

One damp Sunday I sat cross-legged in front of an oak utility furniture bookcase. 'Da-aad,' I drizzled, 'what would I like to read?' He tapped his faintly nicotined fingers on a green book spine, Percy Harrison Fawcett's *Exploration Fawcett*.

'Read this, he is a Harrison,' he said.

'Is he a relative?'

He looked out of the window at the rain, falling on the split paling fence. There was no prospect of going out. 'Yes.'

I pulled out the book. In the front was a picture of a frowning man sporting a hip-length jacket and riding boots, and leaning on a wooden balcony. His propeller moustache waited for a batman to swing it into motion. The chapter titles called to me: The Lost Mines of Muribeca, Rubber Boom, River of Evil, Poisoned Hell, and The Veil of the Primaeval. I strode into the book and came out two days later.

Percy Fawcett made impossible journeys into the interior of the greatest South American jungles, again and again. He walked the frontiers of Bolivia to map them. Maps were crucial; without them the rubber barons would not know whose country they were robbing. He was in the interior most of the years from 1906 to 1913 and met travellers who had seen potions which made rock soften so it could be cut in the butter-smooth joints of the earthquake-proof Incan cities.

I swallowed tales of men who fell out of canoes in piranha-filled rivers, clung to the stern, and were removed at the river bank, skeletons from the waist down. They were killed by anacondas, poisonous spiders, flesh-rotting diseases and the cat o' nine tails. They were sold to pay their own debts. Rubber magnates living on the world's greatest flow of fresh water sent their laundry to Paris and constructed an opera house for Caruso, who came and anchored mid-river off Manaus. A cholera epidemic raged. Caruso walked the decks, and received the daily lists of the dead. Contracts beckoned, time ran out, he went home. Outside the opera house, the curved twin staircases leading up to the classical mezzanine were cleared of cholera victims each day. Dust motes descended shafts of light in the silent theatre.

The book was drafted in note form by Fawcett in 1923. There remained one dream, his search for the lost city of João da Silva Guimarões. In 1743 Guimarões had been hunting only for lost mines. A negro in his party had chased a white stag to the summit of a mountain pass. Below on a plain was a city of some sort. Next day they entered through three arches, so tall that no one could read the inscriptions above them. A broad street led them to a plaza. At each corner was a black obelisk. In the centre rose a colossal column of black stone on which was a statue of a man pointing to the north. The entire city was deserted except for a cloud of huge bats. Nearby they found silver nails lying in the dirt of caverns, and gold dust in the streams.

By 1925 Fawcett, discouraged by his failure to find men of his own invulnerability to hardship and disease, went out aged 57 with his inexperienced son Jack, and Jack's friend Raleigh Rimmel, on one last search for the lost city of Guimarões. Fawcett's last letter to his wife in England read, 'you need have no fear of failure'. They were never heard of again. His surviving son Brian put together the book from his father's notes and published it in 1953.

On another, interminable, wet afternoon in the school holidays, I opened a black book of narrative poetry and read *The Rime of the Ancient Mariner*. The prologue begins: 'How a ship having passed the Line was driven by storms to the cold Country towards the South Pole'.

'Are there any others like that one?' I asked my father, when the other poems in the collection bored me. Thirty-five years on I know the answer.

In my teens I painted, again and again, the spars of the Mariner's un-named ship against livid skies. We moved to Falmouth in Cornwall, where I watched Robin Knox-Johnson tack *Suhaili* into the harbour and complete the first single-handed non-stop round-the-world voyage. It had begun as a race; he won it by being the only survivor.

I left Falmouth Grammar School, and went up to Jesus College, Cambridge to read geography. On the walls of the medieval dining hall were portraits of former scholars. Beneath them, Mr West, the

Head Porter with the cut of W. C. Fields in his flesh and clothes, lectured us on the evils of fornication and drugs. He did not seem heavily scarred by either. Thomas Malthus, author of the essay on population, looked over our heads. Coleridge, opium addict, stared down with great baleful eyes. He had written home, 'There is no such thing as discipline at our College.' That winter I discovered a reprint of Gustav Doré's fabulous engravings for the *Ancient Mariner*. In 1978 I read Chatwin's *In Patagonia* and, looking at atlases, my eyes began to fall south.

In Hay-on-Wye I was trawling the second-hand bookshops for material on Chile, when I found a hank of pages without a cover, which had fallen down the back of the other books. I pulled it out: *An Historical Relation of the Kingdom of Chile* by Alonso de Ovalle, a Jesuit. It had been torn from a larger volume. Although in English, the cover said it was printed in Rome in 1649. It was in such good condition I assumed it was a reproduction. The pages were fresh and white, they were flexible and clean. I bought it and took it round the corner to bookbinder Christine Turnbull. A gravel path led me down an avenue of lavender to her cottage workshop. She looked quietly over it and compared the paper with samples from her cabinets. She stroked her fingers down the spine. 'The English first edition published in 1703. It should be full leather.'

Alonso's report is the first English account of Chile. It was dynamite in its day. The English translator confided that it 'contains secrets of commerce and navigation, which I wonder how they were published'. Ovalle advised speculators that a man with 40,000 crowns to invest, including in slaves, might earn a twenty-five per cent return 'very lawful, and without any trouble to one's conscience'.

I then found Lucas Bridges's book on growing up in Tierra del Fuego as the son of the first successful missionary, Thomas Bridges. After a few chapters I knew I would visit Ushuaia and the bare savage islands of the far south. My great-grandfather had sailed there before the mast on the great square-riggers. My grandfather Thomas Harrison, born in 1896, sailed the Horn in steam and diesel, plying the last of the 'WCSA' (West Coast of South America) trade out of Liverpool. I was the first generation not to sail the Horn or fight a war. Instead, I would go to the end of the world, beyond Patagonia, to Tierra del Fuego. I would do more, I would see the Horn and find lost tribes. The child in me could go even further and sail the waters of Coleridge's albatross and enter the watercolours' blue horizons and sit on Crusoe's imaginary shore. I had imagined these places, they must exist. All I had to do was look for them.

*Rio Gallegos*

By lunchtime I had slept four hours and woken too excited to stay in bed. I went out to look at the town with fresh eyes. I would like to say it helped.

Rio Gallegos was named after the river it stood on, but no one knows where the river got its name. One of the earliest houses belonged to a Doctor Victor Fenton. It was made in the Falklands from a design in an English catalogue, and shipped here, perhaps as early as 1890. It was here before the town, which grew around it during the following fifteen years. It is a two-storey wooden dormer with a long sun lounge running across the whole front. In 1915 it passed into the Parisi family. Señor Parisi's wife was Maria Catalina. She was born one cold snowy August morning in 1860, in her family's toldo or skin tent. They were Tehuelche pampas Indians and lived by hunting with the bolas. She had five daughters and three sons who survived to adulthood. All her life she made a living by native traditional crafts, making guanaco capes, sewing the skins together using the veins of ostriches. Her favourite food was mare's meat with ostrich.

The house is now a museum. The stove has not moved in sixty years, some furniture came from other early houses. The study had three old Remington typewriters. In the lounge a colossal Canadian Victrolla brought over in 1904 played a fine tango on a paste 78. In the kitchen was a washing-machine, hand-cranked and looking like a butter churn with wringers above it. But I was more taken with the story of Maria Catalina. Most of her children would still be alive. I talked to Señora McDonald, now retired, whose Scottish father had come to Patagonia and married a Spanish woman. She spoke English with a strange rural Scots edge to it. 'Are any of Maria Catalina's children still alive?'

She thought for a moment. 'One of the sons, Roberto, lives a few streets away.'

'Is he the kind of man who would mind me calling in for a chat?'

'No, not normally, but his wife died of cancer two days ago.'

This was the dry season; it never rains here in December. But every few hours the rain lashed down like cold nails. People shook their heads and said 'El Niño'. I walked round Rio Gallegos once more and decided to leave. My journey was planned to follow a V shape, moving south to Tierra del Fuego, as far as I could go down the east coast, then to turn north up the west coast. But first I had to backtrack north a short way, to Puerto San Julián. I was sure it would now be a dull town, but I wanted to see it, because it was the scene of treason, bloodshed and executions where tragedy was followed by farce. It was the launchpad for the first two circum-navigations of the world, by Magellan, then Drake. And, of course, Magellan and Drake both met and talked to giants so tall the sailors could not touch the tops of their heads.

*Puerto San Julián*

The bus making the five-hour trip to Puerto San Julián left at half three in the afternoon. This time I rang ahead to book; there were no medium-price hotels. I thought about going to the bathroom in my boots, and booked the one up-market hotel, the Bahía San Julián.

At the travel agents I got on the bus. Everyone else was being picked up from home. Many had been Christmas shopping in Rio Gallegos, and waded on board festooned with bags and boxes. Every seat was filled. When we eventually left town an hour later, the only place left to put my legs was in the aisle. We pulled in at the airport. The driver collected eight large plastic packing boxes and filled the aisle.

The landscape was the colour of burnt grass, stony, empty and huge. The road appeared flat, but was not. After a while the eye learned to see the slight turns, the subtle rises and falls. There were hidden dips betrayed by the road shimmering as a grey soft-edged lens in the air above them. One of the few towns we passed through was named after an early administrator, his whole name: Comandante Luis Pedra Buena! A mid-stream island was wantonly green with trees and flower meadows. Then we entered the great basin where the land falls to one hundred metres below sea level, the lowest in all Argentina. The sun dropped, the dry grass colour turned corn gold and then red gold.

At ten-thirty we rolled into the unmade streets of Puerto San Julián, veering all over the road looking for purchase in the mud. The driver began dropping people off, picking out places where they would not drown walking to the kerb. Eleven o'clock came. He pulled out onto a well-lit dual carriageway, and pointed at me. There stood my brand new hotel. I walked self-consciously onto the thick blue carpets, staring after me to see how much mud I was trailing. A large bar supported two drinkers watching football on the television. The smart receptionist showed me to my room. It looked as though I was the first person ever to stay in it. 'How long have you been open?'

'Not long, two years.'

Early photographs of the town, lining the hotel corridors, had a strange bare quality to them, like a town in a child's dream: big simple buildings, one car, one house, one dog. A single steamer stood at a short pier. Thousands of sheep trotted across an empty square and through a wooden V onto a gangplank and into the hold. One man, stationary on a horse, watched over them. Clutter, the detail that makes life real, had not arrived.

Morning was overcast. I walked down the road at the side of the hotel to see the south end of the bay. Above the high-tide mark was a zone of grassy flats criss-crossed by channels. The bay's circle was wide; low hills came down to grey sandy cliffs. The water was milky blue from fine sediment. As I descended the hill I left the gridiron, the invader's geometry, and entered a barrio of makeshift houses that followed the streams and contours, responding to the land. Each rested at the size it had reached when money ran out. Tiny birds followed me through the scrub, keeping level or just behind. They were rufous-backed negritos, the females dun, the males a shimmer of red-brown and shining blue-black. Perhaps they follow people because we disturb insects for them to feed on, but nobody really knows.

Mongrels, long-haired golden mongrels, squealed and twisted on thin rope tethers, their anguished yelps squeezed from far back in the throat. The plaint of the dogs' barking was blown out to sea by a flat wind. On the wall round the bone-dust sports field lone graffiti appealed: 'Don't fail me.'

I was walking in the steps of Magellan and Drake, I would also be following in the footsteps of a more recent buccaneer, the English bandit El Jimmy.

*El Jimmy*

The writer Herbert Childs came here by boat in the 1930s for his honeymoon. He was searching for an English-born gaucho and bandit who wanted his story written – James Radburne, nicknamed 'El Jimmy'.

Wondering if all the tales of rough frontier life were true, particularly the casual cut-throat violence of the gauchos, Mr and Mrs Childs reached Puerto San Julián, and went ashore to stretch their legs. They found it dull rather than dangerous. Coming back to the ships, they shared the ferry with three gauchos in full rodeo dress. Once on board, a policeman steered them towards third class. Another passenger came up alongside Childs, 'They're going to Rio Gallegos for trial.'

'What did they do?'

'They were in a gang. A fourth one took a bribe and betrayed them to the police. They caught him, skinned him alive, and cut all the skin off his face to make him hard to recognise.'

'Why aren't they handcuffed?'

'They're no danger to anyone else. They only killed because a friend betrayed them. That's not murder down here, they'll get seven years, at most. There's no point trying to escape and giving the police a chance to shoot you and get a reward – not over a little point of etiquette.'

In England, when James was seventeen his father died leaving twelve children. James did not help his mother's desperate plight. Instead he turned to poaching and had an affair. Gossip led to discovery. The girl's furious mother went to court. The judge was swift to reach a verdict, plainly embarrassed by the mother's principal tactic of flourishing the girl's knickers to the courtroom. Time to go. A nearby farmer had shares in a farm in Patagonia. Jimmy did not know where Patagonia was, but he went. After a swift passage of twenty-eight days, he stepped ashore in Punta Arenas on 8 December 1892. He was asked the question all fresh young men from Britain were asked: 'Was it poaching or a girl?'

'Both.'

Jimmy already had the right credentials for Patagonia, and he loved the outdoors and the horses, the hunting and camp life. But in a land of murders and thieves, a mere poacher needed to make a name. He made himself the best gaucho, shepherd, jockey and horse trainer in the district, and one of the best in the region. To his father's fist-craft he added a knife and a gun, and his reputation became an invitation for every hardcase in Patagonia to take a pop at him.

One day, when shearing finished at the Denmark Estancia, he was kept on for a few weeks to cut fence posts and rails in the woods. He saw something which made him tingle, the *toldos*, or guanaco skin tents of Tehuelche Indians. *Che* means 'people' and *tehuel* means 'of the South'. He was to befriend them and live with them, learning their skill and craft, their soft ways of taming horses. They had no bows or arrows, and hunted with the apparently primitive bolas. But in the tall grass of the pampa, the bolas will reach an animal when a lasso will be smothered by the grass, and an arrow deflected.

Two round stones were sheathed in leather, then bound six feet apart with rawhide. A third, egg-shaped stone was tied by a line to the centre of the first line. The throw comprised a combination of horizontal and vertical swings to make them fly in a Y shape and wrap the balls round the neck or legs of a horse, guanaco, cow or ostrich. For ostrich and farmed animals, packed gravel would be used instead of stones, so as not to smash the legs. Charles Darwin was given a brief lesson, swung the stones energetically round, and fell poleaxed as they hit him on the back of the head.

Jimmy, practical countryman though he was, could never make a bolas whose balance he liked as much as the Tehuelche-made ones. Whenever there was a serious hunt, he traded other goods to have an Indian-made one.

The Tehuelche were so famous for their horsemanship that when the St Louis World Fair was held in 1904, the Argentine government wanted to send six of them to compete in the rodeo events. Baller, the local commissioner, was not liked. He gave his son the job of taking the party to St Louis. They didn't like him any better. Young Baller was reduced to picking four men from a group which happened to be camped on his doorstep. Coloko was good at balling ostrich; another, Loco, was a good jockey. Casimiro and another old man were regarded as pretty well useless at most things. The Indians who remained said Baller had picked the most useless men, and then the ugliest women to go with them. But when they returned they brought home the prizes for lassooing and riding, beating all the American cowboys and the South American gauchos.

Not all Tehuelche pastimes were so constructive. One way of killing the time was to catch a viscacha, a cute animal halfway between a rabbit and a squirrel, and skin it alive without killing it. Then they would let it loose in a thicket of thorns and bet on how long it would survive. They could not understand the settlers insisting that they stop this harmless fun. The viscacha has its own strange hobby – collecting hard objects of all kinds to adorn the entrance of its burrow. Darwin heard how one man, riding home at night, realised he had lost his watch. He went back in the morning and, by searching the entrance of every viscacha burrow along his route, soon found it.

After a day at the races Jimmy was caught with a dud cheque and was imprisoned. He promptly escaped but staying anonymous was hard. If ever he got into a dispute, it only needed someone to find out he was called James. There was no other James in the district. He was El Jimmy, the bandit, the jailbird, and the other man had a mark on him. He went native and lived with Chief Mulato in the toldos and fell in love with his daughter Juana. Her father, in a rare drinking session, promised her to the winning owner of a horse race Jimmy had set up. The jockey on Jimmy's horse was Montenegro, a man he had quarrelled with and did not trust, but a natural horseman. Montenegro threw the race in return for marrying Juana. The chief would not go back on his word, drunk or not. Jimmy's enemy Montenegro rode out with his girl.

Jimmy then lived with another Tehuelche woman. She became pregnant. Thirty years later he recalled to Herbert Childs the night of the delivery of his first child.

> 'When the time come, I went outside after getting some other *chinas* (women) to help, telling them to call me if anything was needed, and to call anyway when the baby was born. I'd been outside quite a time and there was no call, though everything got quiet in the toldo. I went and asked if everything was all right and they said for me to come in.
>
> 'I went in. The *china* was all right. I asked to see the babe and they showed it to me, pretty as anything, with blue eyes and white skin. It looked like a proper English baby. I was pleased to see it, but the more I looked, the more it seemed something was wrong. It was so still. I touched it and it was already cold. They hadn't let it live, though it was born all right.
>
> 'They didn't ever think it was right for a child not looking like one of them to grow up with them.'

Jimmy also remembered a winter of such cold that men and animals perished, starved and stranded by the snow. It was 1904 and he was visiting the toldos. When after four days and nights the storm let up, there was seven feet of snow, and it stayed. A skunk came into the tent. They killed and ate it, and two more before the thaw came. 'They tasted like good chicken. I'd rather eat skunk than lots of animals, like pumas; they're awful.'

By late spring most of the horses had died of starvation. They had first eaten each other's tails and manes. 'When I found them first the skin was almost rattling on their bones. I thought it a pity they couldn't eat meat because there was dead sheep everywhere, and men was wool-gathering, plucking wool off dead sheep. This wool does not bring as high a price as clipped wool, but if well plucked, and if it has long staples, it helps a bit if your sheep get all killed.'

They travelled, in part to garner news, but also to feel the space of the pampa again after their confinement. The Megan Estancia of fourteen thousand sheep had one hundred and seventy-five alive. There were circular rings of dead horses where they had walked round and round trying to keep the ground clear, until one fell and stopped the clock for ever. There were some new and grim harvests. Jimmy took four hundred skins from frozen guanacos.

In later life he met Juana again. She had had enough of Montenegro and left him. She and Jimmy ran north and built a farm and a family. It had been a long road, but they were happy. Even here the English owners of much larger neighbouring farms tried to squeeze him out by bribing officials. Jimmy fought them, and won. They lived out their days there.

Old Chief Mulato was not so lucky. Local officials tried to cheat him out of his land and resell it to white farmers. He was now a relic of another way of life, but he still had the deeds to his ancestral land. In 1905 he left for Santiago to fight for his land and prove his ownership. Most of his family went with him. On the way home Mulato's niece died of illness unexpectedly. His son came to fetch Jimmy. Soon after Jimmy arrived at the camp, Mulato's wife died. Mulato himself died at midnight, the son a few days later. In Santiago they had picked up another of the white man's diseases, smallpox. Farmers took the land.

*Rory Wilson*

When I woke up on my first morning in Puerto San Julián, sun filled the streets. In the bright dining-room, two tables away, a tall blond man with a deep narrow chest spoke German to a woman with strong handsome features and long black hair.

I had to find a boatman called Carlos Cendron to take me out to the island where Magellan and Drake held legal trials and executed noble companions amid the burrows of Magellanic penguins. Near the beach I found a corrugated iron house freshly painted in warm pink, and a local woman leaning over a low picket fence, talking to the couple from the hotel.

'I am looking for Carlos.'

The blond man listened. 'Are you English?'

'Yes.'

He put his hand out. 'Rory Wilson.'

I said, 'You're staying at the Bahía.'

'There was someone new at breakfast! I never notice because I am always talking! This is Mandy who has to put up with me.'

'But you were speaking German to each other – I am sorry – travelling alone makes me eavesdrop.' The English are no sooner introduced than they start apologising to each other.

'Mandy's German, we are both at the University of Kiel, we are doing penguin research all down the Argentinian coast. So what do you want Pinocho for?'

'Pinocho?'

'Everyone calls Carlos Pinocho.'

Out of the house came a man with a light fast frame and a lot of muscle. He ran his fingers through tight curly hair and put out his hand.

Rory added, 'It means Pinocchio.'

I said, 'Hello Carlos.'

'We're going to spend a day measuring penguins and packing up our research site on one of the islands,' Rory said. 'Come with us if you want. On the way back Pinocho will take you to Execution Island – here they call it Isla de la Justicia.'

17

Carlos hitched an inflatable to the back of a 1962 American Ford pick-up. Rory and Mandy pulled me up into the truck. Ten minutes later the inflatable was in the water, Carlos gunned the outboard, the bow beneath me kicked, and we planed over the glass of the harbour. The bay was enclosed by low islands and shingle banks. More estuary than Atlantic. Dimples appeared to our left. 'Commerson's dolphins,' said Rory, 'very rare. Very difficult to see them anywhere else. They're *odontoceti*, toothed dolphins, cousins to killer whales. Next to nothing known about them.'

One came round under the bow and blew out water in my face.

'Lovely animal, five or six feet long, a lot of white, each pattern unique, very sociable here.'

Commerson's dolphins were discovered by the naturalist Philibert de Commerson who sailed with Bougainville on the first French circumnavigation of the world of 1766–9. He took his valet Baré along. When they got to Tahiti the natives noticed what his colleagues had not. Baré was a woman, Commerson's mistress.

The dolphin under the bow swam with its back against the rubber. I left the camera in the bag, and the mini-disc recorder with it. I reached out and touched the back of a wild dolphin. Soft and smooth to the touch, neither fish nor flesh. It blew over my face again. Sun on my neck. Bliss.

The tide was ebbing. We came to shallows at the north end of the bay where the water drained, just inches deep, over narrows between island and shore. Carlos lifted the outboard and punted. We came over into deeper water and pulled up under a stilt house at the top of the beach.

'Is this your house?'

'My island.'

'Do you live here during the summer?'

'I come here a lot, three or four days a week if the weather's good. I fish, fix a few things.'

'Who else lives on the island?'

'One hundred and thirty thousand Magellanic penguins.'

They lay on their backs like otters, rolling, frisking, cleaning. They swam slowly to shore and walked up the beach in lines. They stood around in groups of two or three dozen. We beached among samphire, and landed the gear.

The island is low, mostly thirty or forty feet high, and covered in scrub bushes. Penguins come here to burrow and nest, and every footstep I took was within arm's length of a nest burrow. Their territorial call to intruders is like a donkey's bray. Their personal call to identify chicks and partners is a bray with vibrato.

In the hut Rory sorted equipment: stomach pump, bowl, scales. 'They are remarkable birds, nesting everywhere from Cape Horn to near Chiloé, way north up the Chilean coast.'

'I know, I thought I was seeing things.'

'There's a penguin colony even further north nesting on the Atacama coast – the world's driest desert.'

'How long have you been researching these penguins?'

'Penguins? Twelve years.'

'What will this experiment tell you?'

'It's one of a chain down the Argentine coast. The seas along the east side of South America are less rich than the west. All along the Chilean coast the cool nutrient-rich Humboldt Current brings a conveyor of food up from the Antarctic. The coastal shelf round here is not yet badly overfished but it will be. We need to know what they eat and what they need, and where they go for it.

'We spend three weeks running north up the long coast from Cabo Virgenes, at the east entrance to the Magellan Strait, to Peninsula Valdes, where they film the whales.'

He clipped a harness round his waist, and picked up a board like a plasterer's hawk, with a curve cut into one side. Mandy carried a blue plastic bowl, and an orange rubber tube with a bulb pump in it. Carlos studied a clipboard.

Rory outlined the work. 'We've got six penguins out there, each with a thousand pounds' worth of tracking equipment on its back. It's our last day here, I'm hoping to get them all back.' From a bag he took a deep green resin block the size and shape of mackerel head. 'We tape these to the back of the bird; they record the depth, speed and direction of the birds. We download it into a computer and plot where they've been. We pump their stomachs and we know what they've caught, and there's our picture of their feeding needs. My own invention,' he said proudly, and held up the wooden board.

'How are the chicks doing this year?'

He frowned. 'Despite the numbers this isn't the ideal place for them. Their preferred food is fish; further north they get anchovy, here it's sardine, but it's not plentiful, so they have to take a lot of squid, which offers poorer nutrition and takes longer to digest. If the squid is not fed to the chick beak to beak, it will not even recognise it as food, and will let it lie on the floor of the nest. In this part of Patagonia it shouldn't rain at all in December. But this year there was heavy rain. Water ran down the burrows and into the nests. The chicks' down is absorbent, they got wet, so they got cold and died. Some of the first chicks died, and most of the second chicks, which hatch two days later and are often weaker.'

He straightened his back and scanned the beach. 'I think there's one of ours now.' The bird making its way across the honeycomb of paths seemed to know it was being looked at, cocked an eye over its shoulder, and ran off, doing a presentable Charlie Chaplin. Rory disappeared over a low ridge. There was a loud braying noise. He came back carrying a penguin.

He knelt on the ground with the bird upright between his thighs, clipped lines from his harness around each leg and held the back of its head. 'Never hold the flippers or feet; they go berserk, and those beaks are like wire cutters. Imagine putting a Stanley knife on your finger and then putting a seven pound weight on the knife – that's what they do to you. Most researchers use gauntlets. It's just not necessary if you know how to handle them. Of course no system is perfect.' He held out a finger with a deep cut scored along one side. 'That's three weeks old, my own fault. Ever seen inside a penguin's beak?'

I thought carefully. 'No.'

He prised it open with great difficulty. The inside was brilliant pink and the roof of the mouth and the tongue were covered in large strong bristles pointing downwards. 'They eat all their fish head first; these act against the scales, like Velcro. Last sight many fish see.'

Mandy passed him an orange tube like the ones on school Bunsen burners. He slid it down into the bird's gullet.

'How much does it distress the bird?'

'They puke a lot, naturally. They regurgitate for chicks, and a lot of seabirds actually throw up food when attacked, to distract predators. For them it's not a big deal. For us it would be horrible.' Mandy pumped water down the tube, filling the stomach until water spilled from the beak. He whisked it upside down and spilled about a third of its catch into the bowl. The bird kept the rest. 'Besides it's a lot less stressful than the previous technique.'

'What was that?'

'They hit them on the head and cut the stomach open.'

Rory set the bird down and released his grip. It shot away ten yards, drew itself up straight, and walked away with the rest of its catch to its waiting chick.

We poked about in the bowl and began to lay out fish-heads and squid in lines. 'See what I mean about the squid? These fish have been in the gut the same length of time, and are half digested.'

I picked up the squid. 'This is so fresh you could wash it and sell it.'

'And that's what its like for the chick: best part of a day longer to digest it, and poorer nutrition when it does. He pulled out a small green beak. 'Squid beak, stay around in the stomach for months, can't count these.'

A beautiful hawk came over. Excited, I pointed it out to Rory. 'What is it?'

He glanced. 'Don't know, if it doesn't go underwater and eat fish I'm not really interested. Can't help it. Hold this bird a moment.' He gave me an adult. I took the back of its head and pulled it between my legs. It was a ball of muscle, like holding a Staffordshire bull terrier. It stayed perfectly still.

'You've got the hands,' he said. I eyed the beak.

I left them, and went to photograph birds on the beach. There were black and Magellanic oystercatchers; it is unusual for them to be in the same territory. The black ones had a scarlet bill, and orange-red eyelids, and the iris was a startling orange-yellow.

Dominican gulls were nesting, and skuas harried the adults, trying to get at the chicks and eggs. I lay down in the pebbles and waited for them all to get used to me. I was too busy looking inland at the oystercatchers to notice what was creeping up behind me. But when I rolled to face the sea, a group of two dozen penguins had left the water's edge to come and stare at me. After a while, one would lean forward and, after suffering a minute of unbearable indecision, be overcome with curiosity and take another couple of steps nearer. The others would follow, then stop, until the leader began to tremble and, unable to control himself, patter closer. In the end, I bawled out laughing, and they scuttled back to the water's edge.

The wind sprang up and we went in the house to drink scalding maté. Rory scanned the bay. 'There's still a one thousand-pound penguin swimming around out there.'

Carlos said, 'I'll be out here fishing, I know which nest it belongs to, I'll call by.'

We loaded the boat. I looked back at a seventh of a million penguins. 'What's the island called?' I asked Rory.

'We just call it the island. I don't know if it has a local name.'

Carlos nodded, 'It's called Cormorant Island.'

I turned for a last look. A hare sat on the grassed beach top. A hawk stooped.

The inflatable took us across the bay. The evening was growing cold, but before we went back to the mainland I had to visit the place of execution which had brought me to Puerto San Julián, Isla de la Justicia, the Island of Justice.

The low bank lay further offshore than Cormorant Island. The highest point sustained just enough soil to nourish a few thin bushes. The rest was shingle, but it bustled with life: gulls and blue-eyed cormorants were crammed into nesting sites. Our boat bumped gently against the beach and Carlos killed the engine. Wavelets scrabbled in the pebbles, the wind lifted the dove-grey feathers of the most beautiful of all gulls, the dolphin gull. On deep vermilion legs it walked up the beach, looking over its shoulder at us. It picked its way onto grass whose roots curled around the bones of noblemen.

I thought about how this remote shingle islet had dogged Drake on his return when he was attacked by the friends and family of the well-connected man he tried here. It has been called not only the Island of Justice but also the Island of Blood. There was certainly blood, but was it spilled in justice or revenge? When he came to his decision to convict, and condemn, Thomas Doughty, Drake must have been obsessed by the only other commander who had ever trodden this land: Ferdinand Magellan.

*Island of Blood*

Here at Puerto San Julián, on this little island in the bay, nearly five hundred years ago, he and one of his captains, Sebastian del Cano, came head to head, and Magellan showed what he was made of. When his flotilla arrived on the last day of March 1520 to rest his men and repair the boats, he had come too far to compromise his ambition. The shingle banks may have shifted about in the half millennium which now intervenes, but the overall scene would have been much the same The low islands would have killed the power of the waves but offered no shelter from the cutting winds.

He had already sailed off real maps, in among the sea monsters which breached and spumed around their margins. The preparation had been long and meticulous. There would be no adventure like it until Yuri Gagarin went into space, but with Gagarin we knew what was awaiting. For Magellan, the leaving of this meagre harbour was a launch into a totally unknown cosmos.

Magellan had read in Aristotle that the southern hemisphere was a place where no men lived, but he found teeming villages. This was the end of Aristotle. In fact Magellan didn't find just men; he found giants, and so did subsequent explorers, right up to the eighteenth century. With Magellan was Antonio Pigafetta, a young nobleman from Vicenza accompanying the Papal ambassador to the expedition. He was an inquisitive man and a talented linguist.

But one day (without anyone expecting it) we saw a giant who was on the shore, quite naked, and who danced, leaped, and sang, and while he sang he threw sand and dust on his head. Our captain sent one of our men toward him, charging him to leap and sing like the other in order to reassure him and show him friendship. Which he did. And when he was before us, he began to marvel and to be afraid, and he raised one finger upward, believing that we came from heaven. And he was so tall that the tallest of us only came up to his waist.

However, any trouble the giants gave Magellan was nothing compared to what he brought with him. Within two days of arriving at Puerto San Julián there was mutiny. There were men in Magellan's fleet who outranked him socially and plotted against him, perhaps before the expedition had even sailed. On the morning of 2 April Magellan found three of his five boats were now in the control of four rebel officers, Juan Cartagena, Sebastian del Cano, Gaspar Quesada and Luis de Mendoza. Magellan rightly guessed Mendoza was the ringleader. He sent one boat with a messenger to row in full view towards Mendoza's ship, while a second boat came round behind and boarded it by stealth. Mendoza was stabbed to death, and the crew surrendered. A strong tide pulled another rebel ship from its anchors and under Magellan's cannon. It was bombarded, boarded and subdued. Cartagena and del Cano gave up.

Trials were held. To encourage contrition, Magellan first had the body of Mendoza disembowelled, cut in pieces and hung on a gibbet. Quesada was beheaded, disembowelled, quartered and hung next to him. Cartagena had been directly appointed by the King, so Magellan put him ashore, with a troublesome priest, giving them a small sack of biscuit and their swords. André Thevet's 1584 biography of Magellan noted: 'By these means, he softened the others considerably.'

Sebastian del Cano and dozens of others found guilty were forgiven. Magellan simply had too few men to execute all the guilty. By a macabre irony, the next visitor to this harbour on the world's rim would enact another grim piece, a shadow theatre of Magellan's own drama.

## 'With Death or Other Ways'

Magellan's successor in southern exploration was Francis Drake. When, in 1577, he boarded the *Pelican* to begin his circumnavigation, he was thirty-five years old, clear-headed, fiercely loyal to his family, and ambitious. In authority he was ruthless, and had a knack of using his temper to advantage. He was not cruel or reckless; in anger he never forgot what he wanted. When war broke out with Spain, Queen Elizabeth secretly took shares in Drake's proposed raid to enter the South Sea through the Straits of Magellan and plunder Spain's Pacific wealth. She made it very clear that Lord Burghley, who had undermined similar previous proposals, must not know.

On board the *Pelican* was Thomas Doughty, one of a group of gentlemen soldiers, a scholar and linguist, well educated and well connected. He had used his influence to help the expedition gain favour, a point he liked to remark upon. In the beginning he had command of the land soldiers. Drake was Admiral and overall commander, but he was not, in the eyes of a career courtier like Doughty, a gentleman. It became clear that neither officer nor gentleman could quite bring themselves to defer to the other.

There are a number of accounts of the voyage; each one takes sides and makes errors, but it seems certain that Doughty was soon acknowledged as leader of the group of gentlemen, well connected, young, and with too little to do. In the *Mary*, Thomas Drake and Thomas Doughty accused each other of pilfering. Francis Drake went on board and listened to two unsatisfactory stories. To placate Doughty he formally made him captain of the gentlemen soldiers on the *Pelican*.

Doughty thought the new job demanded a speech. He called the crew together.

> My masters, I have somewhat to say unto you. The General hath his authority from her highness the Queen's majesty and her council such as hath not been committed almost to any subject afore this time: to punish at his discretion with death or other ways offenders; so he hath committed the same authority to me in his absence to execute upon those which are malefactors.

This warrant would soon be invoked to secure a man's destruction. But not by Mr Doughty.

Doughty's ship lost contact with the rest of the fleet, Drake suspected deliberately, and bad weather closed in. Drake had had enough; he roamed the deck swearing Thomas Doughty had conjured up the bad weather by sorcery. Magellan's problems had been real-life drama. Drake's now became tragic and even, sometimes, comic theatre. Doughty swore at Drake and was tied to the *Pelican's* mast for two days. Released, he refused to go to another ship until Drake prepared a block and tackle, and threatened to unload him as cargo.

On the last day of June Drake sailed into the bay of Puerto San Julián to prepare boats and crew for the passage into the Pacific, as Magellan had fifty-eight years before. They met giants for a second time. Further north Francis Fletcher had said of them, they 'showed us more kindness than many Christians would have done, nay more than I have for my own part found among many of my brethren of the ministry in the church of God'. Drake gave the giants food and drink. Only once before had the giants seen men like these. Once out of bow-range, one Indian called out in rusty Portuguese, '*Magellanes, Esta he minha terra*' – 'Magellan, this is my country.' A vain and ironically prophetic cry.

They found Magellan's gibbet, a spruce mast, fallen over. The cooper took a piece from it back to camp and from it made souvenir tankards to sell to his shipmates. Digging in the shingle and sparse soil, they found the bones of Luis de Mendoza, Antonio de Coca and Gaspar Quesada. Drake knew the resolute man who put them there was the only one whose expedition had succeeded in passing through the Strait and reaching home. In the twenty years between Magellan's success and Drake's birth, twenty-one ships had tried to follow his course: twelve were wrecked on or near the Strait, and the rest foundered elsewhere, or retreated the way they had come. With those odds stacked against success, there was only one response to dissent.

There are two contemporary accounts of the trial of Thomas Doughty at San Julián. One was written by Drake's chaplain,

Francis Fletcher, who was courteous to Doughty, but his sympathy and loyalties were with Drake. The other, by John Cooke, was hostile. His ship turned for home early, so, writing his version at a time when he thought Drake would not return, he pulled no punches. Looking back, he damned Puerto San Julián as a place where 'will was law and reason put in exile'.

A chair was taken out to Isla de la Justicia and all the crews commanded to attend. In the path of Drake's mighty ambition was Thomas Doughty and his supporters. A game of cat and mouse began. Eventually Doughty made a mortal blunder: name-dropping, he let slip that Lord Burghley knew of the voyage.

'No,' said Drake, 'that he hath not.'

'Indeed he hath.'

'How?'

'He had it from me.'

'Lo, my masters, what hath this fellow done, for her Majesty gave me special commandment that of all men my Lord Treasurer should not know it, but to see his own mouth hath betrayed him.'

The jury found him guilty, and a game of manners followed. Drake asked Doughty, 'Would you take to be executed in this land, or to be set on the main, or return to England, there to answer this deed before the Lords of her Majesty's Council?'

Doughty thanked him for his clemency and asked to answer in the morning. Drake agreed.

Next dawn Doughty dismissed the option of being marooned 'among Infidels'. He also thought no man would accompany him home to England, so he asked to be executed. Drake offered him shooting, which he would do himself, so Doughty would die at the hands of a gentleman. He chose beheading.

The next day Chaplain Fletcher celebrated communion, then Drake and Doughty dined together. No account suggests it was not convivial. Doughty said he was ready for the execution but asked that he might 'speak alone with him some words'. They walked alone along the shingle shore some seven or eight minutes; what they talked about no one knows. When they returned Doughty remarked 'he that cuts off my head shall have little honesty, as my neck is so short'. He laid his head on the block. The axe fell. Drake had needed an argument he would win; his text was Thomas Doughty's head. Drake held it aloft: 'Lo, this is the end of traitors.'

Digging a grave they found a grindstone broken in two, and set one part at the head and the other at the foot.

## Absent Millionaires

In the taxi office at Puerto San Julián I explained that I wanted to go north along the coast, then find Estancia Coronel, the site of a failed early colonial settlement. We negotiated, and I showed a map to the driver – unshaven, five feet nothing, blackout sunglasses and a pack of Marlboro.

The boss came out, Marcello, thirty-ish with clear skin, a thin student beard, and hair brushed back, thinning without retreating from the forehead. We agreed a price. I held out a hand, 'I'm John.' He kept his hand in his pocket. The driver asked, from behind his shield of night, 'So where are we going?'

An enormous explanation followed.

The driver nodded. 'So I am going to take . . .' I lost track of his Spanish.

'No.' Marcello borrowed my map. 'You're going . . .' Another detailed itinerary was launched.

'Understand?'

'Yes. I am going to go up to the top, straight on at the end of the main street . . .'

'No.' Marcello went into the back of the offices. The driver took me to the car, I threw my bag in the back seat. He said 'No'. Perhaps No was the company motto. He asked me to sit in the front. Marcello appeared with Maxi, his six-year-old son. The driver smiled at me, 'They are coming to show me the way.' He was genuinely pleased. At the end of the main street we turned right onto a dirt road and climbed through gentle hills of grasses and low bushes.

The sandy road boiled dust behind us. Silver-leafed, yellow-flowered shrubs lined the track. Low purple flowers with petals halfway between mallows and poppies hid among them, out of the wind. After half a mile there was a fork in the road. We needed to hug the coast, on our right. Sunglasses tried to go left, and at the last minute was corrected by Marcello. The gravel forming a V ridge in the fork machine-gunned the base of the car. This happened every half mile. After a while we came to a junction where all routes were marked right. He steered left. Marcello said quietly, 'It's right here.' I realised that the driver could not read.

We came to what seemed a shallow puddle across the track. He braked to a tyre-screaming stop, reversed, and drove rough country around it. While we did this, an antique Fiat 500 coming the other way skimmed straight through the water. It was nearly an inch deep.

On the shoulder of the hill, with a long open view over the harbour and the low flat islands, was a tomb. Riveted metal bands formed a white picket fence which skirted a small plot. Summer flowers danced on wind-whipped stalks. The grave of Robert Scholl, an officer on Captain Stokes's surveying voyage in the *Beagle*, looks down on Isla de la Justicia and Punta Desengaño, the Island of Justice and Disillusion Point. He died after an illness in 1828.

Around the corner lay the ruins of Frigorifico Swift. In the peak year of 1946, 239,000 sheep were slaughtered here. There was no deep-water harbour. Pugnacious ferries built like Cornish trawlers came into the deep stone basin and butted their way over the shallows to ocean-going vessels out in the bay. The last one sits there now, at the foot of a cliff. From a rusty shed on the cliff top, pipes dangle down like drips disconnected from a dead patient.

We were not the only visitors. At the foot of a wall of one of the sheds, in deep shadow, a fire was lit. Blankets were spread, three women nursed babies or pulled toddlers back to the circle. Four men shouted and then put their shoulders to the ulcerated body of an old Chevrolet. It bumped into thin life; the driver toured the yard and parked it at the head of a downslope. The sun was warm and the low shrubs fragrant in the breeze. They sat and began cooking, twenty feet from a large bed of damp manure.

'Where now?' asked the shades.

'Estancia Coronel.' This was what I had really come for, the site of the forgotten colony of Florida Blanca.

In 1780 Antonio de Viedma came here as part of a Spanish policy to populate Patagonia and defend the Atlantic coast. The Crown recruited two hundred families. According to the advertisement, they would be offered 'transport to the royal hacienda, have their own rooms, be given tools to work their own land, one or two yoke of oxen, enough grain both to plant and to maintain them for the first year'. There were also mineral deposits which would be worked for profit.

We climbed away from the coast. Two ibises flew across our path. We wound inland, then turned through the gates of Estancia Coronel. A long rising drive took us up a broad valley and away from the wide coastal plain. It was one of the few landscapes I saw that looked like anywhere in Britain: it was Mid–Wales on steroids. The estate driveway went on and up until the car emerged into a combe with a fork in the road. We stopped and looked down on two ranges of red and grey farm buildings standing either side of a gravel drive which took a turn round a bank of mown grass. On a tall white flagpole in the middle of the bank waved the Argentine flag.

Marcello pointed. 'The wooden buildings on the right are the old Estancia Coronel. They are nearly two hundred years old. The red buildings on the left are the new estancia, they are all metal.' I took a step forward with my camera.

'No. Stay on the road here, this is private land.'

A small tree like a young willow streamed slim branches from left to right with a drift of romance from a Corot painting. I knelt to photograph the estancia. In the green meadow, sweet buttermilk flowers poured fragrance across the grass. Horses the colour of coffee cream looked up from grazing. Tall trees shaded the roofs. I killed it with a click, put down the camera, heart beating hard. I looked. After taking a photograph you often forget to just look. All stood still. Then the view began to breathe again.

'Up here. We can drive up and look down on the ruins.'

Viedma's project had foundered quickly: no money in the mining, no knowledge of how to farm the thin soil, to milk the short seasons. There was little to see except the beauty of the modern ranch.

'It's Señor Benetton's,' said Marcello, 'he owns all the land for twelve kilometres around here. He owns another ranch, Estancia Sierra Morena, and all the land for sixteen kilometres around that.'

'Is this *the* Señor Benetton?'

Marcello pulled at his own shirt, which was not a Benetton. 'Yes, the clothes, the Formula One. He knows how to choose well. There are many abandoned estancias since the volcano Mount Hudson blew up two hundred miles away in Chile. The ash fell here and burnt the ground and killed the animals. Sylvester Stallone has a ranch too.'

I watched a pale grey mare move onto the shoulder of the hill beneath. A jet black stallion with a flying mane looked at us, bolted a few paces, then stopped, trembling, to look again. 'Does he come here, Señor Benetton?'

'Yes! He came here once.'

'For how long?'

'A day.'

Same as me.

I had an early night; the early morning flight leaving at 6.30am was taking me to the deep south.


*Veterinary Surgeon*

On the flight to Ushuaia I took my seat by the window. A portly man with a fine nose and chin stood aside to show his wife to a window seat on the opposite side of the aisle. We said hello. Within the minute he slid into the seat next to me.

'Allow me to introduce myself, I am Carlos. I am a veterinary surgeon. We are from the north of Argentina, Bahía Blanca. And you are English?'

'Yes.'

'My wife saw you reading Dostoevsky on the bus yesterday and she said, Carlos, you must speak to that man. I said Yes!'

His English was confident but bookish.

'My first language is Spanish but my father was English and sent me to the English School in Buenos Aires. He didn't want me to lose his English. I use it so little now.'

We roared into the sky. 'You are travelling through Argentina?'

'And Chile, I am writing a book about the south.'

'What interested you in Patagonia? There are so many British who came here and stayed. I asked a friend who was from the north of England, your Yorkshire, and he said it was so – my English is so awful – unrestricted?'

'Unconfined?'

'Perfect – the big open spaces. You, of course, have beautiful countryside.' He gestured down at a colossal cliff. 'So like Cornwall. Have you ever been to Cornwall?'

'I lived there as a child.'

He gulped. 'Do you not think a cliff like this is so very like Cornwall? That is how I have always imagined it.'

'In many ways, yes,' I said, thinking of all the other ways it was nothing like Cornwall.

'Good, that is always how I thought of it. And my friend said, We are so confined in England, and here there is just . . .' – he waved his hand at the sunshine and the pasture – 'so much space. Your book, why Patagonia?'

I felt unable to take him through the motivation of rainy childhood days, staring through eyeholes in the condensation on the window pane. 'Have you read the Lucas Bridges book, *Uttermost Part of the Earth*, about growing up in Tierra del Fuego?'

'No, but I know of it.' He made this sound much finer than merely having read it.

'I am going to look for his descendant, Tommy Goodall, on the southernmost ranch in the world. I am also interested in what happened between the natives and the Europeans. Neither had much chance of understanding the other and there's only one script: the economically weaker collapse and die. Even when rare people like the missionary family Bridges actually learned about the natives and tried to help them, there was nothing they could do to change the script.'

'What do you think of Americans? They are very naïve, I always think. Very well-mannered but haven't a clue what's going on outside their own state. What do you think?'

I talked and looked out of the window, flying ever further south, from Patagonia, the Land of Giants, to Tierra del Fuego, the Land of Fire.

# 2

# *Tierra del Fuego*

*No More Tears*

The plane came over the mountains to the north. The view
from the window was of black mountains cut by snow-filled
ravines glimpsed through cloud. They looked malevolent. I felt fear
in the pit of my stomach.

'Welcome to Ushuaia, the southernmost city in the world,' said
the sign. On a snowy billboard a sausage with a green woollen hat
and red scarf ski'd downhill. Why a sausage? No one would say. At
the foot of it a Jack Russell groomed its balls vigorously.

The airstrip was a T-shape newly built out into the Beagle
Channel. A bus ferried the passengers to the low shed where I
waited. My backpack contained extreme-weather clothing and
specialist camping gear for walking in the Andes. Even in midsummer, at heights as low as 5,000 feet, the weather in Tierra del Fuego
can kill. In winter the land closed down. At one time I had hoped
to go further south, right down to Antarctica, but the only trips I
could find started at £5,000 and I did not have that kind of money.
Waiting for the bags I stared longingly south towards it.

A decommissioned bread van pulled up and two thin men in
blue overalls moved luggage from it to the single luggage carousel.
I looked out through its rubber flaps and saw the snow on the
mountains of Isla Hoste, the only land of any size between us and

Cape Horn. People collected their bags and left. I waited for my backpack. It had taken six months to choose and buy the contents. The carousel rotated. The van returned with six more bags, none of them mine. Everyone left. The carousel stopped, the rubber flaps closed and hid Isla Hoste. The thin men with thin shoulders shrugged, and shut the rear doors of the van.

The representative of Aerolineas Argentina was a woman in her thirties with black shining hair. Imagine a tight-head prop forward with maroon lipstick. I explained the problem and she listened thoughtfully, shrugged and walked away. I explained the problem to another man in uniform. When I finished, he said, 'I do not work for the airline, I am customs. But I think it is in Rio Grande. We will telephone now. Please come again in the morning.'

The Governor's bungalow pictured, in Lucas Bridges's time, on a cart track on the shoreline, was still recognisable near the traffic lights at the dock gates. This spot was Alacushwaia, the bay of flying loggerhead ducks. The corrugated homes of the first settlers are now crisply painted and surrounded by cottage gardens whose plants fly like troubled dreams through the swift spring, bursting into flower, nursing their seeds to ripeness in the last warmth of March. The roof of this cottage was red, its walls grey, and its windows and shutters picked out in white, like the picket fence. They are now local landmarks, or earn a living as museums or libraries. Lace behind the panes, the house name on the trunk of a cedar, gorse flaring yellow by the gate.

I checked into the Hotel Alakaluf. The hotel reception was on the first floor where grandfather was playing with a little boy of about two-and-a-half. Patio doors, leading onto a narrow balcony over the main street, were fully open, leaving a space wider than the balcony, through which you could fall out into the street. The grandfather was glued deep in the soft upholstery of an ancient sofa. The toddler ran around.

The room was plain and comfortable. Raúl, from reception, pushed his black hair back from his eyes. 'It is very nice, own fire. Gas, easy to light.'

'Show me.'

He knelt. 'It will be warm when we light the fire which is very simple.'

'Let me watch, just to be sure.'

After five minutes he was very red and the fire had not changed colour. He stood and stretched and looked round the room, and saw my small day-bag. 'You don't have much luggage.'

'No.'

'How long are you away?'

'Three or four months.'

He nodded, impressed. We both knelt in the corner and followed what was left of the polished-away instructions. They were simple but useless. When I stood up and stopped watching he got it to work. I went out to look round the town, leaving the fire on. If the hotel burnt down, I would not lose much luggage.

The buildings, taken one at a time, were mostly ugly and functional. Side-walls were bare breeze-block with fat slugs of cement oozing from the joints. But opposite the Hotel Alakaluf, Gonzalo's shop front exploded with Jamaican colour. It sold teddy bears, electrical goods, whisky and toiletries, watches, penknives and pipes. Prices were marked in pink hand-cut cardboard bells. I bought a key ring showing the extent of Argentina's Antarctic Territory.

The town was full of curiosities, narrow two-storey log houses shaped in a flat-topped A, and tiny cabins, bachelor-snug. The Banco Nacional de Argentina, on Avenida San Martín, was modelled on a ship's bridge, and fabricated in yellow cladding as brilliant as the gorse. The whole vessel squatted down, head-butting the mad westerlies with bravado. The architect had made one bad slip. For the name of the bank he chose free-standing letters pinned to the north wall. The week had been calm, nevertheless the sign read Ban:o Nacio:al de Arg:nt:na.

Avenida San Martín was clogged by dusty cars with cracked windscreens. Grilles like fencers' masks covered the front lights. The best models had bullet-like holes in them and crazed spider webs exploding away from them. There were American four-wheel-drive monsters with balloon tyres and stainless steel gallows behind the cab. Boys on ball-wheeled quads, or scrambling bikes with blown exhausts, mowed down the middle of the street. The star was Angel, a lad of seventeen with gold in his left ear, driving something which looked like an oil rig on wheels. He spent all afternoon and early evening waiting for chances to blast twenty yards through the traffic, then to sit trapped and crackling, hustling for the next gap. He was a one-boy noise weapon.

The strip was garish, loud, unplanned, full of goods and big brand-names. But because the building plots were packed tight, it lacked that sprawling feel of a small downtown in the USA, full of aimless spaces which no one finished off or looked after, and which made you feel, when you crossed them at night, that someone was training an infra-red sight on your shoulders. Ushuaia was brash and energetic. On Saturday night when the music shops leave their doors open and push their stacks onto the veranda, there is fun at the end of the world. I walked the boards, had my hair cut, and bought a bottle of shampoo. Not reliably knowing the Spanish for lanolin-free hypo-allergenic, I saw No Más Lagrimas for babies and bought that. No More Tears.

*Fat Fat*

In the morning I made coffee in the kitchen overlooking the Beagle Channel and pictured Darwin's boat moored here when it was the biggest man-made object in southern Argentina and Chile. The kitchen had three fridges full of bags and boxes, and two saucepans of mutton stew, stuck with their owners' names; but I never saw anyone cook there. The gas stove had a saucepan to boil water for tea. I turned on the tap and air locks blew out in a long artillery barrage.

Waiting for the water to boil, I walked into the dining room next door. A very fat man sat at a trestle table watching television with two even fatter cleaning women. He might have been married to one of them. I made the coffee and took it to my room and drank it with bread and cheese.

Later I returned with the washing-up. The two sitting women had slaughterhouse bodies with slabs of flesh applied to all parts of their frames. They now sat with stone legs planted open and unbuttoned blouses revealing hanks of breasts divided by chasmic cleavages, as if ready to feed the melancholy man whose face said, Look at me, you can see I am too fat to work. His shirt was unbuttoned belly-low, and he ran a finger under his collar, and round through the hair that hung over it. While he sweated about the lack of work commensurate with his size, one of the women filled the sink with pots. Elbowed in suds, she held them under for cleaning. Black polka dots on purple nylon stretched across the Jupiter's meridian of her back. A lattice of thin shoulder straps pinched tightly into flesh: a boned rolled joint.

As she scrubbed, her heavy breasts flew over the sink. 'Money, there's never any money.' Her voice was metal and full of starlings; she shouted like a radio.

The man's eyes rolled down his face, sad as a basset-hound. 'Work, I can't find work. There isn't any work. You show me where there's work.'

Her hands flew and the polka dots were flecked with suds like insects in cuckoo spit. 'Never any money for the likes of us. The boy needs shoes.'

'No work.'

'Clean, clean, clean, and no money.'

He sagged so his whole body looked like hounds' ears. 'No work here at all.'

I was frightened she would talk to me. I pictured the man being breast-fed, the women feeding each other, until they were too fat to leave the room. One would spend the afternoons washing her breasts in the sink, while the man's eyes followed the football on the grainy television. I stood a few minutes, my dirty plates in my hands. I returned to the room and cleaned them with Travel Wash in the bathroom sink.

Raúl's sister Estella ran me down to the airport. Maroon lipstick gave a flame-thrower glare and retired to pluck and sandblast her eyebrows. Estella spoke. 'A missing backpack from yesterday's afternoon flight?' The bag appeared from an office. So simple. Smiles all round. I smiled at maroon lipstick. She showed me her fillings.

Bags unpacked, I went out. The main street didn't look much but when you started to walk it you found it was long, and you lost your sense of how far along it you were. At first the Banco del Tierra del Fuego seemed a useful landmark. After two days I was sure that they moved it each night.

A poster advertised an exhibition of photographs of the 1914 Shackleton expedition, in a hotel at the back of the town. A taxi dropped me off in front of a massive new timber hotel in the forested hills behind the town. The reception staff shared four things in common. They were young, good-looking and had not heard of an exhibition, or of Ernest Shackleton. I wandered off and found an empty lounge, where a log fire blazed in a walk-around fireplace. The photographs of the most remarkable escape in the history of exploration were on the walls.

### Out of Whose Womb?

In August 1914 the *Endurance* was anchored in Margate ready to sail for the South Pole. The expedition's objective: an 1,800-mile crossing of the Antarctic on foot, going over the South Pole. In the morning paper its leader, Ernest Shackleton, read of the general mobilisation. He telegrammed the Admiralty offering the ship and crew for war service. The one-word reply: Proceed.

His photographer was the Australian Frank Hurley, who also took an early cine-camera. He sported curly hair, and an open face. In a self-portrait he stares at the lens with unassuming eyes. They do not hint that he was a man who took perfectionism to the borders of fanaticism, tying himself to freezing masts to secure precisely the photograph he wanted.

The advertisement for the expedition had been brief and to the point: 'Men wanted for hazardous journey. Small wages, bitter cold, long months of complete darkness, constant danger, safe return doubtful. Honour and recognition in case of success.' No one would complain about the accuracy of the job description. The *Endurance* was frozen into the ice before they could begin their land journey to the Pole. Hurley photographed the long escape from disaster, as the ice holding the boat drifted northwards. He wound the handle on his cine-camera as the ice crushed the hull of the *Endurance*. Shackleton watched helplessly as the mast fell towards the photographer, crashing down ten feet from him. Hurley did not miss a turn.

The exhibition showed new prints taken from the original glass plates. It contained most of the best shots. My favourite was a floodlit view of the *Endurance* at night. Each dog was sponsored by a public school. They would later kill them to save meat rations, but for quite some time no one had the heart to eat the dogs themselves. Eton wasn't eaten.

They looked to Shackleton. Sir Edmund Hillary, the first man to cross Antarctica, said of the great Polar leaders, 'For scientific discovery, give me Scott; for speed and efficiency of travel, give me Amundsen; but when disaster strikes and all hope is gone, get down on your knees and pray for Shackleton.'

Once the *Endurance* had gone, the only hope was to man-haul two ship's boats to open water. They aimed for Paulet Island 560 kilometres to the north, a speck of land off the fingertip of Antarctica. Shackleton lectured the men. They could carry little that was not vital. He took out his gold watch and laid it on the ice. A handful of gold sovereigns were flung down after it. Then he took from under his coat Queen Alexandra's farewell gift of a Bible. He tore out and kept her inscription, and a page from the *Book of Job* which read: 'Out of whose womb came the ice? And the hoary frost of heaven, who hath gendered it?' God joined Mammon on the ice.

The lesson served. Hurley and Shackleton went through the six hundred or so glass photographic plates, choosing the best. They smashed all the others, so they would not later be tempted to come back for more. They tramped north until the ice broke up and they were floating on a piece of ice just sixty metres across. An unknown current bore them away from Paulet Island towards the open ocean. They launched the boats and made it to Elephant Island off the tip of the Antarctic Peninsula. The men clutched handfuls of stones, the first land they had known for nearly a year and a half. One boat was upturned for a hut for the twenty-five men who would remain here while Shackleton, Worsley, Crean, McNeish, Vincent and McCarthy set out in the *James Caird*, a seven metre-long leaky open boat, for the island of South Georgia, 800 miles away across some of the cruellest water in the world.

They accomplished the second longest voyage in an open boat. The only one longer was made by Captain Bligh after the mutiny on the *Bounty*, and his men began the voyage fit, warm and well-provisioned. Shackleton had made land, but on the opposite side of the island from the only habitation, a whaling station. In between lay an unmapped mountain range.

The journey that the three fittest of them would now make would emerge in literature in a curious place, set in another kind of desert:

> Where the hermit-thrush sings in the pine trees
> Drip drop drip drop drop drop drop
> But there is no water
>
> Who is the third who walks always beside you?
> When I count, there are only you and I together
> But when I look ahead up the white road
> There is always another one walking beside you . . .

Published in 1922, just three years after Shackleton's account, T. S. Eliot's *The Waste Land* drew on an experience from their walk across the jagged pitiless whitescape to the whaling station on the other side of the island. Shackleton had written:

> I know that during that long march of thirty-six hours over the unnamed mountains and glaciers of Georgia it often seemed to me that we were four, not three. And Worsley and Crean had the same idea. One feels "the dearth of human words, the roughness of mortal speech," in trying to describe intangible things.

I left in a thoughtful, almost sombre mood. I did not suspect that in less than two weeks I would bump into a memento of their rescue in the only town in the world south of the city of Ushuaia.

*Allen Gardiner*

Ushuaia was founded by missionaries, and the last book I read before I left Britain was a slim maroon volume from 1887, a book with gilt-edged pages and soft tissue covers to the illustrations. The frontispiece is an engraving of a man with hair curled tightly around a long head. A strong straight nose leads to a firm thoughtful mouth. The capped epaulettes are pale and wispy, like jellyfish trailing his pale arms below. He is Captain Allen F. Gardiner, and his signature is neat and determined. He was one of the first missionaries to attempt to work with the natives around here, following earlier disasters, and he was a walking evangelical catastrophe.

The death of his wife tipped the mind of this popular athletic captain into a masochistic brand of religion. Forty years old, he retired from the Navy and dedicated his life to teaching the Gospel to the heathen. Something extreme in him called out for the ultimate, for the end. His eyes settled on Tierra del Fuego. What happened was an object lesson for those who followed. The lesson was: don't do it like this.

His first attempt failed when incompetent planning found him in the wrong place, in bad weather at the start of winter, being greeted by hostile natives. Gardiner recorded: 'The character of the natives has undergone some considerable change, a Fuegian mission must of necessity be afloat – in other words, a proper mission vessel, moored in the stream.' This plan forgets that the Yámana were canoe Indians.

Back in England he declared that the recent attempt was not failure but reconnaissance – a view few shared. He toured the country lecturing, but money came forward very slowly. The brigantine, which could be moored in safety, became two twenty-six-foot boats which would be beached. This compromise contradicted all his own previous arguments on how the settlement and mission could be safely established. The party to go to Tierra del Fuego included a Staffordshire surgeon, Richard Williams, and John Maidment, a young man commended by the Young Men's Christian Association for his piety, trustworthiness, humility, faith and hardihood. All these virtues would be hard-tested. Three Cornish fishermen – John Pearce, John Badcock and John Bryant – brought seamanship and more piety. A carpenter called Joseph was the last.

They sailed in the square-rigger *Ocean Queen* with their own boats as cargo. They carried with them stores for six months. Fishing lines, guns and ammunition would help them live off the land. On 5 December 1850 they arrived at Banner Cove on Picton Island, at the eastern end of the Beagle Channel. Next morning they began building a gated fence between themselves and the souls they had come to save. The following day Yámana appeared and walked into the tents taking what they wanted. They probably commented on the appalling manners of the white men in turning up and not making an exchange of gifts. But Gardiner would not have known. Neither he nor any of the others had learned a word of their language.

The *Ocean Queen* stayed a while, sailing on the nineteenth. Gardiner then looked for the guns and ammunition. The main store of both had carelessly been left on the *Ocean Queen*. In two weeks, not one of them had checked that they had unloaded the weapons on which all their calculations for survival depended. They had only the guns and shot that each man had about him. Unable to defend their island camp without violence, they decided to find a base on the north shore of the Beagle Channel. But they had to alert their supporters to their new location. On a large rock, at the entrance to the cove where they had been left, they painted

DIG BELOW

GO TO SPANIARD HARBOUR

MARCH

1851

In the sand beneath they left messages in bottles. Spaniard Harbour is on the eastern tip of Tierra del Fuego Island. This was Aush Territory, a sub-group of the Selk'nam. Spaniard Harbour was so remote that there was little chance of contact with the heathen souls they had come so far to save.

In March scurvy appeared. Without local food they would run low two months before new supplies could be expected. They split into two little groups, one living in a cave, the other in an upturned boat. By the end of June relief was a month overdue. John Badcock was suffering horribly from respiratory problems. He asked Richard Williams, who was lying near him, to sing him a hymn. When he had finished Badcock repeated one verse with an eerily loud voice, and died. Gardiner wrote a letter to his son. He gave advice about choosing a profession, commending the missionary life 'which is indeed a delightful one'. There was no missionary work to be done here. Just the strange working out of a need to serve and suffer. One by one, they all perished.

The journal ends on 5 September, exactly ten months after they had arrived. Gardiner's short entry reads

> Great and marvellous are the loving kindnesses of my gracious God unto me. He has preserved me hitherto, and for four days, although without bodily food, without any feeling of hunger or thirst.

Twenty days later the *John Davison* sailed into Banner Cove, and Captain Smyley saw the white painted message on the rock, and found the bottles. In a rising gale he ran the ship over to Spaniard Harbour. His diary reads: 'Went onshore and found the boat with one person dead inside, another we found on the beach, another buried. These, we have every reason to believe, are Pearce, Williams and Badcock. The sight was awful in the extreme. The two captains who went with me in the boat cried like children. Books, papers, medicine, clothing and tools were strewed along the beach. But the gale came on so hard it gave us barely time to bury the corpse on the beach and get on board.' He later added, 'It is the opinion of myself and also of Captain Nicholls that with proper management they might have gone with safety to the Falkland Islands, Port Famine, or the Coast of Patagonia. I have even done more than this in a whaleboat at different times.'

The dead men's diaries speak of many things, but never of escape. Like a modern sect, there was a closure against the outside world, a contempt for merely physical solutions. Patagonia, like the

Terra Australis Incognita in the time of Aristotle, was a metaphor for the unattainable. Gardiner and the surgeon, three pious fishermen who lived together in Cornwall in Christian community, and the man from the YMCA and a carpenter: they all used it as a forge to test the worth of their souls. In this at least, by dying at peace and in faith with their God, they succeeded.

In Britain, news of the discovery of the bodies of Allen Gardiner's party provoked letters to *The Times*. What, spluttered one correspondent, was the worth of 'the dreadful sacrifice of fine Englishmen for the sake of some miserable savages?' But among the many who might have done more to ensure Gardiner had an adequate vessel at his disposal, the disaster pricked consciences.

In 1854 a Dartmouth schooner rolled off the stocks and was sailed south by George Packenham Despard to pick up the torch of the Gospel. With him went his family and two adopted sons, one of whom was Thomas Bridges. Young Thomas Bridges would at last bring his talent for good planning and judgement to go with the piety and courage of his predecessors. The schooner was christened the *Allen Gardiner*.

## *The* Monte Cervantes

To meet the descendants of Thomas Bridges I had to get eastward down the Beagle Channel, and the easiest way was by boat. The Channel is generally very deep, but rogue peaks climb up from the depths to pierce the surface in low, bare rock islands. All navigation here is perilous. If a man falls in and takes all the right precautions, retaining his clothes, keeping still to conserve energy, he may survive as long as eleven minutes.

All the wildlife that can swim or fly nests on the tips of these mostly submarine mountains, out of the reach of terrestrial predators. The catamaran *Luciano Beta* slid by a rocky islet. At one end was a pepperpot lighthouse, its red and black paint bands blistered by the weather. Clouds of South American terns clamoured above, their wings like the arc of a bow, their fork tails pinning the air in twisting flight. Erect cormorants and torpid seals lay squeezed together. A few white pigeon-shaped birds picked their way round the ledges scavenging: they were snowy sheathbills. These spotless birds – their Spanish name means Antarctic dove – hurry the food chain along by pecking nesting seabirds on the backside to get hot guano. The rocks writhed with life. Skuas relentlessly harried the nesting birds to steal their eggs. In the Selk'nam language, the month of January was called 'the moon of broken eggs'.

Monica Perez, a local wildlife guide, slid in beside me. She had a high thin voice and the careful neat hands of a bank clerk. 'Here on this rocky island was the most famous shipwreck of the passenger ship *Monte Cervantes* carrying thirteen hundred passengers which hit this rock and sank. Only one man died and that was the captain. He insisted on being the last man to leave the ship, but when everyone else was in the lifeboats he could not be persuaded to leave and he went down with his ship.' I stared out at the stone pepperpot marking the Ararat on to which he had sailed his boat. Unable to leave her, he had sailed down the mountain with her.

'This was taking the responsibilities of captain too far?' I suggested. 'All boats sail downwards without help.'

'Not at all: he was a proud man.'

The Hamburg-South America Company chartered the smart cruise ship *Monte Cervantes* to promote a new type of tourism: luxury cruises to frontier country. They sailed from Buenos Aires on 15 January 1930. They coaxed senators, generals and society families to promote the very first trip. Young men and women played poker, the loser bought the champagne. They called for smart cocktails and laughed at the German barman struggling to concoct them.

On the evening of 19 January, before they reached Ushuaia, Doctor Alfredo Segers, voted president of the cruise's Glee Club, gave a lecture entitled 'A Cruise to the South'. Forty-four years before, his father Polidoro had come with the expedition of Ramón Lista in 1886. It was shipwrecked. The next year Alfredo, as a young boy, had come south on the *Magellanes*, a 400-ton transport bringing mules, sheep and prisoners to Staten Island Jail. At Puerto Deseado, at the east end of the Magellan Strait, they had foundered. Passengers trying to launch the lifeboats floundered among marrows and fodder brought for the animals. The captain bellowed for order. They rallied. All but two were saved: one disappeared, and one went mad.

You might think a cruise lecture from a hereditary Jonah would not be first-choice entertainment, but the lecture was a huge success. Besides, those were the amusing old days. Today, here on the 14,700-ton *Monte Cervantes,* it was another age: modern-day safe ships. They held races: egg-and-spoon, threading needles, and eating cakes in one bite.

On 22 January at 12:45 passengers were ready for the second sitting for lunch. The *Monte Cervantes* steamed eastward out of Ushuaia harbour before turning round the rocky islets in the entrance and continuing west. The wind began to blow from the south west. Pilot Rodolfo Hepe was on the bridge. He asked Captain Dreyer for charge of the ship, and suggested he go to lunch. Dreyer declined. In a while Hepe sang out, 'Giant kelp close on the port'. He later recalled: 'As no rocks were marked there I thought it was floating weed. Before the ship could change course, we were in the weed, there was a faint creak, and we were on a rock. The bow went up, then we tilted to port.'

But the local Governor wrote: 'I have had access to all the local reports; the accident was due to ignoring the fact that it was dangerous to make that passage with a ship of that draught.' Locals, watching horrified through binoculars from the shore, agreed it was taking the wrong course, and even before the ship sent out its SOS, they ran to their boats to mount a rescue.

The quiet collision made several holes 300 feet long. The holds and cabins flooded immediately. Dreyer quickly ordered bulkheads and hatches sealed to buy time. An oil tank exploded, passengers panicked, three young women were crying.

'What's the matter?'

'We have left our life jackets behind.'

'Why?'

'Because the fasteners were mouldy and would stain our dresses.'

A Spaniard called Beldo Barco took out a hand-held movie

camera and began to film. A magazine photographer began taking pictures as passengers were evacuated to lifeboats. One indignant subject demanded, 'And are those for the magazine too?'

'Certainly not! They hired me to take pictures of a cruise. Shipwreck wasn't mentioned in the contract. If they want these, they can pay gold dust.'

A flotilla of fishing and sailing boats, launches and tubs from Ushuaia soon reached the foundering liner and its VIP passengers. The last were not ashore till 2 am. They made their way to the houses, shacks and cabins of Ushuaia. The *Monte Cervantes* slipped lower and lower: all of a sudden she turned painfully over to starboard. Everyone was safely off except Captain Dreyer. Some said he jumped as it slid under. Others thought they saw him return to the wheel. And though the papers speculated and the beachcombers searched the shore, his body never appeared.

The visitors doubled the town's population in a day. At the jail, they opened up the warders' houses and spare cells. Food was short and prices rocketed. The prisoners voted to give up half their daily ration to help feed three hundred of the new colonists. Or so the prisoner governor said.

A call went out to the *Monte Sarmiento*, a sister ship sailing for Europe, to turn round in Montevideo. Six days later she sounded her siren in Ushuaia Bay. Its blaze of light whispered of Buenos Aires, warm nights, crisp sheets. Spirits revived. They did not tell the rescued passengers that its own predecessor had sunk here in 1912.

One of the humbler government functionaries remarked on how swiftly the appetites of the rich revived once they started lodging insurance claims for lost luggage. 'From the amount claimed I wondered if I had been travelling with ordinary civil servants like me, or maharajahs and sultans.'

*Harberton*

I was on the *Luciano Beta* to visit the farm at Harberton where the Bridges family had moved to Ushuaia. Thomas Bridges was spending too much of his time looking after the physical welfare of the natives, said the Patagonian Missionary Society, snug in its Brighton headquarters. The members endorsed his twenty years of selfless dangerous work in a land where every previous missionary had fled, starved or been murdered, by recording he had been 'instigated by the Evil One to his ruin' and was 'a rat deserting a sinking ship'. But one of the Society, Captain Willis, five feet high and four feet wide with a home-trimmed moustache, thought differently. He lent Bridges his whole life savings of £700.

Bridges named his new home Harberton after his wife's pretty Devon village, near Totnes, where her father owned the smithy. I had visited the West Country churchyard one still late-afternoon in summer and found her family graves, the Varders, which lie on the top of the tump of land below the east window, the elegantly engraved slates transformed by brilliant sidelighting into poems of light and shadow. The forge stream still runs underneath Mary's old home.

We cruised east down the channel. A house with cream corrugated walls and red corrugated roofs stood on a lawn at the water's edge. An Argentine flag hung from a flagpole, a door was open. It looked like the army barracks in toytown. I imagined a man in dark trousers, braces and a collarless white shirt coming out each evening. He would stiffen into a ramrod for ten seconds, salute the sunset, and draw down the flag, quartering it across his chest, mechanical folds, blue white, blue white, into a triangle. This place was Remolino, where John Lawrence, a nursery gardener, came as a missionary at the turn of the year 1869–1870. His family would marry into the Bridges.

It was here in 1912 that the *Monte Sarmiento* sank next to their garden, the passengers dutifully evacuated. It is still there, sleek and rusting in the shallows, its empty davits hooked into the evening.

Thomas Bridges's friends in the Falklands advised him not to leave Ushuaia. It was madness; the government would not give him the land; if they did, he would be bankrupt within the year. Bridges talked to his friend Dr Moreno at the La Plata Museum in Buenos Aires, who introduced him to his uncle, Antonio Cambaceres, the

President of Congress, who led him to ex-President Bartoleme Mitre and finally to the man himself, President Julio Argentino Roca. As his son Lucas Bridges noted, 'In some respects they were not unlike each other: about the same height; both lean and wiry, with small, eager, almost hungry faces surmounted by broad high foreheads, both neatly trimmed with beards and moustaches.' But Roca had been a soldier and led a campaign of genocide against the natives of northern Patagonia. Bridges had been told the Argentine government would not consider giving a grant of land to a foreign missionary society. He had six children to care for, and a missionary society which did not believe in his vision. He had already resigned from the mission on the strength of his confidence that Roca would understand where the way forward lay, and help the natives adapt. His life lay in Roca's hands.

Roca quizzed Bridges endlessly about the land and his work. It must have seemed that he wanted to find fault. Abruptly he asked, 'How can my government compensate you in some measure for the life of self-sacrifice you have led, and the humanitarian work you have accomplished?'

The land Bridges needed was his. He searched the coast and settled on one bay, before changing his mind. He moved one bay further east, to a place which the Yámana called Ukatush. A word whose meaning even the Reverend Bridges did not manage to untangle. And it was this he called Harberton. Within it he chose a cove the Yámana called Tuwujlumbiwaia, or Black Heron Harbour, to build his house. The first site became Thought Of Bay.

One morning in 1873 a party of Kawéskar canoe Indians came to Thomas Bridges from the wild, western channels. They looked down on the Ushuaian Indians who kept to the sheltered waters, calling them Creek People. Among them was a short stout woman with a wide mouth and few teeth. When she saw Thomas Bridges's children she astounded him by pointing to them and saying, in English, 'Little boy, little girl'. This was Yok'cushlu, who had also been given an English name, Fuegia Basket. Not only could she speak some English, she had been to London and met the King and Queen.

Yok'cushlu remembered the man who had taken her to England to be educated – Captain Fitzroy and his ship, the *Beagle*. Fitzroy aimed to civilize them, and return them to Tierra del Fuego to do the same for their fellow Indians. Instead, they returned almost immediately to their traditional culture. She remembered the young Englishman who had accompanied them on the journey back, Charles Darwin. She recalled the English words for knife, fork and beads, but when someone brought a chair, she squatted down on the floor next to it. She had forgotten what it was for. She had married a Kawéskar man from the west, and now spoke both native languages, but her English was soon exhausted. Thomas Bridges talked to her in the Yámana language, Yahgan.

She related her extraordinary story.

## Three Fuegians

Captain Robert Fitzroy was a high Tory and defender of slavery. He held to a deep and fundamentalist religion and saw things as black or white, believing in the literal truth of the Bible. It is the profoundest irony of the whole Darwin voyage that Fitzroy eagerly expected to gather proof of the historical reality of the biblical flood. Darwin, on the other hand, at twenty-two, was on his third career, having evaded both the Church and medicine. By modern standards, he had not done enough to get into a good university.

Fitzroy had three strange passengers, native Fuegians brought to England on his own initiative, and maintained and educated at his own expense. In a brilliant miniature, Fitzroy's patrician project for these natives encapsulates the failure of understanding, and the impossibility of cohabitation when two cultures collide. His commonest justification for his action was the one he gave the Admiralty: 'I hoped to have seen these people become useful as interpreters, and be the means of establishing a friendly disposition towards Englishmen on the part of their countrymen.' There was also a religious motive. He was concerned for the eternal souls of these people who had never heard God's word; and indeed another of his passengers was Richard Matthews who had volunteered to go with the Fuegians and begin the mission. But the natives were never asked whether they wanted to go to England, for Fitzroy's first motive of all had been to seize them as hostages in reprisal for the theft of one of his boats.

The small whaleboat in question had been exploring the land around Navarin Island, and the crew slept on shore. In the morning their boat was gone. They spent weeks chasing round the native camps, finding a mast, a line and other gear, but never the boat. They seized hostages. A muscular young man of about nineteen was taken. His name was El'leparu. Some women and girls were held on board; however, all but one, a smiling girl of nine or ten, slipped away and swam to the shore. Her name was Yok'cushlu. Later a youth named O'run-del'lico stayed willingly on the *Beagle*, after some sign language and the gift of a pearl button to his father.

As an aristocrat, Fitzroy saw these alien people through his own monocled vision. 'Their rough, coarse and extremely dirty black hair half hides yet heightens a villainous expression of the worst description of savage features.' He went further, calling them 'satires on mankind' – they were not part of his world, but, reflecting as a Christian, he thought they might be made so. It is interesting, although little discussed in all the literature, that the sketches and engravings of Fuegian natives bear little resemblance to the photographs of them taken just a few decades later. The faces are drawn squat, partially negroid, and very black, whereas actually their features and colouring are much more like those of high-cheekboned North American peoples. But Victorian European eyes saw a lower race, and drew them using their own racial vocabulary for debasement.

They skeletonised another native who had been killed. Museums liked to measure man to study him objectively. In London's Natural History Museum lie the relics of seventeen thousand people, a population the size of a market town, collected from all cultures and histories. The anonymous Fuegian is there among them.

Before the *Beagle* sailed out of sight of their home, the captives had begun a journey of change far more profound than their physical one. What went on in the minds of the Yámana we cannot know, but we can perhaps guess a little better than the men on the *Beagle*. The sailors imagined that O'run-del'lico's father sold him for the button, but Lucas Bridges said that selling a child was unthinkable. This was just a gift which took place at the same time, unconnected in the minds of the Yámana.

Nevertheless the youth became Jemmy Button. El'leparu was named after a prominent rock in the vicinity, christened York Minster by Captain Cook. Thus a church became a rock which became a man; the life of St Peter in reverse. Yok'cushlu's new name may have come from the contraption which the crewmen of the stolen boat put together to get back to the *Beagle*. She was called Fuegia Basket. They took one last hostage, a young man seized from a canoe, and called him Boat Memory, a haunting name lapping across the ocean of the years. He was the only one whose real name was not recorded.

In October 1830 they sailed into Falmouth Harbour. The punctilious Fitzroy knew how easily natives fell prey to contagious diseases not known in their own land. He took them to a farmhouse and had them inoculated against smallpox. In spite of this, Boat Memory caught it, was admitted to the Royal Naval Hospital in Plymouth, and died, leaving Fitzroy pained and remorseful. Having hated the way the natives had constantly pilfered his goods, he must now have wondered what he himself had taken from them.

Jemmy, Fuegia and York were taught Christianity and some English, and dressed in English clothes. Jemmy grew plump, and took to admiring himself in the mirror and sulking if his shiny shoes were smirched. Fitzroy noticed how, in accordance with his own theories, education improved their features and made them less savage. At St James's Palace they were presented to King William IV and Queen Adelaide, who gave Fuegia her lace bonnet and a ring. York, already a young man, could not, like his younger companions, step into a whole new set of behaviour. He began to be jealous of attention given to Fuegia. She enjoyed attention so much that on one occasion others had to intervene to prevent her and York having sex.

So the first Fuegians that Darwin saw were Fuegia Basket, then about eleven, York Minster, around twenty one, and Jemmy Button, in his late teens – all freshly laundered and ready to go home and spread civilisation. They were tailored, trimmed, and the two younger ones spoke good English. In their luggage were many unopened gifts from Christian well-wishers, most of which turned out, on arrival, to be tea-sets. Darwin mentions York's intention to marry Fuegia but spares his readers the facts of their ages.

Once again anchored off Wulaia Cove on the west of Navarin Island, they put ashore Richard Matthews and the Fuegians. Matthews married Fuegia and York. Hundreds of Yámana began to arrive but showed little excitement. Darwin saw his first Fuegians in native state and was appalled. Having regarded his three travelling companions sympathetically as individuals, he now reverted to Fitzroy's inability to accept other cultures, different lives, and slipped straight into racial stereotyping. 'I could not have believed how wide was the difference between savage and civilised man. It is greater than between a wild and domesticated animal' and 'It is a common subject of much conjecture what pleasure in life some of the less gifted animals can enjoy: how much more reasonably the same question may be asked with respect to these barbarians.' Only when faced with a particular enigma – the failure of the Fuegians to appreciate how firearms kill at a distance – does he approach an insight which might have helped: 'We can hardly put ourselves in the position of these savages, and understand their actions.'

They sailed away from Wulaia Cove, apprehensive about the four who stayed. The issues were central to nineteenth-century views about the improvement of mankind and his upward progress. Would the civilised homecomers influence the others, or fall back? Would the next generation inherit the civilisation? Fitzroy and Darwin returned a month later and found out.

As they approached Wulaia they saw various items of Matthews's clothes on passing natives and feared the worst. It turned out that Matthews was still alive, but at the end of his tether. Despite pleadings from the returned Fuegians, the rest of the tribe systematically plundered and threatened him. Fitzroy told him to come home and Matthews gladly accepted, dividing his things between Fuegia, York and Jemmy. The rest of the tribe promptly began stealing them. Jemmy watched his own brother take things. 'What fashion call that?' he asked. He looked at his countrymen: 'Damn fools.' In all the time they had known him it was the first time he had ever sworn.

The *Beagle* called by again a year later, in 1834. A canoe approached bearing a thin long-haired man, dressed only in a rag, washing paint from his face. Not until he was close did they recognise him. Said Darwin, 'I never saw so complete and grievous a change.' Jemmy Button came on board, switched over to his English manners and handled a knife and fork with grace. He said that York had spent a lot of time making a large canoe. One morning Jemmy found out why. York had piled all their possessions in it and paddled away with Fuegia.

Twenty years later Captain W. Parker Snow met Jemmy and, taking out Fitzroy's book of the 1830s' *Beagle* voyage, showed him sketches of himself, York and Fuegia in native and civilised condition. Jemmy laughed and looked sad in turn, but he did not ask to return to England with Parker Snow. On 19 February 1883, the year after Darwin died, Thomas Bridges was in the western channels, on London Island, when he caught news of Fuegia, now known as Yok'cushlu again, and went to see her. It was ten years since they had first met, and the little girl had outlived the great names in distant places, but she was now about sixty-two years old, weak and unhappy. Bridges tried to revive in her failing mind the Christian promises which she had heard in smoky London town. The light of Bethlehem shone in his eyes. Impassively she heard him out, then left.


*Tommy Goodall*

The catamaran was passing Gable Island, named after the roof-like patterns in the bleak cliffs. Behind it snuggled Harberton. A silhouette with the unmistakable beak of an ibis flew across the light.

At a time when the Reverend Bridges's finances were at a low ebb, he risked money chartering a schooner, the *Rippling Wave,* to bring 1,500 sheep from the Falklands. The money was partly his own, the rest was a share of the faithful Captain Willis's life savings. They were brought here to the largest of the islands, where they could be contained without the labour and cost of fences. Bridges knew there were many of the massive Fuegian foxes on the island. The farm once packed three hundred skins to London, where, because of their size, they were mistakenly sold cheaply, as wolf-pelts. They were trained in killing by their parents. Bridges once shot a vixen and found a nest of chicks in her mouth which she was taking home for her young to kill. He was naturally very nervous about the damage these could do to his investment.

The sheep spilled on to the shore after their long sea voyage. The big foxes took one look at them, broke cover and ran down to the beach. Panic-stricken they swam the quarter mile to the mainland, to escape. Small groups of rocks in the channel were strewn with exhausted foxes resting.

Animals in isolation develop behaviour devoted only to their past range of experience. Charles Darwin found that the Falkland Islands fox had no experience of being hunted. He obtained his specimen by walking up behind it and tapping it smartly on the head with a geological hammer.

On the mainland the Harberton foxes found more sheep and took time to size them up. It was twelve years before a fox was seen on Gable Island again. By then they had learned they could seize the strongest sheep by the neck and kill them with ease.

Our boat came into a small sheltered bay in the centre of which stood a group of low buildings with corrugated white walls and low-pitched red roofs. Wooden landing stages limped into the still waters of Estancia Bay and a launch was hauled out on the grass above the shore. The ship's horn filled the bay with a mournful bellow. A man of middle age stood alone on the jetty in a blue jersey and bibbed denim overalls. He had a thick mop of dark hair and a greying beard. One arm waved aloft briefly. It was Tommy Goodall, the great-grandson of missionary Thomas Bridges.

The launch reminded me that one of the Bridges sons, Despard, had built his own boats and raced them against visiting crews. He and Lucas made a formidable team. Lucas's fighting weight was more than fourteen stone. But this was at the turn of the century. It was impossible that any of their craft had survived these seas and the climate for so long.

The landscape was intimate and green after the raw majesty of the strait. The long line of the main house had an English-style cottage garden below it, with a lawn and flowering shrubs. There was a gate in the split paling fence. Above it, making a giant wishbone, were the jawbones of a whale. On the wall was a pair of home-made snow-shoes, white plimsolls tied to a wooden frame with a string mesh. Behind the estancia a brown horse with white socks galloped over a flower-sprayed meadow.

I walked the estate with Nicola Forster, a young American woman. 'How did you come to be down here?'

'I moved to Buenos Aires two months ago and I saw an advertisement in the paper to be a general help around the farm.'

'Must have been some advert.'

In the middle of the wood was a replica of the old Yámana huts. They were crude shelters of branches with brushes of beech leaves stuffed into the gaps. It started to rain. We went inside. It was raining in there too. The natives ate great quantities of mussels, and they threw the shells outside the door. The door was moved around as the wind changed, and a circular midden of rubbish grew up. Seeds took root. Eventually Calafate bushes colonised the calcium-rich waste, and provided sweet berries and protection from the wind. These circles lie all along the shores of the straits.

We came back to the estancia and the shearing shed. 'You've got 50,000 acres but I've hardly seen any sheep.'

'They spend most of the year away out there,' she waved a hand at the mountains, 'but they are rounded up and put in that shed to wait for shearing.'

'Why do you need a special building for that?'

'It is practically impossible to shear a wet sheep. Until 1978 the estancia had its own team of shearers, then there was a dispute with

Chile. A lot of the shearers were Chilean and they were all sent back. Since then, like many other estancias, we use a *comparsa*, a group of travelling shearers that make their way through Argentina.' (*Comparsa* is a nice word for any kind of jobbing work – it can also mean a movie extra.) 'The men who come here start in the north of Patagonia at the end of September or the beginning of October and they work their way south. As this is a relatively small estancia, and is as far south as you could possibly get, it's the last one they come to in all Argentina. They don't get here until about February. There are stations for six shearers: Harberton is a small to medium-sized outfit; the biggest, Estancia Maria Behety, has forty. In February the floor is slick with lanolin, and boys collect the fleeces and cut the dirty wool away from the bellies, then it's burnt on the beach. Until 1978 the bales were taken by boat to Ushuaia, but they built a road and lorries are much cheaper!' She lengthened her stride, 'Come in here, this will surprise you.'

We walked across the yard to a long low building with double doors on the end. Nicola had to lift one to creak it open. I peered into the gloom. Filling the shed from wall to wall was a whaleboat. In the dark air above it flew two condors. I ducked. Her laugh rang out in peals. 'They're stuffed!'

I opened the other door to let in more light. She pointed to the nearer one, its wings hanging down sadly. 'Yes, he's seen better days. This was found dead on the road forty years ago.'

'He looks like he started on the wrong drink and kept going.'

'The other was found a few years ago by Tommy's daughter Abby, still alive. It had been hit by a car. They fed it blood and raw meat but it died after a week.'

Its wing span was wider than the boat, which I now looked at properly for the first time. She said, 'This was built by Despard Bridges.'

It was a long slim skiff, clinker built, with a slender handsome swell to its waist, about twenty feet long. Two pairs of metal rowlocks still sat ready. Lucas's brother Despard was the carpenter of the family. Eventually he built a whole ranch house at Viamonte on the Atlantic coast. As a boy he had asked his father's permission for time and materials to make a full-scale boat, instead of just models. His father also needed him for work on the land, and he told Despard it would be a waste of time, boards and nails. 'To undertake such a work, you would need at least a year's apprenticeship under an expert boat-builder.' Despard offered to pay for the copper nails, and to saw his own boards from logs without taking any of the native labourers from their jobs. His father relented. With Lucas, he dug a saw pit and Lucas would handle the bottom end of the heavy pit-saw and Despard the top. Every slim plank of the clinker boat was hand-sawn from logs, planed smooth, steamed and formed to the boat. After several months watching Despard at work his father said, 'I shan't need you again, Sonny, till that boat is finished. It will be a good one and I hope you will let me use it sometimes.' The boat, the *Esperanza,* was the first of many. The largest was an eight-ton lighter capable of carrying a hundred sheep to and from their islands. But the most famous was the one he made immediately before this, the racing boat they used in regattas, modelled on a whale boat. The boys used to race the ratings from the Argentine navy. They never lost. The navy blamed the boat. It was too good.

'It was built in 1901, and last floated in 1960. They found it was in too poor a condition to use again, but no one wants to get rid of it.'

We walked through the whale jaws and up to the house for coffee with Tommy Goodall. The house is the oldest in Tierra del Fuego, and one of the world's first prefabricated houses. It was made of pine, in Harberton, Devon, and sheathed in corrugated iron to lessen the fire risk. It was shipped in numbered pieces, then reassembled in Harberton, Tierra del Fuego.

Bridges chartered the *Shepherdess,* a 360-ton brigantine which he rashly agreed to pay for by the day – fifty shillings. The captain belonged to a fanatical religious sect, which he joined after giving up the bottle and signing the pledge in a flood of tears. Fortunately the sect was very open-minded about milking a good contract and the captain took a leisurely 108 days to saunter to Harberton, Tierra del Fuego, thanking the Lord each dawn that he was two pounds and ten shillings richer. The cargo of bricks, coal and limestone was topped by a young South Devon bull, four Romney Marsh rams, two pigs and two collies. The passengers included two Devon carpenters and Edward Aspinall, the Missionary Society's replacement for Bridges at Ushuaia.

Because of the delay, the winter of 1887 was upon them before they could start work. The perishable goods had to be stored before anything else was done. The crew would not help, the natives quickly became bored with unskilled labour. Bridges, although only forty-three, was already ill and weak. The sons had to shoulder most of the work. They had to use some of the precious prefabricated house timbers to make a provisions store, and the house could not now be built as designed. They sawed their own wood to replace the wood used for the store. For a whole bitter winter they lived in a one-room hut built from corrugated iron and borrowed waste wood. It was a year before the main house was completed.

Tommy is the fourth generation of the Bridges dynasty and is bilingual in English and Spanish. He speaks English quietly with an unplaceable accent.

'Who are your nearest neighbours?'

'The coastguard, sixteen kilometres to the west. My nearest civilian neighbour is my cousin Martin Lawrence, fifty kilometres east. They are also descendants of Thomas Bridges.'

'How often do you leave Tierra del Fuego?'

'Well the last time I took a vacation was 1986, except for a ride on the *Pacific Princess* from Madryn to the Falkland Islands, about a three-day trip last year. Usually we go the States; my wife Natalie's family come from Ohio. We always take our vacations in winter time, and try to make sure it's a vacation in the northern hemisphere.'

'Do you ever feel trapped down here by the business?'

'Occasionally, it has its problems,' his voice slowed, 'but so has life everywhere. It's hard to get spare parts for machinery. But we don't have much machinery – just shearing generators and pick-up trucks. We get parts from Buenos Aires or the USA.' I had meant was he lonely or bored, but he talked about machine parts.

'What are the winters like?'

'1996 was a good winter. In 1969 we had snow on 4 September, it was gone in four days. That was all the winter we had. The worst was 1995. We had snow in late May, and you couldn't even get round on horseback again until September. We lost about eighty-five per cent of the animals.'

'They were killed by the cold?'

'No, not cold, snow. They couldn't get at the ground to feed.'

'Can you weather such losses?'

'It's going to take us ten years of very good winters to get back just to where we were before, without selling anything.' He was calm about this prospect.

Lucas Bridges recalled his father's first conversations with the Yámana Indians. The old men talked of cruel and killing winters of long ago. They said that in their youth the channels had frozen over and made it impossible to launch canoes to catch fish – their main food. The beach was an iron pan of ice covering the mussels and limpets. Guanaco herds starved and froze. So did the Yámana.

Years went by and Bridges saw no weather like this. He dismissed the old men's tales. Then one year it came again, as bad as everything they had said. First October brought a false spring. Trees were in leaf, birds nesting, sheep heavy with lambs. On the sixth came three feet of snow, then the murdering frosts, and a persistent south wind from Antarctica blowing straight into the bay at Harberton. Of four thousand lambs, fewer than four hundred survived. Song birds fled the snow-sodden forests and fell exhausted on the shore. The incoming tide lifted them and bore them away in rafts. Others fled to a cave in the neighbouring Cambaceres Harbour where they died in flocks until they carpeted the whole floor.

We looked out over the placid silent bay. When this was the most remote farm on earth, Lucas Bridges left for a hut in the middle of Selk'nam territory. Every Fuegian tribe feared them as murderers. He had a hut, but he used it for stores and slept outside. After a time he put off going back to the bustle of the farm at Harberton, surrounded by people. When he had to go to Buenos Aires on business, he was scared stiff.

'Lucas Bridges would never have wanted another life, would he?'

Tommy said, 'There was a saying in the family that when someone put glass in the windows of his house, he moved on.'


*Paachek*

Next morning Ushuaia harbour shook under a blustery wind as Greenpeace's *Rainbow Warrior* sailed in to anchor. A creaky veranda took me to the door of the Fuegian Museum. A bell danced on a spring, and a tall stooped young man spilled his limbs down the wooden stair and greeted me with shoulders bobbing forward and his long arm extended for a handshake. 'I'm Jorge.'

In the upstairs study of the little house he showed me a copy of the famous Bridges Yahgan/English dictionary. It is hard to imagine it could have been completed in the lifetime of one person. It runs to 665 pages. If Bridges had not compiled it, the language would have vanished, leaving only the trace of lyrical and descriptive place names: Ushuaia itself (Ush, as in bush, why-a) means inner harbour to the westward. Tushcapalan, the site of Thomas Bridges's house, was the kelp island of the flying logger-head duck.

When the previous missionary sally had met with disaster, two Yámanas, Okoko and his wife Gamela, had been left in the Falklands. Gardiner had planned to teach the natives English. Bridges determined to learn their language. The two men, the two methods, personify the old colonial approach and the new anthropological one. When he and the Reverend Whait Stirling of the Patagonian Missionary Society later went to Tierra del Fuego, the Yámanas approaching in their bark canoes heard, for the first and perhaps the only time in their history, a white man hailing them in their own tongue.

Whatever the physical labours of the day, Thomas Bridges spent the evenings of nearly four decades probing endlessly to test and distil meaning. The dictionary grew, accompanied by bundles of notes and annotations in his clear neat hand. In 1924 Samuel Kirkland Lothrop was sent by the New York Museum of American Indians to spend three months studying the ethnology of the natives. He called the dictionary 'probably the most extensive study of primitive linguistics ever carried out'.

Bridges laboured to connect seemingly unrelated usage of the same word, and to record the imaginative extension of words to other actions or feelings. *Mötŭõ-skulata* – 'to go or come in and ventilate a room by letting the wind blow freely into it and through it' – came also to mean to grow into perfect manhood, to become a thorough man.

*Guta* means to crack, hole, puncture, fracture, and also to catch as a cat or hawk does, a bird or mouse in its claws. From this idea of a cluster of points, it comes to mean to sew up little tears in a canoe.

Some of the definitions read like miniature poems. There is a word *gamoo*, which is about fetching things. *Gama möni* means 'to gamoo standing, to gamoo frequently or always. To be in, as clay or other loose matter, in a cart or box or barrow. To search for anything by torchlight.' There were words of minute scope: *luakuci* means to take or fetch or bring into any canoe or boat, in the mouth of any living thing, as a dog does its pup.

The study of these cultures was a race against time; faster and faster the outside world caught up on them. The very south-east of Tierra del Fuego was inhabited by the Aush, driven into a corner from better land by the fierce and murderous Selk'nam. Lucas Bridges cultivated two of the Aush, Yoyiimmi and Saklhbarra, and began learning their language. He stopped when he found that fewer than sixty people still spoke it.

The last full-blooded Selk'nam, the museum exhibition said, had died recently. He had lost his own name, Paachek being changed to Pacheco, to be easier for Spanish tongues. He appears in photographs as a great bear of a man in a guanaco coat. He spent his life shearing sheep, taming horses and riding. He had to. Selk'nam did not build canoes or fish; most could not swim; they hunted guanaco.

The settlers drove the guanaco away and raised sheep. The Selk'nam were not farmers and did not understand that animals could be owned. When they shot sheep, the settlers shot the hunters.

In those days sheep were wealth. Tierra del Fuego is too far away from world markets to make much money from sheep any more. Now it is oil and tourism. Americans and Canadians and the other great travellers, the Germans, New Zealanders and Australians, come here to see the end of the world. The rich pay up to $45,000 to fly to the South Pole. They go home, they do somewhere else. Unlike in the last century, authentic Indians would now be worth much more than the sheep.

One of the last full-blooded Yámana was Granny Rosa who died in 1983. She was probably the last one of all. Her old age is preserved in a portrait photograph wearing a collared shirt and a cardigan, her face unreadable. Paachek's Selk'nam race suffered most, because they were hunters and it was inevitable that they would come into direct conflict with agriculture. His family and tribe died out. They were shot by bounty hunters at £1 a head, the same rate as for a puma. Payment was made on production of the Indian's ears. There was a bonus payment for the ears of a pregnant woman with those of her foetus. Children were inoculated with diseases and returned to their families. There was a trade in large mastiffs from Europe to hunt them down. They were shot with the latest long-range rifles. The naked Indians shot back, with their bows and arrows. European scientists bought their skulls to measure and classify.

The tribes died from despair, from drink and the quarrels which lay in the bottom of each bottle, but most of all from the easiest of ways to kill strangers: diseases like measles, to which they had no resistance.

At the end Paachek could only speak his native language with one other person, the half-blood Segundo Arteaga, 85 years old. He chose not to speak it much. He spoke little at all and was rude when it suited him, and it suited him often. All he owned were his clothes, his knives, some photographs and a silver straw, called a bombilla, to strain and drink green maté tea.

Paachek died, in silence, in hospital; his handful of relatives started to make their way south to say the old burial service over the last true Selk'nam. But the hospital ordered his immediate burial. There had been two other deaths and the old man's might have got in the way. The other two deceased were both white. His belongings went missing. Some reappeared. The knives and silver bombilla did not.

His name was Paachek, his father was Khooyn, the magician and medicine man, his land was Karukinka, his tribe was Selk'nam. They are all gone.

## Stone Age Perfection

I slipped inside the tall heavy doors of Ushuaia's larger museum, on the old waterfront road. The reception was sombre and churchy. There were beautiful displays of the Stone Age hunting tools of the natives. I would later see captions in Santiago's Pre-Columbian Museum which described a type of bone harpoon as being in use between 4000 BC and AD 1900. The melancholy postscript added, 'The only cultural way of dating when such objects were made is that the more carefully made and fully finished objects were almost certain to be old.' This lack of technological ambition appalled Victorian travellers. Part of Darwin's disgust for the Fuegian natives arose from his realisation that the canoes which came to beg from them, and the clothes and weapons the people had, were unchanged since the first reports 300 years before. It is reminiscent of Livingstone's despair of Africans who lived within sight of the vapour rising from Victoria Falls but had never troubled to go and see what it was.

In front of me was one of the objects which disgusted Darwin and the Victorians because it had not 'evolved' in five hundred years: a Selk'nam bow. It was made only from the dwarf deciduous beech, *Nothofagus pumilio*, which takes hundreds of years to creep to its full size, when its trunk will still be little more than a foot in diameter. The heartwood of the tree is red, but this is inferior. In between it

65

and the bark is the white wood they coveted. A tree straight enough and large enough to extract a bow from was rare. A log over four feet long was cut and then split, then they looked for a length unblemished by knots or red wood. The grip of the bow would be fashioned from the side nearer the heartwood, the newer, more springy wood formed the tips. The bow was extremely complex in section. The initial shaping produced a triangular section with the apex at the back, facing the bow-string. This was then refined to a section the shape of an elongated pear measuring two and a quarter inches front to back at the centre, and an inch and a quarter at the tips. If it was made by an expert bow-maker, or *k-haäl-chin,* the pear-shaped section was not smooth, but composed of twenty-five tiny, flat sides, each tapered equally towards the tips of the bow.

The bow-string was made of twisted sinew from the front part of a guanaco's foreleg. A wet string is useless so they were carried in the same waterproof bladder as the hunter's flint and tinder.

The bowstring could chafe if it was attached directly to the wood of the bow. So sinews from the back of a guanaco were bound tight around the tips to form a softer bed for it. The wood was finished with a white paint made from clay and water. Both string and bow were greased frequently to keep them supple.

The manufacture of the arrowhead and the shaft were equally painstaking. Feathers from the left wings of birds were preferred for the flights, because the slant of the base of the feather's spine differs from wing to wing, and a right-handed man can make a neater job of binding a left wing feather to the shaft. Every detail has a rationale born of experience. A piece of fox fur would be used to hold each arrow shaft against a polishing stone. When it was nearly done, the stone would be put aside and the final polishing done with the fur, now full of very fine dust. While the man worked, he chewed a small piece of black mastic in his mouth, picked up from the beach, which the natives called whale dung, not knowing they were nodules of ship's pitch, washed ashore. It was smeared, with ash, round the bottom of the shaft to give finger grip.

When given a new material they soon found how to use it to greatest advantage. Arrow heads were made from stone until the

Europeans came, then with glass, the sculpting done, as it is with flint, by pressing on it, not by blows. They worked on several at a time, keeping the others in their mouth because they were less brittle when warm. Ideally, they were thinned down to one sixteenth of an inch.

They had not changed because they didn't need to; they were perfect. It was strange that Darwin did not recognise the survival of the fittest design.

Rounding a corner I was face to face with the young Picasso. A second look: the face in the photo was thin, awkward, short-haired, wide-eared. But it wasn't Picasso. In his sulky face much was simply withheld. He was not looking at me, or at posterity. Or even at the cameraman. The young woman from the reception appeared at my side.

'He was prisoner No 90, the Jug-Eared Dwarf.'


*Lighthouse at the End of the World*

Both the Chilean and Argentinian governments believed the only way to settle the south was for convicts to build the infrastructure of a town, and for settlers to follow. They began in Punta Arenas. In 1842 it had six hundred people. Most of them were convicts and the prison officers were soldiers posted there to guard them. In 1851 there were 248 prisoners and families, 144 soldiers, and 44 civilians at liberty. The prison consisted of log huts surrounded by a wooden stockade, and control over the convicts was precarious. When a new governor, Bernardo Philippi, was sent from the north the next year, he found ashes and skeletons, but not a single survivor.

A new prison settlement was formed, but in 1877 there was another uprising, the guards joined in, and convicts were scattered throughout Patagonia. If the men were prepared to run off, Tierra del Fuego was obviously too cosy: somewhere really unpleasant was required. Six years later the Argentinian government founded a new military prison at San Juan de Salvamiento, a bare rock harbour on the cold hell of Staten Island one hundred miles east of

Cape Horn. Men from the vast sunny plains of northern Argentina were brought here to suffer ten feet of rain a year.

The next April they saw six naval ships anchored in the bay of San Juan de Salvamiento. Soldiers trooped ashore with wood, canvas and building materials and took them to a three-hundred-foot cliff on the north of the island. There are twenty-one known shipwrecks at the foot of it. They built a low ten-sided pavilion whose roof came to a central point, topped by a segmented globe with a cross on the top. It looked like a seaside bandstand.

It was finished on 25 May, a lighthouse to guide ships through the Le Maire Channel and round the Horn. Its beam could be seen fifteen miles away. One hundred soldiers remained to assist ship-wrecked sailors, maintain the light, and ensure no other nation came and claimed this splintered corner of oblivion for themselves. Six of them persuaded women to share their lives there.

In 1899 the prison was moved across the island, to the slightly less exposed site of Puerto Cook. There were now fewer than fifty prisoners and the number of guards was reduced before, in 1902, it was abandoned out of pity. The men were to be transferred to a new jail in Ushuaia, which was to merge with the civil prison. However, the appearance of boats meant one thing to the prison-ers, an opportunity to escape. The convicts ran riot and overpow-ered the guards, killing some. They took guns and set off in boats to the mainland. Forty landed on the eastern tip of Tierra del Fuego. The nearest settlement was the Bridges family estancia at Harberton.

In Ushuaia, Governor Esteban de Loque responded by making Lucas Bridges Honorary Commissary of Police, and ordered him to use the Selk'nam to track down the criminals who had arrived in their homeland. Bridges spoke to a party of Selk'nam who were close by. Tininisk the medicine man was their spokesman. He will appear again at the end of this book, a dark figure who appeared in a photograph just before I made a discovery which stunned me.

Tininisk said, 'We have no quarrel with these strangers. They have not killed our friends and relatives, and we care nothing about other people they may have killed in their own country.'

They would only help on the basis that they tracked the men but did not attack them. Nearly all the criminals were recaptured.

Jules Verne's last manuscript was *The Lighthouse at the End of the World*. He never saw the only light between the River Plate and the South Pole, but the idea of this glimmer, at the world's rim, consumed him. The novel was published, after his death, in 1905.

But sailors complained about the light. It reflected off a nearby cliff wall, and captains saw the wrong one, or both. When the soldiers left, it was abandoned. Within twelve years the Panama Canal was open and steam ships were carrying most of the world's trade. The trial of rounding the Horn could be left to a dying breed of men carrying heavy low-value goods, like guano and copper ore. On the unlit decks, they once again peered into the dark and looked and listened for Staten Island. Twenty miles separated it from the east tip of Tierra del Fuego, but in Cape Horn weather navigators might go weeks without sight of sun, moon or stars to fix their position. If they made it, they saved one hundred miles. In the dreadful weather of 1905, when five per cent of all British ships were lost, the four-masted barque *Bidston Hill* had her first sight of Staten Island when the crew looked up to see what was knocking her spars and mast down.

In 1993, another Frenchman, a tousle-haired La Rochelle sailor called André Bonner, read Jules Verne's novel and decided to go to Staten Island and look for the lighthouse. He left his companions on board and jumped into four feet of snow. He lost his way, and wandered. His companions gave him up for dead. Five days later he came back, wild-eyed. 'I found the lighthouse! And I'm going to rebuild it!' He did. The Lighthouse at the End of the World Association has one thousand paying members and forty sponsors, including Electricité de France. Bonner has rebuilt the lighthouse. It serves no purpose whatsoever.

## Ushuaia Jail

The morning was bright and warm, a military band wheeled out of the naval base and up the hill, the music coming fitfully on the stop-go wind. It was a nice day to visit the biggest building in Ushuaia, the jail. It is on the east side of the town next to the naval base, and is now a museum. Like much else in early Ushuaia it was built by the prisoners. They quarried the stones and mixed the clay to make the bricks. They felled the trees to saw the planks and beams.

In town they built the streets and bridges, the telephone services, the fire station, and laid the water supply. They built the stone pier which brought more prisoners down from Buenos Aires. Up went the first printing press, producing the first newspaper. They built the railway along the sea shore which brought the stones and lumber back to site. Along it bounced the little 0-8-0 steam engine maintained by the Bonelli Brothers, who had formerly maintained a money exchange where rich clients were retired beneath the basement's concrete floor, while their funds steamed into the Bonelli account.

For most Argentinians, Ushuaia was Patagonian for jail. In 1919, the priest and anthropologist Martin Gusinde found 1,050 citizens in Ushuaia of whom only 500 were at liberty. They were selected from prisons in the north, re-offenders, violent offenders. The chosen prisoners were told to gather their possessions and stand in a yard where they were body-searched. Then they were marched into a hall where a blacksmith waited with a lump hammer. In a box were iron U shackles, and iron rods half an inch across and fifteen inches long. In another box were fixing pins. The prisoners were brought forward one at a time, still swaggering at being singled out as hard cases. Three blows locked a pin in place. When the convict went to walk forward, his swagger was reduced to a hobble of eight inches.

The prisoners were taken in police trucks to naval transports, where they were stacked like slaves. Martín Chaves was appointed prison guard and had to go south with the prisoners. He recalls, 'The voyage lasted twenty-nine days. One day I went down between decks to see my convicted co-passengers. I'll never forget that shock. Here was a hell. Humidity, heat. In Bahía Blanca they had delayed the sailing to take on board coal, which was put in the hold underneath the deck where the prisoners were held. The coal dust crept through on to the fettered men. It stuck to their faces, they breathed it, they spat it. It made their faces into masks, accentuating the ears.

'Phantoms, spectres, I don't know what I saw. I left that charnel house, saddened to the soul, asking myself if the prison directors, judges, ministers had any idea about that hell-ship.' At Ushuaia they fell blinking and lamed by ulcers on to the half-built pier they would now have to help finish. The prison was laid out in a giant semi-circle. A central tower commanded five radial pavilions, two storeys, three hundred and eighty single cells. At times six hundred men were crammed in there.

Today, it is a museum, in reality, two. The first rooms house a collection about early maps and sailing ships, with models of Magellan's *Trinidad*, the three *Allen Gardiner* mission vessels, the *Beagle* and Scott's *Discovery*. Beyond were the two-storey galleries of the prison cells. I have been in a number of different prison cells. But I do not know what it is like to walk in and not expect to walk out. The materials are usually concrete and steel. Here the doors were solid, not bars, the window too high to see out of without climbing. Climbing was forbidden. Each cell was the same shape and size as my room in Rio Gallegos, and had similar furniture. The concrete floor was broken and damp.

Who came here? Mateo Banks came from an Irish family who settled in Azul, in the province of Buenos Aires. Born on 18 November 1872 he had four brothers and sisters who looked forward to inheriting the livings of the two family estancias, El Trébol and La Buena Suerte.

On 18 April 1922 he staggered into Azul police station. He described how two disgruntled workers had tried to poison his family, then run amok. But the police sniffed Banks, and smelt a rat. They began digging. On 1 April Rettes Pharmacy had sold strychnine to a Mr M. Banks. On 12 April he bought a rifle. A week before the killings his brother Dionisio's signature had been forged on sale certificates for fifteen hundred cattle, in favour of Mateo Banks. One of Mateo's brothers had found out and challenged him.

His excuse was weak and they all suspected him. When a meal tasted bad, they stopped eating, and Mateo began firing.

The trial was over when Banks insisted that he had been shot in the foot defending himself. He held up the boot. There was a bullet hole in the top, another in the sole, but his foot was untouched. He couldn't face the pain. He had shot his empty boot.

Señor Herns was better known as 'The Handsaw' or 'The 'Quarterer'. He was a man who bitterly resented not having studied medicine. When he murdered his business partner, and cut him into four pieces, he did not know that lungs would keep a ribcage afloat. The chest section appeared, bobbing on Lake Palermo. In the prison he worked as a butcher. He could quarter the heads of cattle faster than anyone had ever seen.

Convict No 295 was Bigfoot. He was also Vicente Gianatempo, Claudio Cerdeira, and Erasmo Fabeile. He was a Mexican who entered Ushuaia Jail on 19 April 1919, sent from Tucumán sentenced to twenty-five years for grievous bodily harm and murder. In jail he fought recklessly against discipline. He led the mutinies and took it as a solemn duty to provoke all prison staff without discrimination. He blocked his cell window and lived in darkness. He took his pan of food and spread it on the floor to eat. He lived naked. Towards the end, he spoke to no one. He growled at sentries and barked all night. When originally sentenced, it had counted against him that he had pretended to be insane. He died in 1932.

In 1931 Señor Cernadas was appointed prison director. His assistants Faggioli and Sampedro turned the regime into one of continual terror. When Aníbal del Rié interviewed Faggioli in 1933 he was indiscreet: 'Look, why beat about the bush? Here it's just not possible to keep control without a club. They died quicker, but they were good-for-nothing.' Deaths had previously run at six a year. Now the little burial cart ran once or twice a week across town to the cemetery.

Convicts were punished for the offences of talking in line, arriving late for parade, and answering back. They were held down and beaten with heavy iron bludgeons, or one-pound iron balls tied to steel cables. It was best to lose consciousness, because the beating stopped. If you stayed conscious you were hosed with cold water and left in the snow, or left naked in a cell with bars on the window but no glass. At other times prisoners were starved for days, then their arms and legs were beaten and broken.

Abruptly all prisoners were told that serious faults would be punished by summary shooting. A coffin was always present on a table for the next inmate. Punishments were always carried out at night, when the prison was quiet and the sound of screaming carried through the empty galleries. The prisoner was taken out of his cell at midnight and run between two lines of warders with clubs and bludgeons. There is a picture of prisoner B95 taken on Halloween 1930. He is haggard, shaven-headed, white-bearded. His eyes are round and hopeless. He is thirty years old. The truth about Cernadas's regime gradually leaked out. He was driven out of post, but not punished. Many thought he had done a good job.

On Sundays the prison band went into the town to play. Mario Guido, President of the Chamber of Deputies, wrote, 'They go out to offer the neighbourhood the joy of music. A contradictory and pitiful show. I cannot understand how the people can bear it.' No one talked to the man who played the bass drum. El Petiso Orejudo – The Jug-Eared Dwarf. I stepped into his cell. On the wall was a picture of him tying the special knot he used to strangle children.

## El Petiso Orejudo

In September 1904 in Buenos Aires a seventeen-month-old baby boy, Miguel Depaoli, was abducted. He was found near the foot of an agave cactus. They grow twelve feet high and have sword-shaped spiked leaves. The baby had been beaten and stabbed on the cactus. Miguel was badly hurt but survived.

On 9 September 1908 Zacarías Caviglia walked into the yard of his property at the corner of Victoria and Muñiz. He found a toddler lying half dead in his horse trough. A skinny young man stood by, as if about to help. Caviglia pulled out a two-year-old called Severino González Caló, and brought him round. The helpful teenager gave a fair description of the woman who had brought the boy there.

Six days later at 632 Colombres, Señora Botte came out into the yard to find out why twenty-two-month-old Julio was crying so. She found a youth bent over him, carefully burning his eyelids with a cigarette. He ran off. The attacks continued until the assailant's luck ran out. When he tried to seize eighteen-month-old Ana Nera, a policeman was nearby, and caught a thin uneducated boy with a weak constitution and ears like a wing-nut. The sixteen-year-old Cayetano Santos Godino was arrested at 1970 Urquiza. Someone, police or press, styled him El Petiso Orejudo – The Jug Eared Dwarf.

He explained himself at a press conference. 'Many mornings, after a talking-to from my father and my brothers, I went out looking for work, but if I didn't find any, it was good to kill someone. Then I looked for someone to kill. If I found a youngster I took them somewhere and strangled them.'

He posed for pictures to show the knot he used to strangle children. The loop is in his right hand, the free cord in his left, and he is tightening the short end between his teeth. He looks to his right, as if for confirmation that the choice of knot is appreciated. I am standing in the cell where he spent more than thirty years. In this room was the twisted mind of a boy in the body of a man. He became older but he did not grow. It was the only room where I thought about whether the door could accidentally close behind me.

Other souvenirs of the trial include a photograph of a set of kitchen scales. On them sits a black rock, maybe a piece of coal. It weighs two pounds nine ounces. He used it to hammer a nail into the head of one of the children.

He was too young for the death penalty and there were no proper asylums, so he was sent to Ushuaia. In prison he gradually became less violent. He attended school lessons, but the report on his studies read 'Knowledge acquired in the establishment: none.' He underwent other courses of improvement. On 4 November

1927 an operation was carried out on his ears, to correct the likely source of his evil.

In 1936 he applied for parole. The psychiatrists couldn't make their minds up: 'He is either an imbecile with anti-social tendencies, or a hereditary degenerate and instinctive pervert. His pathological psychology has no cure.'

He wrote regularly to his family although they never replied. At first he worked chopping wood or breaking stone, until the doctor certified him too weak for heavy labour, and he became a cleaner in the prison. Earning 20 centavos a day he saved 800 pesos. He never took money out, remembering that his father and brothers had once ridiculed him for not finding work and earning money.

One day Godino caught the prison cat and began his games. Other inmates heard the cat's screams, lured Godino into a trap and beat him to death. Not a soul attended his prison burial, warder or convict. The gravedigger worked alone.

When I stepped outside the air smelled very sweet.


*Fat Thin*


In Ushuaia's main street a slim woman was sticking strips of paper across the window of the travel agent. I was noticing that Ushuaian women came in two sizes, slim and immense. She was slim. The little banners said Antarctica $1,100. The dollar symbol was a classical design once stamped on pieces of eight. It began as a drawing of a scroll and the Pillars of Hercules, and ended up as a motif. It was in wide use in Central and South America for the peso, long before Thomas Jefferson proposed it for the new US dollar in 1784.

The rate of exchange was a straight one peso to the dollar, which flattered the peso, made Argentina much more expensive than Chile, and drove American tourists wild. I did not have $1,100 spare dollars, but I desperately wanted to get to Antarctica, and I had big new credit card limits in case of emergencies. Antarctica seemed like a good enough emergency. I went in.

'Why is it only $1,100 dollars?' I began.

'It sails tomorrow and there are empty places. This is a special price. It is a $4,000 trip in the best cabins. Sometimes they sell off at $2,500, even $2,000. But I have never seen it this cheap.'

I thought, what is the worst thing I would want to find out about a cut-price trip to the most dangerous ocean in the world: 'It is a Russian ship?'

'Yes.'

I thought of Aeroflot. Then I thought of icebergs.

I imagined the reasons it might be cheap. Each speculation finished with me subsiding pitifully into ice-filled waters while the vodka-sodden captain defended the only life-jacket with a revolver.

I booked it.

I crossed the street to a new pizza place. It was bright and spare and Formica-shiny. The ghost of Edward Hopper sat at the bar. I sat, back to the wall, and watched the customers. Two sisters sat in the window seat. One was thin and librarian-looking with wing-framed spectacles and a navy cardigan over a beige nylon polo-neck. The other was exactly the same height. She looked as if there had once been two more sisters but she had eaten them both, to punish them for being thin.

The thin one took out a baby teddy bear and put it on the table. She took out postcards and wrote on them intently in minute handwriting. They ordered mineral water which they drank in tiny bird sips. The fat one read the menu. From time to time they spoke to each other, mouthing the words but making no sound. No one must hear. After forty minutes the thin one finished writing and picked up the teddy bear between her finger and thumb. She spoke to it and put it in her bag. She took the menu from her sister and read in a low passionate voice: 'Chocolate roulade, Black Forest gâteau, fruit sponge, chocolate-covered cherry cake.' The fat one lit a cigarette. When her sister finished reading they left. Two half-glasses of mineral water trembled on the Formica.

Next night I walked eastwards along the coast road, to try to see the land as the Bridges had seen it, raw, untouched. The houses petered out. The road led out past the naval fuelling pier, where a small grey gunboat was moored. Kelp gulls fed on the shore. Now houses began again. None looked as though it had the courage to stay there. They were home-built, most were ramshackle, all had ill-tempered dogs. Vegetable plots were coaxed towards fruit. Flowers were stabbed into bare earth alongside drives and paths. The beds looked like fresh graves. By the gravel loop where the buses turned stood a low red shack. An old man with broad shallow shoulders worked beneath a naked light bulb dismantling a stove. In two places I could see straight through both planked walls and out the other side. He saw me looking and glared. He called in a grandchild and spoke to a dog. It tore to the end of its lead and launched itself into space at me. I stood still and it fell short, in foaming fury.

The still evening beauty of the Beagle Channel: Navarin Island was sidelit, a stark and simple block of mountain. A forest of beech rose up a thousand feet. The bare top was bathed in a lemon light. I decided that one day I would climb it.

I walked back. Tomorrow, Antarctica.

# 3

# *Antarctica*

*Drake Passage*

The Russian vessel *Akademik Sergey Vavilov* was a business-like white ship about six and a half thousand tons designed for research work in polar waters. The mate Sergey Korolyov took us through lifeboat drill. The lifeboats were orange steel bombs with two hatches like square drain covers to get in and out. I sat inside, in near-darkness, imagining it in use, full, knee to knee, smelling of diesel, vomit and fear: blind, no view out, just the noise, the thin yellow electric lights, and the hand of the ocean on it, clumsy as drunken gods.

The *Vavilov* moved to the bunkering pier and took on oil. The ship's horn bellowed and bounced off the hills. At sunset we sailed east down the black artery of the Beagle Channel, its dark blood bringing the night. 'Beyond the city,' said Aristotle, 'there are only beasts and heroes.' The flanks of the hill darkened, the tousled forest canopy bulged, the great woolly shoulder on a sombre bison. We sailed east, into the waters where Coleridge's poetic albatross was shot, for real. East, into the widening channel and the rising choppy swell. East, into darkness.

The morning brought long rolling swells fifteen feet high. I put on waterproofs from head to foot and went out to the stern rail. Land was well out of sight. Six hundred miles wide, the Drake

Passage is the bottleneck of the Southern Ocean. Low pressure systems march through the landless latitudes of 50° and 60° south like a procession of flagellants, each lashing the back of the one in front. The water beneath them is pulled with them, thirteen miles a day. The break-up of the ancient supercontinent of Gondwanaland sent Antarctica slipping, for forty million years, down through the Roaring Forties and on to the Pole. Since then, nothing but the sullen advance of the ice, in the recent Ice Age, has stood in the way of their fury.

To survive down here different birds have developed quite different strategies. There aren't many ways of succeeding, but the environment is rich, and the rewards huge. Antarctica has only thirty-nine species of bird but they number seventy million individuals. Behind the ship were three which represented one, extreme solution.

The wings of a high-performance glider are eighteen times as long as they are wide. So are the wings of a wandering albatross; the lift they generate is forty times as powerful as their friction through the air. When the wind exceeds eleven miles per hour, they only need to move their wings to steer. One bird tagged on remote Crozet Island travelled nearly 9,500 miles on a single feeding trip of thirty-three days. They can continue feeding at night, flying hundreds of feet above the surface, watching for the squid's pale internal luminescence.

Very few seabirds specialise in gliding; the costs, like the benefits, are extreme. Albatrosses struggle to take off in light winds and often crash-land. They don't like to stand up for long. They are truly at rest on the wind, and they live in a world where the winds seldom stop.

The two southern giant petrels came back and forth, gliding high across the wake, falling low into a trough to one side, and kicking up off the wave high into the air. They are very large brown-and-white birds which are closely related to albatrosses and fly like them. Waves and wind seldom run at the same speed, so even in light winds they can use the air pressure which is created on the face of the water to create lift. A black-browed albatross stayed further back, sometimes advancing parallel with the ship six hundred yards off, vanishing behind the bulk of the big rollers. I followed it forward up the ship to the bow, where it cut across our path and drifted away.

Beneath me were small dark brown birds from the same taxonomic order as the albatross and the giant petrel, but adopting the opposite strategy. They are the shrews and mice of the ocean birds, hyperactive, energetic; it takes three hundred of them to balance the scales with a single albatross. They hunt the surface inches of the sea for krill and tiny squid, up and down the faces of the grey-beard waves, their wings a blur of motion. Sailors saw their feet pattering on the water and called them petrels – after St Peter. There are thought to be about one hundred million Wilson's storm petrels alone, perhaps the most populous bird on the planet. I grew dizzy trying to track them in and out of the waves.

Away to port, a school of Minke whales surfaced. These nine-ton creatures were not hunted until the bigger whales were butchered to the edge of extinction. In the meantime Minkes had prospered on the riches once eaten by monsters ten times their size. But now, restricted hunting is allowed, and they do not linger near the sound of ships' engines. We were sailing at twelve knots. Within minutes they passed us and were gone.

The weather calmed and hourglass dolphins appeared. The long evening took us into the middle of the Drake Passage. In the early hours of the morning the air chilled. We had crossed the Antarctic convergence, the frontier where the icy waters of the Southern Ocean butt up against the warmer waters of the South Atlantic and slide down under them. The Antarctic water is driven down to the blind black depths of the ocean floor and creeps slowly north. At the surface, each ocean is different, but every ocean floor on the planet is the same. The Southern Ocean floods the basement of all the other oceans. Traces can be detected off Labrador, having taken perhaps ten thousand years to reach there. We had crossed the convergence. We were in Antarctica.

Antarctica

*Sergey Vavilov*

The public address was pure M★A★S★H. 'Just – er – a little reminder that the 2:30 lecture on plate tectonics will begin in about fifteen minutes. Right. That's it. See you in fifteen minutes. In the lecture theatre, Deck 6.'

Our expedition leader Bill Davies was a brawny Canadian with a Yul Brunner haircut. He told us, 'You can't really tell Canadians by the way they said aboot instead of aboot. Americans love telling us we say aboot instead of aboot, but we really say aboot.'

I asked Bill what our chances were of making a landing on the continental mainland.

'You simply can't tell till you get there. One season, one visit, the wind blows the ice out of a harbour and it clears early. Another season, nothing doing. No one knows till you get there.'

'Not promising.'

'Listen, soon as we cross the convergence you're in Antarctica. The islands are the real Antarctica too. If you went to Manhattan Island you wouldn't feel you hadn't been to the USA just 'cause it's an island.'

'Good point.'

But I still wanted the mainland.

*Giving Birth to the Ancient Mariner*

The most famous albatross of all was seen and shot in these waters. The story begins over two hundred years ago. On 21 October 1772 a boy was born, the youngest of ten in the house of the vicar and headmaster at Ottery St Mary in Devon. Samuel Taylor Coleridge was large and fat and greedy, and stared at the world with huge grey eyes and his mouth slightly open. He would never breathe easily through his nose.

At three he went to school, devouring books and food in equal measure. When he was eight he fought incessantly with the next youngest, his brother Frank. Their nurse favoured Frank, their

81

mother favoured Samuel. He took his sulks to the tumbled grave-stones across the sunken lane and fought out revenges among the coats of arms, the stone animals. On Ottery's ancient church clock, the golden sun and the silver moon chased a star in orbit.

Samuel read *Robinson Crusoe*, published just sixty years before, in 1719. It was based on a real-life mariner, the argumentative sailing master Alexander Selkirk, who had himself marooned on the Juan Fernández Islands off Chile, because he thought his vessel the *Cinque Ports* unseaworthy.

*Robinson Crusoe* sold hugely and was pirated. Eight years later, in 1727, appeared *Philip Quarll, The English Hermit* telling the fictional adventures of a man 'who was lately found in an Uninhabited Island in the South Sea, near *Mexico*; where he has liv'd fifty Years unknown and remote from humane Assistance, and where he still remains and intends to end his Days.' *Philip Quarll* is now a forgotten book, but as boys both Coleridge and Wordsworth read it again and again. Its author is given as Edward Dorrington but no such person is known, either as a real name or a pseudonym. Quarll harboured one great regret. He made a bow and arrow and shot a beautiful seabird, perhaps a frigate bird. 'I have destroyed that as was certainly meant for Nature's Diversion.' Young Coleridge read with open mouth and rolled his grey eyes over the oceans of words.

Fifteen years passed, and Dorothy Wordsworth's diary for 20 November 1797 recalled a walk with Coleridge a week earlier: 'We had been on another tour: we set out last Monday evening at half past four. The evening was dark and cloudy; we went eight miles, William and Coleridge employing themselves in laying the plan of a ballad.' William Wordsworth later reminisced: 'In the autumn of 1797, he [Coleridge], my sister, and myself, started from Alfoxden pretty late in the afternoon, with a view to visit Linton, and the Valley of Stones near to it; and as our united funds were very small, we agreed to defray the expense of the tour by writing a poem. . . . Accordingly we set off, and proceeded, along the Quantock Hills, towards Watchet; and in the course of this walk was planned the poem of the *Ancient Mariner*, founded on a dream, as Mr Coleridge said, of his friend Mr Cruickshank. Much the greatest part of the story was Mr Coleridge's invention; but certain parts I suggested; for example, some crime was to be committed which should bring upon the Old Navigator, as Coleridge after delighted to call him, the spectral persecution, as a consequence of that crime and his own wanderings. I had been reading Shelvocke's Voyages, a day or two before. While doubling Cape Horn, they frequently saw albatrosses in that latitude . . .'

In 1726, Simon Hatley was an officer on George Shelvocke's voyage around the world, and near Cape Horn the weather began to oppress him. They were heading toward the edge of the known seas of the world. Shelvocke wrote:

> We all observed, that we had not had the sight of one fish of any kind, since we were come to the Southward of the straits of *le Mair*, nor one sea-bird, except a disconsolate black *Albitross,* who accompanied us for several days, hovering about us as if he had lost himself, till Hatley, (my second Captain) observing, in one of his melancholy fits, that this bird was always hovering near us, imagin'd from his colour, that it might be some evil omen. That which, I suppose, induced him the more to encourage his superstition, was the continuous series of contrary tempestuous winds, which had oppress'd us ever since we had got into this sea. But be that as it would, he, after some fruitless attempts, at length, shot the *Albitross,* not doubting (perhaps) that we should have a fair wind after it.

'Suppose,' said Wordsworth, 'you represent him as having killed one of these birds on entering the South Sea, and that the tutelary spirits of these regions take upon them to avenge the crime.'

> At length did cross an Albatross,
> Through the fog it came;
> As if it had been a Christian soul,
> We hailed it in God's name.
>
> It ate the food it ne'er had eat,
> And round and round it flew.
> The ice did split with a thunder-fit;
> The helmsman steered us through!

And a good south wind sprung up behind;
The Albatross did follow,
And every day, for food or play,
Came to the mariners' hollo!

In mist or cloud, on mast or shroud,
It perched for vespers nine;
Whiles all the night, through fog-smoke white,
Glimmered the white Moon-shine.

'God save thee, ancient Mariner!
From the fiends that plague thee thus! –
Why look'st thou so?' – 'With my cross-bow
I shot the Albatross.'

These lines close Part I. From now on, all will be different.

And I had done a hellish thing,
And it would work 'em woe; . . .

There was more than one myth about shooting albatrosses. Some sailors believed it was bad luck to shoot them on the voyage out, and good luck on the voyage home. Others believed it was always bad luck.

One morning at half past six I stood at the stern of the *Vavilov* as we neared the South Shetland Islands. I was alone on deck watching through binoculars a wandering albatross, *Diomedea exulans*, two hundred metres behind us. There is something consistent through time in man's reaction to these birds. The Latin name was given in the eighteenth century by Linnaeus who called their genus *Diomedea*, after a Greek hero at Troy. Diomedes captured the palladium, the sacred image of Athena, goddess of wisdom. His companions were transformed into birds at his death, accompanying his winged soul.

This albatross cut wide arcs to either side, moulding three metres of wing to the slate blue water, then using the air pressure to bounce up, giving itself height which it hoarded, now using the wind to keep effortless pace with our fourteen knots. When it wanted speed it surrendered the height and glided up to the stern rail in a few seconds. On it came. We were the only two living things outside. Now it floated above the side rail and I could see its size, the great hook of its beak.

Herman Melville writes of the albatross in his chapter on the horror of the whiteness of Moby Dick. 'Bethink thee of the albatross: whence come those clouds of spiritual wonderment and pale dread, in which that white phantom sails in all imaginations.'

The wandering albatross becomes whiter and purer in colour as it matures. There was a saying that no whale-boat ever saw a pure white one, but it was near these same waters that Melville, on a whaler, saw his first albatross, grounded, like a medieval king captured in battle.

> It was during a prolonged gale, there, dashed upon the main hatches, I saw a regal feathery thing of unspotted whiteness, and with a hooked Roman bill sublime. Wondrous flutterings and throbbings shook it. Though bodily unharmed, it uttered cries, as some king's ghost in supernatural distress. Through its inexpressible, strange eyes, methought I peeped to secrets which took hold of God. As Abraham before the angels, I bowed myself; the white thing was so white, its wings so wide, and in those for ever exiled waters, I had lost the miserable warping memories of traditions and of towns. Long I gazed on that prodigy of plumage. I cannot tell, can only hint, the things that darted through me then.

The bird floated closer to me and drifted above the deck of the *Sergey Vavilov*. I pocketed the binoculars; it was now too close to need them. From five metres away it looked at me for some time, ghosting forward and back. Its large eyes moved over my body with intelligence and curiosity. They live as long as elephants, sixty to eighty years. I felt fear. Its wings reached out either side of me, the head I could scarcely have held between two hands.

Bruce Chatwin made much of choosing which albatross Hatley might have shot. The bird whose range suits the position best is the light-mantled sooty albatross, a beautiful bird, subtly coloured in dusky greys, which I saw join us from the mist as we crossed the convergence of the Atlantic and the Antarctic waters and sailed on towards the South Shetlands. The description of a 'disconsolate black albatross' gives further reason for thinking that the bird shot in the version Coleridge knew was *Phoebetria palpebrata antarctica*. It is also, Chatwin thinks, much smaller and more portable as neck-wear.

He misses the point. The image had been with Coleridge since childhood. A child identifies profoundly with innocence treated cruelly, feeling the hurt as if it were inflicted on them. He had read Quarll and thought long about this 50-year recluse, who was damned in his own mind for one sad day, shooting his home-made arrow through the breast of a great sea drifter like the frigate bird. When, fifteen or so years later, Wordsworth suggested the use of Shelvocke's story, Coleridge seized an idea which already had a home in his imagination. Quarll was a man innocent enough to kill, guilty enough to pay. Coleridge certainly tracked down the original Shelvocke account and read it for himself. He uses further details in the poem which appear in no other account. When John Livingstone Lowes had finished his draft analysis of this part of the poem he wrote to Joseph Conrad, who replied

> Dear old Coleridge invented the Albatross of that tale. There can be no doubt of that. A very fine piece of work – about as fine as anything of that kind can be – and so authentic in detail that it might have been told by a sailor of a sombre and poetical genius in the invention of the phantastic.

I think a sailor would also have given the Ancient Mariner's ship a name. Conrad did not mean Coleridge conjured the bird from nowhere; he meant he applied it to his own purpose. At the time he wrote the *Rime,* the longest sea voyage he had made was to cross the River Severn at Aust, a journey you can now complete in sixty seconds by driving over the old Severn bridge at Chepstow. Coleridge was not David Attenborough; he wanted a symbol. For instance, Coleridge's description of the bird's stay on the Ancient Mariner's ship is quite fanciful.

The magical bird perched on the ship for 'vespers nine'. The big albatrosses are among the largest flying birds; they weigh twenty five pounds. Apart from being the size of the biggest turkey in the shop, albatrosses have webbed feet. They fell off rigging, if they ever tried to perch on it at all. Sailors used to catch goonys and other big seabirds for food by letting them alight on the deck and leaving them there for ten or fifteen minutes. Goony was an English dialect word meaning simpleton. Unused to the motion of boats, they became seasick and the sailors could walk up and throw them into the pot. So it would have gone with the albatross.

Significantly, the keynote of Coleridge's story is not vengeance, such as the Hatley episode might have suggested, but remorse, like that which gnawed at the solitary Quarll for half a century. The Ancient Mariner's redemption is secured in the moment that he, in a fit of melancholic reverie, blesses the water snakes simply because they are 'happy living things!' around his ship of death.

Coleridge saw that modern epics could rely on real journeys which had reshaped the mind of man. These could replace classical myths as the skeleton of literature and liberate it from repeating classical models, while still providing equivalent weight and structure. Voyages were the documentaries of the day, and had common currency among the educated. Knowledge of science, anthropology and psychology could underpin drama based on new self-knowledge, and mankind's expanding awareness, his wonder at the world. It was an insight which Coleridge himself valued as highly as any he had: that no other animal, only man, had a capacity for wonder.

*The Ancient Mariner's* lack of classical structure or references makes it very immediate to modern readers: most of us have no education in the classics. Coleridge employed two animal images: the killing of the albatross, for sin, and the blessing of the water snakes, for redemption. He used them in an utterly modern way to affirm that all life is part of one physical and moral system, a kind of moral ecology, before the word ecology was even coined. But he could not take his Age with him. Coleridge's educated contemporaries, including friends like Wordsworth and Southey who should have known better, saw no classical foundations and thought the structure lacked real substance. The poem was too radical to be widely understood by his contemporaries, and was not richly appreciated until the era of psychoanalysis. His own publisher, Cottle, griped:

'How much it is to be deplored, that one whose views were so enlarged as those of Mr Coleridge, and his conception so Miltonic, should have been satisfied with theorising merely; that he did not, like his great Proto-type, concentrate all his energies, so as to produce one august poetical work, which should become the glory of his country.' None of them knew.

I went on the rear deck with the *Sergey Vavilov's* ornithologist, Californian Stephen Spittler, veteran of two seasons in the Southern Ocean. Out of the worst of the weather, we watched for nearly an hour. Sometimes obvious questions get interesting answers. 'We throw nothing overboard, so why do they follow the ship so long?'

'The boat stirs things up. Turbulence brings creatures nearer the surface where they are more easily seen. It may be that birds like albatrosses used to follow the whales for the same reason they now follow clean boats, the turbulence. Before man hunted them, whales moved round the globe in huge schools churning up all kinds, particularly when feeding. You've seen the humpbacks feeding co-operatively, encircling shoals of fish and blowing streams of bubbles to funnel them together. There would have been rich pickings for birds. By comparison, a ship is a poor substitute.'

'Did they follow the early sailing ships?'

'It would appear so; some of the very early accounts describe being followed. Given there were no boats in the southern oceans for years at a time, that suggests the birds followed instinctively, there was no chance to learn by trial and error. If you're a sixteenth-century seabird seeing your first tubby sixteenth-century sailing ship, thinking it's a new kind of whale isn't such a dumb idea.'

The sea was rising and growing colder. Long waves twenty-five-feet high were bearing down on the stern of the ship which rose at the last minute just as it seemed the wave would break over the deck. Twice we went running for something to hold on to but the ship stayed on top of the advancing wave.

Conrad wrote: 'The most amazing wonder of the deep is its unfathomable cruelty.' Squalls lashed the spray over us and the cold got through my four layers of clothing. Suddenly the albatross fell from the sky and crumpled on to the sea. It was a meeting of two worlds – the hard beak of the feathered spirit meeting the alien beauty of a squid. The beak rose with the great-eyed killer of the southern waters writhing in its grasp. Its beak sliced and it would return five hundred miles to a single downy chick. Quickly it fell astern, and when it swallowed the cold live gelatine, the white marvel was already lost in the curtain of grey behind.


## A True Case

I kept my eyes trained far out in the grey. Before me were the colourless foredeck, the sea, sky and tabular icebergs big enough to land a 747. As we came closer, toothpaste blue shone in the clefts.

A plump American man nuzzled alongside. 'I have a friend, a spiritual adviser and guide. She was arrested and put in Holloway for no reason.' His hair was wispy and confined to the sides of his head. 'It was the second biggest LSD haul in British history. I visited her with an ex-inmate. She was just staying in a house where a man renting a room received a whole load of stuff. Of course when she knew, she left and the dealer helped her to the taxi carrying her suitcase. The police surveillance saw all this and arrested her. Of course if you are arrested in the US they have to bring you to trial in ninety days, but in England – are you from England? – well, the only fingerprint they had was on a piece of paper and she had to move this piece of paper to go to the john. That was all the evidence they had. They had no evidence at all.

'She had legal aid. Five of us gave evidence. The judges wore wigs. Shit! It's like the Middle Ages. Do you have shit! Barristers can't talk to witnesses, so if your solicitor is an idiot. . . .

'I work in the justice system back home as an expert witness – here's my card – and the judge took notice of my evidence. When summing up he said "Remember Mr Steenberg said this, remember Mr Steenberg said that."'

His waistcoat was woolly. He wore steel-rimmed glasses and sat in a low chair while I leaned on a rail on Captain Beluga's bridge.

One hundred feet above the water, the windows had rubber wiper blades to move the water when the Southern Ocean blew up.

Without looking at it, I held his card in my closed fist, and gently shut my eyes. 'Are you from California?'

'Hey! Yes I am! Are you psychic too?'

## The Last Continent

John Mandeville, the fourteenth-century author of a fanciful book of travels, knew the northern polar area was named Arctic after the Greek word ἀρκτικος for the constellation of the bear. Coining a name, the opposite pole must be the counter-bear, or Antarctic. This was the first use of the word.

Most maps of the world reduce Antarctica to a ribbon of white at the foot of the page, as vague and insubstantial as the old Terra Australis Incognita, but the land and sea below the Antarctic convergence cover one eleventh of the planet. About half the permanent surface has land below it but only 2.5 per cent shows above snow and ice whose average depth is well over one mile. It has the highest average altitude of any continent. It is also new.

The earth originally had no polar ice. In the last 150 million years, since the middle of the dinosaur era, the average temperature of the earth has dropped from 30°C to 10°C. During that time, the old supercontinent of Gondwanaland has drifted into the pattern of the modern continents. In the last 50 million years, a final parting of it cleft Australia, and the footloose piece settled over the South Pole, butting up against a much younger block of land detached from the southern tail of the Americas.

This badly hampered the ability of big ocean currents to move heat round the globe and smoothe out differences in temperature. The North Pole became practically an inland sea, ponding up cold water. Now that there was land at the South Pole, snow and ice could be trapped instead of blowing north and melting. Once snow began to settle, it reflected more and more heat back into space. A freezing engine was installed in the world's basement, and the temperature differences between the hot and cold parts of the world grew wider. By 4 million years ago Antarctic glaciers reached the sea, and all over the planet the ice and cold advanced.

Beneath all this lie footprints of life in tropical Gondwanaland, memory traced in sand. Salamanders and lizards left their impressions in mud, a few quick steps preserved for us for ever from the antique light of a forgotten afternoon. In 1981 the 40 million-year-old jaw of a marsupial was found on an island in the ice of the Weddell Sea. It was an opossum which lived when Australia and Antarctica lay side by side in the temperate southern seas.

In the afternoon of our third day at sea the weather became clearer and calmer. The southern horizon lightened, suggesting ice just beyond. Soon a tabular iceberg came into view. The sides were ice cliffs, a hundred and fifty, maybe two hundred feet high, pieces broken away from the vast ice shelves on continental Antarctica. This one had come from the Weddell Sea, from 1,000-foot-thick shelves. In a few hours we could see the first land, the bleak north coast of King George Island in the South Shetlands.

This group of islands was discovered by an English merchant-man, William Smith, who was blown off course. The log of the *Williams* for 19 February 1819 laconically records 'land bearing from SSE to SE by E, distance about ten miles'. Eerily, he found his wasn't the first ship to reach here. On the north side of Livingston Island, just to the north of Deception Island, he found the remains of the *Sant' Elmo*, a Spanish galleon abandoned, dismasted, at 62°S in the Drake Passage. Smith was unsettled by the wreck, with no sign of bodies. He was the last man in history to discover a continent, but he found a ghost ship waiting for him there. He had the stock of its anchor made into a coffin. When he went home he found his partners were bankrupt. He died a pauper.

King George Island appeared as a low range of hills rising straight from the water. In just a few places black rock showed through. We turned south west and came round into Admiralty Bay. Because the island is easy to service it is busy with research stations. Brazil's base is easy to spot – it has a football pitch. We anchored off Point Thomas, and Zodiacs, fast inflatables with outboard engines, took us through the brash ice to the Polish station, Arctowski, named after their countryman Henryk Arctowski, who was a member of Adrien de Gerlache's *Belgica* expedition.

A spit of grey shingle ran out to a dark rock. I bumped ashore next to it beneath a statue of the Virgin, in a rock niche. I stepped on to Antarctic soil.

On the beach to the right stood a large yellow cabin on stilts. We walked away left along a beach of round stones. Out of the shallows plopped little Adelie penguins, their flippers out after a swim. At some point everyone looks at a bird or animal and asks 'Don't they get cold?' Stephen Spittler had the best answer: 'If they were cold, they'd be dead.' Their insulation is so good that when they have caught all the food they need and come out of the water, they have to hold out their flippers to cool down.

In the stones was a pair of feet from an Adelie, attached only to bare leg bones. The toes were pink and lay close together, hiding the webbing. The nails were long black ovals, a hank of feathers remained on the ankle. It looked disturbingly like an old crone's hands reaching from fur cuffs. Adelies are hunted by leopard seals who shake them hard enough to skin them. This had probably been a victim.

At the far end of the beach female elephant seals were wallowing in a mud patch between the rocks. They come ashore pregnant in spring, give birth and lose up to 650 pounds of fat, weaning their pups and fasting. A group of ten lay close together, occasionally opening a red eye, or yawning. Patches of old brown fur were moulting, exposing a new greyer coat. A young male, too small to have bred this year, lolled in the shallows. Their oil was regarded as equal to whale oil and they suffered terrible losses. They now prosper on most Antarctic and subAntarctic islands.

I went back to the other beach and saw a tall man walking, hands clasped behind his back, cheeks and nose raw in the circle of his tightly drawn jacket hood. I knew Bernard Stonehouse by reputation. He was spending his fiftieth summer of research in the Antarctic. We introduced ourselves. He took us through his research programme. 'I'm working on tourism and human impact, with the Poles; it's easier than working with the Brits. I'm based with the Scott Polar Research Institute at Cambridge, we're an independent unit and this sometimes makes for difficulties with the Foreign Office. The Poles are very interested in tourism. They've always been very hospitable; Arctowski is the one station that never turns down a tourist ship. They say, these are the public, these are the taxpayers, paying for scientific research in Antarctica. They have a right to come here and be treated well – a view I share very strongly.

'I've been helping the Poles to develop their station to include a tourist centre where you can get information about what science is going on down here. That's the one thing every tourist I've spoken to says is missing. At the same time I am able to do my own research on the scientific impact of people on the animals.'

'And the results?'

'We've had a seven-year programme and we've been testing some of the assumptions, often voiced, about what happens when people go ashore in Antarctica –

'They trample the vegetation – well no, they don't, they don't normally go anywhere near vegetation.

'They frighten the animals – no, they don't. The animals are usually very interested in what's going on.

'They behave badly – no, they don't, they behave extremely well.'

'Really?'

'Yes, on the whole they behave far better than the scientists and their support staff. The tourist industry began with the idea that the visitors were intelligent people who realise they are going into a wilderness area and want to keep it intact. They get lectures and briefings on the way down. This helps sell tickets to the right kind of people. Now you've never had that strength of principle applying to scientific stations. It does now, since a protocol was added to the Antarctic Treaty, but tourism took the initiative long before there was any Antarctic Treaty.

'You go round Antarctica and see where the mess is, see the piles of forty-gallon drums, and you see the abandoned navigation beacons, and you see the abandoned huts, the rubbish tips. Tourists haven't contributed one thing to that.'

'Why didn't scientists want to set an example?'

'It's never paid the scientific industry to do so in the way it paid the tourist industry. The big American base at McMurdo Station was an absolute mess, everybody said so, even the Americans. In 1968 the first tourists went there, rich, very influential Americans, and they were appalled. I'm told they stormed up to the Admiral's cabin and said, "Look, we haven't come here, all this way, and spent all this money, just to see rubbish dumps. Get 'em cleared up."'

'People had complained before, but the answer came back very pat: "I've got all the dollars in the world to take stuff down to Antarctica but I don't have a single dime to take anything out." These visitors were VIPs, they mattered, and the clearing-up began.'

'So before this, empty planes flew back north?'

'Empty planes, empty ships. It takes time to put things in ships. If that time wasn't paid for in the contract – and it wasn't – they didn't do it. Pilots going to the South Pole don't even stop the engines. You off-load, turn round and fly out as soon as you can.'

Bernard stooped twice in quick succession, cupping a small green flower from the wind. 'Antarctic pink and Antarctic hair grass. In a few yards you've seen the only two flowering plants which grow in the whole continent. They grow only in the maritime Antarctic. Devon Island in the Arctic – just one island – has a hundred kinds of ferns and flowering plants, including shrubs and trees. Antarctica has just two. The weather here is so extreme it's constantly removing the materials for life.'

In the stones to our right lay the skull of a great baleen whale. The shore and headland were free of snow. Thin green colouring showed where plants were scraping a living, growing lush in the rare sheltered pockets. We went into the research station, taking off our boots. The scientists, nearly all male, had just arrived, relieving a group who had spent a whole year, overwintering. It was a wood-lined bachelor-pad. Most men had, or were starting, beards. Walrus moustaches flourished. Books lined the walls, adding five more inches of insulation. Small musical instruments, a squeezebox, a mandolin, lay on chairs. There was a games box, as in a holiday cottage. People seemed to be everywhere. I asked Bernard 'What's it like trying to cope with the mixture of crowding inside the base, and total isolation outside?'

'Well, I never overwintered in any research station where there were no dogs. That was like having another hundred people round the place. Dogs are banned now, as an alien species. I can't imagine that even the friendliest tractor is quite the same. No one has ever found a good way of choosing the kind of people who will cope with the conditions and get on with one another.'

'Didn't one Russian axe another one to death over a game of chess?'

'So they tell me. When it became a mass operation down here, the psychologists were called in to have a say on selection. The results were no better than just having three or four chaps in an office saying "He'll do. No I didn't like the look of him. Yes, let's have him – no I didn't like his face." Of course many camps have women now, the Australians were the first, surprisingly. On the whole I think it's worked very well. Women are far more civilised.'

## Whiteout

I asked Bernard 'When did you first come down here?'

'In 1946. I was a meteorologist and second pilot. The Americans pulled out of the Peninsula in 1940–41 when the US entered the war. The Argentines went down there putting up signs, which annoyed the Brits who maintained claims based on their administration of whaling down there. So a British expedition went down there in 1943–44, Operation Tabarin. Port Lockroy was Base A, Deception Island was Base B, and so on.

'Things were pretty basic. One time we had flown east across the Peninsula and were trying to get home. We were staggering back into bad weather, and had got over the central ridge. The carburettor was freezing up, and because of headwinds we were running out of fuel. We had to land in a whiteout. We landed on the sea ice but hit a bit of brash ice we couldn't see, and turned the whole thing over. It was a very light plane, a little Auster Autocrat, far too light for the job really. We were lucky.'

'Had you been able to radio ahead to say you were in trouble?'

'No.' He laughed quietly. 'The radio had packed up early on. It was steam radio, a long time ago. You take good communication for granted now. In the 1940s you could hardly rely on radio at all. If your radio was reliable it was too heavy to cart around on a sled. We had these hand-cranked things they'd invented towards the end of the war.

'We had got ourselves into a pretty difficult position. We were about eighty miles from the station. We had one very small tent and hardly any food. We started walking on sea ice which was probably moving faster than we were. We didn't know if we were going to be ten or twenty days, so we planned for twenty. You feel tired, constantly tired. It becomes difficult to concentrate. Your body is whispering, Look, sit down, rest, go to sleep. You are using energy far faster than you are replacing it, so just camp down.'

'If you are caught out now, it's not a bad strategy. Stick at the site. Where we were, that wasn't a possibility. We wouldn't have been found. So, like Scott and his crowd, we had to keep moving. You become irritable, unable to use your faculties properly. I think that's probably what gets most people. It all depends on when you start to feel it's not really worth going on. I take my hat off to the people who did, in the old days, just soldier on, putting one foot in front of the other. You realise what an effort of will that is.

'The principle of survival is that you have to be pretty well convinced that it's worthwhile. I remember thinking at one stage, well this is bloody silly. I'm only twenty. I'm not giving up, I have a life to live. There's all kinds of things I haven't done — that kind of thing, which sounds a bit trite, but was very important at the time. That lasts you for a time, then you have a rest. You get yourself in that frame of mind again. If you can't do that, if you don't have that sense of conviction, then I don't know what you do. You may rely on the Good Lord, you may rely on luck, you may rely on whatever people rely on. Somehow, at that age, I got this idea that I had to rely on myself.'

'Did you talk to each other much?'

'No. Hardly exchanged a word. We didn't have that sort of energy. In the morning we'd say, Which way are we heading? And later, Are we keeping on the right track? and we'd look back and see we were making a curve. We were not going along making jolly conversation to keep each other going. All three of us had the same point of view, that you saved as much energy as you could. One of us was having a harder time of it than the others because he wasn't quite as well dressed. The other two kept an eye on him, but it wasn't a matter of chivvying him or anything. If he was beginning to lag a bit you waited for him and then walked with him and that got him moving again. None of us was in the frame of mind where we had to sing "Onward Christian Soldiers" to keep going.'

'Did you ever feel you were distancing yourself from the others, knowing how personal the ability to survive was? When Scott was retreating, a callousness appeared towards a member of the team once they saw he would be the next to fall and die.'

'No, but that's an extreme stage. We were not near that extremity – at least I don't think we were. I am perfectly certain you could get into that frame of mind and it would be very sensible to do so. You'd have to work out what you were going to do, when someone, one member of the team was breaking down irrevocably. You can spend a certain amount of energy chivvying him along, but there must come a time when you say that's it. If we spend more time or care on this one, he's going to prejudice the team, and then you would have to make up your mind.'

'How many days were you walking?'

'Only about nine.'


*Deception Island*


The *Sergey Vavilov* turned out of Admiralty Bay and slid south west down the south side of King George Island. Late in the evening

I went up on deck as we were turning into Maxwell Bay to drop off stores for the Uruguayan Artigas base. One of our Zodiacs cut a wake to a soft necklace of yellow lights. It went quiet. Two Russian crewmen came up from the sauna and jumped into the little swimming pool, newly filled from the icy sea.

Three humpback whales must have swum past the *Vavilov* and into the natural harbour. I saw the tails first. In the middle of the bay, encircled by a low arena of hills, they stopped to play, crashing their flukes down. At midnight when just the rags of daylight remained, they left the bay and the *Vavilov* turned and followed them south into the last darkness.

The morning was grey with a stiff breeze. Off our starboard were the grim cliffs of Deception Island. We were below Bailey Head and a colony of hundreds of thousands of chinstrap penguins. The ship began to swing right, heading directly at the cliffs. On our left, on Ravn Rock, a twist of girders were the last remains of the whaler *Southern Hunter*, wrecked here on midsummer's day 1956. It had turned the same colour as the rocks; Antarctica was already absorbing it. On the right were the six-hundred-foot cliffs of Cathedral Crags. Slowly, in front of us, a cleft in the rock opened out, a gap between cliffs just six hundred yards wide, a navigable channel less than two hundred yards wide. We were sailing into a volcano eight miles across.

Deception behaves like an island created by a magician; boats have come here and found icebergs blocking the entrance. They have sailed in and had icebergs lock the door behind them. They have sailed into this channel, Neptune's Bellows, and been met with a wall of water coming towards them as earthquakes dropped or raised the harbour floor.

Men came here to slaughter their way through the natural riches. The waters teemed with so much life that the first ships found it hard to row their boats as the oars struck the backs of seals and whales. The very air was foul with the stench of whales blowing. They killed the seals on land. Men killed them in the breeding season, and killed all the animals they could handle. They did not kill pups, but the pups were not weaned so they starved anyway. Some of the animals' natural behaviour told against them. Male fur seals would stop their harem of females escaping back into the sea. So the sealers would blind a male in one eye, and leave him alive to keep on shore the females on his sighted side. Meanwhile they butchered the others on his blind side. The sex-starved sealers thought it especially funny how males would still mate with freshly killed females.

In the summer of 1820–1 British and American crews fought a battle with blade and club to dispute the right to take seals. The next year it mattered less. The seals were already rare. Six years after the discovery of the continent, the Antarctic fur seal was nearly extinct. As one site was exhausted, the captain would climb to the highest point of land and look for the next islands. In 1820 a group of Connecticut sealers were ready to move on from their anchor near Livingston Island in the South Shetlands. Captain Pendleton sent nineteen-year-old Nathaniel Palmer to look for a better harbour and new sealing beaches. It proved a short hop to Deception Island and next day his boat, the *Hero*, nosed into the concealed channel and, listening to the wind sighing through the rocks, he named it Neptune's Bellows. When he climbed the hill to look for new sealing grounds, and collect bird eggs for food, he gazed to the south east and saw new land, perhaps, and – the arguments go on – the first sight of the Antarctic mainland, the last continent.

The *Vavilov* sailed through the Bellows and into a harbour only slightly smaller than Rio de Janeiro. We bore to starboard, anchoring off Whaler's Bay. The island is a volcano whose centre has dropped. The sea flooded in, and the land that is left forms a stone horseshoe bent until it has nearly closed. In light snow we went ashore. The island is warm enough to make its own weather, cloudy and sunless. Hot vents still provide warm pockets where green vegetation prises a toehold. The vents smoke faster when air pressure falls, warning of advancing storms. The rocks are so rich in iron that departing ships often found their compasses were deranged. It may also interfere with the human body's natural magnetism. Long-term residents are said to suffer from a nervous disease and become incapable of being at ease.

Whaler's Bay was the only area not mostly snow-covered. The

beach was fine, dark grey volcanic gravel with a matt surface that swallowed light. The shore was dominated by the rusting remains of the whaling factory. Domed steel fat-boilers thirty foot high sprouted a topknot of valves and pipes. One chimney stood, another had fallen. Oil storage tanks like gasholders surrounded them. One was canted at an angle and patched with graffiti. Steam hung eerily over the shallows, where volcanically heated water from beneath the iron permafrost flows to the surface, usually at a balmy 13°C. This was much hotter. I bent to warm my hands in the rivulets running down the beach, and found they were too hot to keep my hands in. Another eruption seemed to be brewing.

The Bransfield Strait between here and the Antarctic mainland has the best waters for krill in the southern hemisphere and, following them, the richest concentrations of big whales. The whalers would tow the carcasses into the Deception's harbour and anchor. In the nineteenth and early twentieth centuries, the market was for oil, so only the whale's blubber was used. Flensers moored a small boat alongside the body and cut away the blubber, then it was hauled into the ship to be boiled down into oil. This was the way Herman Melville would have known in the 1840s. The rest of the leviathan was pushed out into the bay, swollen with the gases of corruption. The wind blew them to shore. If there was no wind they rotted where they lay. A young man called Thomas Bagshawe described this harbour in 1921.

> The carcasses and other refuse were allowed to float around them. The stench from the masses of intestines, stomachs and livers was too revolting to be described, and the water around the ships was discoloured with the oil and blood. The shore in the neighbourhood was hidden by an accumulation of meat and bones in various stages of putrefaction. Some of the flesh was a relic from previous seasons, so that, when getting ashore from a boat, one was liable to find oneself wallowing in old whale flesh instead of stepping upon solid ground.

Bonuses to the men were paid per whale, not per barrel, so quick, crude, wasteful flensing paid better. In 1929 shore factories were built and the Hektor Station constructed a slipway to haul out carcasses for thorough flensing and efficient processing. The British officials who administered the island during the whaling heyday, from 1910 to 1931, gave the Hektor company the right to all abandoned carcasses in an attempt to reduce the waste. It brought improvement in two ways. Not only did Hektor mop up what others left, but its competitors now flensed more thoroughly to deny the company easy money.

The head of the beach is a springline where each company built a little wooden hut or shelter over its own freshwater spring. You can still see them. A few miles north, at the head of the bay, the water is heated to bath temperature. Occasionally it hots up and boils the feeding krill, attracting clouds of Dominican gulls for their first cooked meal, and forcing starfish out of the water and on to the beach.

A steel winch lay in the ash. A small tractor called a Clectrac, with milled steel wheels like those on traction engines, was embedded up to the seat, a fossil of the last big eruptions in the 1960s. A single Weddell seal lay in the centre of the beach and yawned pink when I passed. A few tilted crosses marked the old cemetery, overcome by hot mudflows in 1969. These lonely corpses suffered first burial, then cremation, and now the weather is slowly uncovering the graves again.

At the head of Whaler's Bay I walked round the corner of a large hangar and found an orange wingless plane (the wings were inside). It was an old British Antarctic Survey De Havilland Beaver brought out in boxes and assembled on the beach. The first Antarctic flight was made from here in 1928, just one year after Lindbergh's solo flight of the Atlantic. The newspaper monster William Randolph Hearst sponsored Hubert Wilkins and co-pilot Carl Eielson to fly a Lockheed Vega. There is a photograph taken in front of a tough-looking monoplane standing next to an Austin Seven. The Austin and the Clectrac were brought in to smooth out an ash runway. Wilkins flew south to Mount Jackson. Hearst got his story.

I turned and walked back. The south end of the beach was strewn with whalebones and barrels, half buried and burst open like daisies. The cold and the wind abraded bone and wood to a near identical grey, so the long rectangle of unused barrel staves looked like the skeleton of a wooden leviathan awaiting resurrection. Small boats, fully decked, which used to lighter the barrels full of whale oil from shore to ship, made beautiful pointed ellipses in the sand.

I began a long climb up the hill to look out over the Bransfield Strait to Antarctica, from the very spot where Nathaniel Palmer took what may have been the first look at the mainland of the continent.

## Neptune's Window

The ridge above was the rim of the blown-out volcano. The dramatic bite out of it gave views towards the mainland. That was where I had arranged to meet Brian Shoemaker. Brian was a retired US Navy pilot lecturing on the *Vavilov*. He flew the first full aerial survey of the whole of Antarctica. The plane sent down two signals at different wavelengths. One reflected back off ice, the other passed through ice but bounced off rock. Flying two sets of lines, the second at right angles to the first, they put together the first three-dimensional picture of both the land and the ice. He is inclined to describe the work as boring flying, but the commonest cause of death in Antarctica is plane crashes.

We perched on a ledge above six-hundred-foot cliffs. 'Nathaniel Palmer was told by his boss to come down and scout out the territory to the south of Livingston Island for new seal colonies. He came round the west end of Livingston Island and went north east, and past Hannah Point, named after a Liverpool sealer *Hannah* wrecked there on Christmas Day 1820, and discovered the seal rookery there. Then he turned south and saw this island – you can see it clear as day from Hannah Point, even in bad weather – and he came down this side of it.' Brian pointed left. 'He came down here and saw these cliffs, then he saw the entrance of Neptune's Bellows and saw it was a caldera, not a simple island, and called it Deception

Island. He sailed in and parked here, looked around, collected some eggs to eat. He did go back and get the American sealing fleet, and they made this place the centre of their operations.

'Palmer came up here, right where we are now. He saw this view, just as we see it now, and named it Neptune's Window. You can bet your bottom dollar that if he saw something he would have gone to take a better look. He wasn't searching for a continent; they didn't pay. He was looking for seal rookeries. The mainland is seventy miles away. From this place, on a good day, I have seen the whole middle of the Antarctic Peninsula laid out. From higher up you can see even further south.'

Today the cloud rose and fell but we couldn't see more than fifteen to twenty miles. 'And this was the first claimed sighting of Antarctica?'

'He didn't claim that; the US Government made the claim. He didn't know this was a mainland. Thaddeus von Bellingshausen, commanding two Russian navy ships, was here at the same time. His men had sighted something from the masthead a short time before; he didn't know it was a continent either – in fact he thought he might be seeing an iceberg. But his ship's log shows he was in a position, and looking in a direction, where he would have been able to see land.'

Brian pointed. 'Out there, is where young Nat Palmer, nineteen or twenty years old, encountered in the fog an answer to his own bell. He met Thaddeus von Bellingshausen, went aboard his ship, and compared notes, and that's recorded by both men. Bellingshausen had, shortly before, run into the continent on the other side of the Weddell Sea.'

'Who was first?'

'I think we have to give the nod to Bellingshausen. That was determined by a very distinguished panel of experts – one American, one Brit and a Russian – in a pub near the Scott Polar Research Institute in Cambridge, called the Panton Arms.'

'I know it well.'

'In the back research room.'

'That was an international panel with no bias?'

'No bias at all, we eliminated our bias by taking aboard liquid drugs. It's called bias elimination. Before that, however, we had used the same drugs at research parties, but in incorrect doses, and they devolved into shouting matches.'

'The ritual tearing of national flags becomes very important at that stage in the research.'

'Absolutely, but' – Brian pointed into the channel – 'that meeting did take place out there, and you can still see the wake, and if you go there you can feel the spirit of Nathaniel Palmer because this is where his life changed. He became a responsible man and evolved instantly from a young boy to a great man. Later on he was the father of the American clipper ship and a founder of the China trade from San Francisco and he lived into the 1870s, a very wealthy and powerful man.'

Light poured down through holes in the cloud. Nesting seabirds clamoured on the rocks above. Turning round I could see across Whaler's Bay and discern the full ring of the island, and the whole harbour.

'A more dreary or more cheerless scene cannot be imagined, than that which Deception Island of Shetland presented. . . . Here all is joyless and comfortless, huge masses of cinders and ashes lie strewed about,' wrote the surgeon of the *Chanticleer* which spent fifty-four days here in 1829 doing state-of-the-art research on gravity and magnetic fields. But they noticed that they remained very healthy during their stay, which they attributed to the cold weather and the hot sulphurous gases. To test whether it favoured the dead as well as the living, they opened the grave of an unknown sealer and found his body intact.

At the farthest end the *Chanticleer* carried out her observations on magnetism and gravity. At the end of the summer of 1829 the crew were happily preparing to leave what one midshipman called 'the last place that Nature made'. They left a maximum and minimum thermometer on the beach. For seven days they failed to beat the weather and the ice, eventually getting out of the harbour on 8 March. Stopping for fresh provisions in the Caribbean, Captain Foster's canoe turned over in the warm blue waters and he drowned. When the *Chanticleer* returned to England it was allocated to newly appointed Captain Fitzroy, but was found unfit for service without a refit. Instead he got the *Beagle*, and Darwin.

Thirteen years later a man from the sealer *Smiley* saw the thermometer, bent down and read a minimum temperature of −21.3°C, the lowest temperature ever recorded at that time. He then picked it up, and lost the maximum.

A geological fault runs round the whole shore with a weak spot at Neptune's Bellows. At any time the entrance could either drop deeper or close up entirely. In 1820 Robert Fildes sounded the centre of the harbour at 1,080 feet. Nine years later, Kendall could find no more than 582 feet. Both were reliable observers. It is highly likely that there was a major eruption in the years between. In 1921 the whalers at anchor found the cold and gloom relieved by warming air. They soon saw why. The sea around them steamed and began to boil, and before they got out the paint had blistered from the sides of the ships.

In the twentieth century the island was a research base for Britons, Chileans and Argentinians. From 1912 the whaling station had a post office, a magistrate and a customs officer. The magistrate tried the only civil law case in Antarctic history. The sled dogs were fed on penguins. On 2 April 1953 Able Seaman Francis McNally did not kill the penguin first. Fined £2.

The island boasts another first. On 5 February 1948 the crews of HMS *Snipe* and the Argentine ship *Seaver* played a football match, the first international on the last continent. One nil to *Snipe*: the usual drab England–Argentina encounter. No crowd trouble reported.

In the winter of 1967 there were 341 earth tremors in one month, and all three bases were alert to the need to evacuate quickly. At 18:54 hours on 4 December 1967 a cloud was seen, then jets of steam and ash burst through the sea ice covering the north of the bay and visibility fell to twenty-five yards. Ash began falling nine minutes later. The Chilean base was being destroyed and its scientists headed for the British base. The water in the whole of the huge harbour was rising and falling five feet about once a minute.

Triggered by the rising hot air, a severe electrical storm began and giant hailstones fell side by side with hot ashes.

There was no word from the Argentine base across the bay. At ten to three in the morning the Chileans arrived, tortoised under a sheet of board to stop burning ash setting their clothes alight. The twisted metal frame of their hut was now all that remained. Forty-two men now huddled in the British hut, listening to earthquakes tilt and topple the old steel whaling chimneys and shake the rusting drums of the storage tanks like theatrical thunder machines. After four o'clock the Argentinians came on the radio to say they were unscathed. By midday the Chilean ship *Piloto Pardo* was bearing them all away. Dust and ashes rose thousands of feet above the mountains behind them. When they returned, there was a new island in the bay.

For two years researchers came back to continue work and were driven away again. In 1968–69 there were light tremors throughout the summer. In February they intensified, and by 21 February they were continuous. The east side of the island blew. Five men from the British Antarctic Survey were thrown from their beds and lay, ears to the ground, listening to the earthquakes roar through the earth towards them. A three-mile crack opened up beneath the ice on Mount Pond. It was five hundred feet wide and three hundred feet deep. The meltwater tore down the hill, fifty feet deep, and mixed with the ash to form scalding mud slides. The unmanned Chilean base was destroyed.

The British retreated to Neptune's Window, where one man was felled by falling bombs of hot ash, and their portable radio was knocked out by a direct hit. They crouched there for three hours until the eruption eased. Under cover of a metal sheet torn from the wall of a hut, they battled back to camp to try to start the generators and call for help on the main radio. It was full of mud and debris. The Clectrac had become archaeology.

They got away by helicopter at 16:30. Since then Deception Island has only been sanctioned for specialist research at the Spanish and Argentinian stations, and only in summer, when workers can have reasonable hope of evacuation.

We crunched down the hill, through gravel and ash, and along the shore. It was not lack of whales which closed the station; the slaughter went on. It was a man called Peter Sörlle who in 1922 invented the stern slipway to haul whales straight from the ocean into the ship. With condensers to make their own fresh water, they could now hunt without land stations like Deception.

For twenty years this small dangerous island was the home of brutalised men. They boasted, 'Below 40°S no law, below 50°S no God.' They worked eighteen- and twenty-hour shifts through the seamless summer days and nights. In 1911–12 10,760 whales were killed in the South Shetlands, South Georgia and the South Orkneys. As one species was wiped out they changed to another. Alan Villiers went whaling in the Southern Ocean in 1923. When the weather was cold 'the whales froze as they lay belly-up in the water alongside, before they could be flensed. When this happened the blubber could be cut only with axes. Even the blades of our steam saws (which were meant for bones) could not handle it, and broke.' When it was a little warmer, 'The flensers and the blubber-cutters kept the frostbite off by dipping their hands into the warm whale's blood. Sometimes the whales became putrid and, first distending like barrage balloons, would explode with a dreadful mess of mile-long innards and a stench which penetrated even our defences.' The gulls and skuas grew fat.

I looked at the different ruins, the scoured whalebones and bleached skeletons of boats and buildings. A lone gentoo penguin, with a brilliant orange flash on its bill, looked up and down the beach, like a patriotic reveller who had lost the parade. The Zodiac bore us back, skimming above a sea bed carpeted with the bones of the largest creature ever to live on earth.

Tomorrow we would attempt to land on the mainland.


*Port Lockroy*

The night did not grow dark, and at six-thirty in the morning the cabin was flooded with sunshine. The ship was moving forward very gently, the sea calm and still. We were sailing south west down the Gerlache Strait named after the *Belgica* expedition leader. We slipped between the Antarctic Peninsula and the big islands of Brabant and Anvers, then little Wiencke. The view from the top deck was one of cold pure beauty. The sky was a blue so bright and clean it etched itself into your heart. To the left was the Antarctic mainland. Ice cliffs met the water, above them smooth flanks of pure white snow rose steeply, up and up, five hundred, seven hundred feet. Above the nearest, three rock towers clawed them-selves out of the snow and rose through a horizontal girdle of mist and up into clear sky above. At fifteen hundred feet the peaks of the stone pinnacles were once again cloaked in snow, rags of thin smoky cloud rolling in the turbulence around their heads.

Ahead lay the narrow Le Maire Channel between the mainland and Little Booth Island which mirrored its majesty. I went to the bow where Bill Davis was examining the sea ice and broken bergs through binoculars. The ice began to strike the hull with a clang and drag down the side. Middle-sized pieces are called growlers from the noise they make against the ship. The sea was filling with the small brash ice, and a lid of cloud seemed held over the Channel by the peaks of the mountains. An iceberg the size of a big car bumped past, looking as if it had been designed in a psychotic 1950s Detroit style-shop.

Bill peered anxiously ahead, a spotted red scarf knotted over his bald head. He raised his binoculars and frowned. He flung out his right arm and said 'No', looking to see if the bridge had seen him. The bow thrusters kicked in and turned the *Vavilov* hard to star-board. 'There's no way through.'

'No landing on the mainland?'

'Not today.'

But, I consoled myself, visiting Manhattan Island is still visiting America. Then I thought 'Bollocks'.

We turned right round and headed for the narrow Neumayer Channel between Anvers and Wiencke Islands. Wiencke is another name from the *Belgica* expedition, a sailor lost overboard in the Drake Passage. A berg like a Neolithic tomb sloshed by, a cap of ice on dwindling pillars. The larger ones coloured the sea around them a brilliant cold green. But occasionally truly green icebergs occur, coloured by minute organisms. Coleridge:

> And ice, mast-high came floating by,
> as green as emerald.

We came to a sheltered bay off Port Lockroy, the first permanent station in Antarctica, established by Winston Churchill in 1944 to secure the harbours and fuel stores of Antarctica against use by German warships. For many years it lay derelict. The old radio antennae were snaring and killing shags. Asbestos and broken glass littered the ground. Penguins, always curious, became trapped in the rubbish and died. Eventually the British Antarctic Survey decided it was too historically important to let it fall apart. For several summers, David Burkett and an assistant – this year it was Nigel Price – have laboured to return the huts to spick-and-span condition. Black walls and roofs were picked out with red and white trim. A Union Jack cracked in the wind.

A wooden ramp led up to the front door. Right next to it a gentoo penguin had built its nest of small stones. Two of the rooms have been restored to how they were around 1962, with valve radios, kerosene lamps and English tinned goods lining the kitchen shelves. Port Lockroy is the most visited tourist destination in Antarctica, receiving 6,000 of the total of 11,000 annual visitors. David and Nigel live in the hut and run one room as a post office and souvenir shop, with the profits going into the charitable trust which now runs the site.

David Burkett and his assistants have also been carrying out a long-term study of the impact of tourism. The results at Port Lockroy confirm the curious conclusions from other sites. At some sites there is no impact on breeding success, but at others tourism definitely has an effect – the number of birds goes steadily up, and no one really knows why.

Gentoo nests were on every piece of rock. Their Latin name reflects a labelling error made on a crowded research trip. *Pygoscelis papua*, the world's third largest penguin, would cook in its own insulation if it ever went near Papua New Guinea. These penguins share the incubation. One sits tight on the nest while the other feeds. The nests are built just far enough apart that they cannot peck their neighbour without getting up. The returning bird makes its way back, trying on the way to steal a stone from another nest to present to its mate. There are only so many stones; they make their way round and round the colony. The remaining bird defends the egg against skuas.

The word skua is very ancient, deriving from a word in the Faeroese language of the North Sea, *skúgvur*, whose origin is now unknown. One pair will defend a territory of about ten thousand penguins, and hunt co-operatively, one harassing the penguins with swoops, while the other lunges for the egg or chick. Snowy sheath-bills waddled between nests pecking at penguins' rear ends when they thought the supply of guano was falling short.

A penguin flew in to land behind me. A bird with a white front, black back and narrow tail. After all these years they had cracked it – flying! I followed its flight into the middle of the gentoo rookery, to a small group of imperial cormorants, white fronts, black backs, which had made their home among the penguins.

Back in the *Vavilov* we sailed back into the Gerlache Strait, then across into Anford Bay. Captain Beluga was trying to make it across into Neko Harbour on the mainland. We might yet join the club. However, when we got there large icebergs from the glaciers were mixed in among tabular bergs from the ice shelf. The sun came out and we lowered the Zodiacs. Through thin brash ice we headed for a beach at the head of a U-shaped sound filled with loose ice. The Zodiacs made several aborted attempts to land on a beach awash with sharp blocks of ice debris. Suddenly there was a break. The propeller cut through the slush, making a noise like a giant cock-tail-shaker. I could feel bumps through the rubber side tubes on which we sat, as we rode right over the smaller pieces. I tried not to think what noise a ripped and deflating Zodiac would make.

When we swung our boots over the side we were ashore on mainland Antarctica. You can still fit all the people who can say that into a big stadium.

The head of the sound was a wall of fissured ice where a short steep glacier was calving into the sea. On the shore watching us stood little chinstrap penguins, all black and white except for their pink feet. A thin black line across a white throat gives them their name. A large Weddell seal lay on a snow ledge above the beach. It took one look at the thin red line of approaching Gore-Tex and decided to make for the water. A crewman was crouched down on his heels photographing the chinstraps when one thousand pounds of nervous seal lolloped within a yard of him. The danger was passed before he had seen it. When he took his eye from the viewfinder and realised how close it had been, he keeled slowly backwards over his heels.

I climbed the hill behind to about five hundred feet, sweating with the effort in soft deep snow. Turning round, I had to look hard to see if the black commas on the shore were people or penguins. The eye of the imagination, voyaging south from here, would pass over the ridge of mountains which lie down the west side of the Antarctic Peninsula. It would fly over the Larsen Ice Shelf in the Weddell Sea, which sends huge tabular bergs out into the Drake Passage. It would rise over the Eternity Range and on over the Ronne Ice Shelf. Thirteen hundred miles into its flight it would meet the Pensacola Mountains passing just to the right of Mount Hawkes, 12,000 cold feet high. It would take one thousand eight hundred miles to reach the South Pole. But everywhere that rocks broke the surface, and thin ice could create a miniature greenhouse, there might be traces of life in the surface of the stone. At the instant of passing the Pole, the course changes from due south to due north. The map is empty. Two hundred miles to the left is the Russian Vostok Station, which recorded the world's lowest temperature, 67°C colder than the one recorded on the balmy shores of Deception Island.

Three thousand two hundred and fifty miles into this imaginary flight, over Wilkes Land, even in summer, the coast would still not be in view. In winter, the edge of the pack ice would be another five hundred miles north.

Five thousand six hundred miles in a line from where my feet were planted in the snow was the first land without ice, just south of Perth, Western Australia – a journey as long as crossing America coast to coast and back again. In all probability, the group of scientists at the South Pole would be the only human beings in the whole journey. So hostile is its environment that Antarctica was first crossed only eleven years before man stood on the moon.

That night I was still too excited to sleep and got up at one-thirty to walk round. The sky was pink above a line of rounded hills. There was a beautiful soft light. It might have been sunset, sunrise or moonrise. Bill was sitting on the rear deck smoking a cigarette. He never seemed to sleep. 'You made it,' he said, 'the mainland.'

'The Manhattan Island argument is good. But I still wanted the mainland.'

He smiled. 'Everybody does. Welcome to a very small club.'

In the morning we edged into the Errera Channel, a fjord-like strait near Couverville Island. We then headed in a Zodiac towards a gentoo rookery, when a long black back with a small flat fin broke the surface a hundred yards away. Humpback whales. At first I thought there were three, but what I had counted as two separate animals was the head and tail of one huge forty-ton adult. Sergey Korolyov turned the Zodiac parallel to the pair. They swam on the surface maintaining easy speed with a stately rhythmic motion. The black head shone like wet rubber and was stubbled with round knobs. It was not until we could hear their breathing that the size and the very liveness of these mammals came home to me. It seemed impossible at first to believe something so big could be a live mammal, like me. I thought of a line on whales from Dylan Thomas: 'Jericho is falling in their lungs'. The large adult raised its fluke, white-streaked and feather-edged, and dived. The water closed. We waited. The channel now felt strangely empty. Two minutes later they surfaced a quarter of a mile away. For half an hour they sported around and blew, while we held our breath.

We continued to the shore where the gentoos making their way from nest to sea and back had worn trenches through the snow, faint pink with krill-rich guano. By weight, penguins comprise 70 per cent of all Antarctic birdlife. It is possible there are now so many penguins in the world because there are now so few whales; in

Antarctica they eat much the same food. The food chain of baleen whales like the humpback is the most extreme in the world. It became possible about 140 million years ago with the appearance of diatoms. These are deceptively advanced tiny plants which start to appear in the geological record around the same time that flowering plants appear on land. They comprise one single cell, and are invisible to the naked eye.

The productivity of this simple direct ecosystem beggars counting. Diatoms are eaten by krill, a shrimp-like creature which sieves the diatoms from the water. The dominant krill species, *Euphausia superba*, is the Methuselah of the zoo-plankton world. They may live seven years, and each summer, as the sun returns south, the ocean seethes into fecundity. Krill are the most successful animals on earth. Every year they grow by a weight which exceeds the mass of the whole human population of the world. The biomass of all the world's krill is the greatest of any animal – greater than locusts, wildebeest, cattle or rats. In 1981 researchers off Elephant Island at the tip of the Antarctic Peninsula sailed into a shoal of krill which coloured the sea pink. They estimated it held 2.5 million tons of krill, moving in a single group, heads and tails aligned, turning in unison. In biomass terms, it was the equivalent of a surreal encounter in which Salvador Dali, accompanied by the entire population of Spain, performed synchronised swimming. In its life, a krill will eat its way through ten million, million, million diatoms. This is a number similar to the number of stars in all the universe, or the age of the universe in milli-seconds.

The biggest whales eat three to four tons of krill a day, all summer. A year's feast is built on a number of diatoms expressed as five with twenty-seven noughts after it. That is the whole food chain, from an invisible single-cell plant to a hundred-ton whale, in two giant steps.

Once whales were so dense that they bumped against full-sized sailing ships. Now the krill-eating seals and penguins benefit from the scarcity of whales. Crabeater seals which, despite their name, are mainly krill eaters probably exceed ten million in number, making them the most populous marine mammal in the world.

In the evening there was a barbecue for passengers and crew on the rear deck of the *Vavilov*. Steaks and sausages left the flames sizzling hot, were placed in warm bread, and were cold in two bites. 'Congratulations!' declared Bill to everyone. 'You are all now members of the Canadian Barbecue Club.' One of the Finnish passengers wanted to go for a swim. A young Frenchman offered to join him. The crew lowered an access ladder to water level. The Finn dived in, swam out to a piece of ice and came back. The Frenchman dived in, surfaced facing the ladder and shot straight back out.

I asked the Finn, 'Why?'

'My grandfather and father lived in a village where there was a tradition of winter swimming; they'd cut holes in the ice to swim on Christmas Day. I wanted to do something similar.'

I asked the Frenchman, 'Why?'

He couldn't speak.

## Cape Horn

Bill was poring over a chart, plotting a course back to Ushuaia. 'I'm thinking of persuading Captain Beluga to stop at the Melchior Islands.' He pointed out a tiny cluster of points on the chart, off the Gerlache Strait, between Anvers and Brabant Islands.

'What are they like?'

'Don't know. None of us has been there. Captain Beluga has never been there. I'd like to check them out.'

We slid into the lee of the islands and launched the Zodiacs. The light was subdued, the cloud base a few thousand feet. The islands' coasts finished in sheer walls of glacier ice over a hundred feet high. Rocks in between the islands snagged and held passing icebergs. We wound our way through the channels between them, out of sight of the *Vavilov*. When we cut the engines the quiet was unnatural. There was little wind, and the ice damped down the waves to ripples just a few inches high. We came through a channel twenty yards wide and into an enclosed pond between icebergs and an islet. It was like a set for *Superman*.

When seawater begins turning to ice, salt is left behind and the remaining water becomes too saline to freeze. It forms pockets and worms its way down through the ice until it appears scored full of bubbles, and much bluer. It looks quite different from the compressed glacier ice. Snow which settles and freezes has its own bedding planes, sometimes curved and sculpted by the wind. As they float, the sea erodes much more ragged contours. Each berg is a palimpsest of its own formation and destruction. The enclosed bay was like a sculpture yard. One low berg rose up nearly vertically at the end nearer to us in what looked like a pinnacle, but as we drifted past was revealed as a blade. Round the next corner a leopard seal, the great predator of penguins, lay on a raft of ice, turning his eyes slowly to follow us.

We weaved on for an hour, magical, silent, alone.

Our return crossing of the Drake Passage threw up some long rollers and squalls. I tried to stay on deck bird-watching, but it became hard to stand up and chew gum at the same time. Stephen Spittler came out, laughing. 'Cold enough yet?'

He pointed to a group of birds the size of a small gull. They were white underneath with deep brown heads and upper sides. The tops of the wings, back and tail looked as if they had been sprayed with white, to mimic snow patches. '*Daption capense*s used to be called Pintado Petrels, still are to me. Spanish for "painted petrels", beautiful birds. They got renamed: cape pigeons. I refuse to call a bird that beautiful a cape pigeon. You want to catch one?'

'No.'

He laughed. 'You got to do it at night. You shine a big torch on them, it stuns them. But you better have a net ready. Next thing they do is fly straight at the torch and vomit over whoever's holding it. Never tried it myself.'

As we came up just west of Cape Horn the wind fell, the sea dropped and the hatchet head of the cape came into view. Peale's dolphins picked up our bow wave. Shearwaters scythed across the wave tops. We turned east of the Horn where the coast is savage. Each little headland runs lower and lower into needle-edged rocks, reefs, row after row, never giving up.

In name, I was rounding the Horn, but I thought of my great-grandfather clawing his way round in square riggers, and my grandfather in the engine room, stoking, his hands so calloused that when he stroked my head he scratched me. I have seen him light cigarettes by flicking a coal from the fire on to his palm and holding it for everyone to use the red ember. They would not have felt glad that I had been able to come comfortably, as a passenger. They would have called me a fool for coming at all. But as they turned this corner on the homeward trip, they knew the worst of it was over. They were Liverpool bound.

I sang the shanty to myself:

> Were you ever off Cape Horn
> Where it's always fine and warm?
> Where there's a king with a golden crown
> Riding on a donkey.
>
> Were you ever in Liverpool Bay
> Where the girls all shout Hooray!?
> Here comes Johnny with his six months' pay
> Riding on a donkey.

Eight days on board the boat had produced a pleasant infantilism in me. Instead of packing and unpacking being an almost daily routine, my laundered and ironed clothes were neatly stowed in cupboards in the cool grey cabin. I liked its anonymous feel, and the economy of space. After meals I left the dishes on a tray and walked away. When a landing was planned, a Zodiac appeared. Tomorrow, early, I would be deposited on Ushuaia dock again, and I would have to get back to my planned route, starting with the great old sailor town of the south, Punta Arenas, across the border in Chile. I had appointments there, with the living, and the dead.

# 4

# *Punta Arenas*

*Cape of Ten Thousand Virgins*

U shuaia's neat new airport building was empty and locked. No one else was there. I sat on the grass. Loggerhead ducks sat on the tarmac. A black bird of prey danced about in low reconnaissance. Another taxi drew up. It was Robert. He had been on the Antarctic trip and had asked a question about Admiral Byrd's winter alone at 80° south. It had something to do with whether the CIA and the KGB had collaborated to work with extraterrestrials. The lecturer had replied in the negative. Robert wore stonewashed denim and a T-shirt hanging like a curtain from his beer-belly. He was travelling for four months but carried only a light hold-all and a small haversack. He saw me sitting on the grass and nodded. He tried the locked door. 'Is it open?'

In half an hour staff arrived to open up. We boarded a smart jet, taxied to one end of the tarmac and made it into the air just before the water at the other end. In half an hour we came out of the cloud and over the Magellan Strait. When Thomas Cavendish came through here in 1585 he wrote: 'There remains no reason of any kind, whether of utility, or of expediency, or of policy, to compel anyone to renounce his own country and undergo the severe punishment of settling in the Straits of Magellan.'

Today the water was combed by a flat fast wind into low spray-filled turbulence. This was the channel Magellan sailed through in thirty-eight days. He thought it was tough sailing; the experiences of those who followed proved how fortunate he had been. Of the next twenty-one boats to attempt the new route to the Orient, twelve sank off Tierra del Fuego. It was some time before they realised that the consistently unlucky weather from April to September was caused by the reversal of the seasons in the southern hemisphere.

Below us, in the eastern jaws by the Cape of Ten Thousand Virgins, a cargo vessel specked the immensity. We dropped over Porvenir. The Strait here turns nearly north to south and we cut across it to Punta Arenas. There were small whirligigs of rainbowed spray scudding over the channel. The plane repeatedly plunged vertically down or slithered sideways. I was sure we would pull out of our descent and turn round. The ground made another muscular effort to jump up and land on us. We banged the tarmac, and stuck to it. The airport buildings appeared deserted. We watched litter play at tornadoes in the angle of the door. A stairway on wheels was pushed towards us by three men. When the wind gusted they went backwards. Welcome to Chile.

I found a minibus, asked the fare, and sat inside. A large young Texan joined me. The driver closed one door. Robert appeared. He got half in. 'Anyone asked him about the fare? These guys are always on some kind of scam. I got a taxi in Ushuaia, cost me two and a half times the right rate. They're all in it.'

'Flat fare three dollars,' I said.

'US?'

'US.'

'That's good. You sure?'

'That's what the man said.'

'He did?'

'Twice.'

'If you're sure.'

There was room in the minibus for two more people. A short and very round local woman with four large bags of shopping got in, and we were full. Her clothes were shabby and she was sweating warmly. She sat looking at her feet. I spoke to her and she smiled shyly, spoke too quietly for me to hear, and showed a gold tooth and four black gaps. The driver slammed the back door, took his seat and collected the fares. 'Three dollars flat, you're sure,' said Robert.

I gave the driver three dollars. 'Yes.'

Robert gave the driver five dollars. 'I want change, yeah? Two dollars.' To help, he put up two fingers. The driver gave him two dollar bills. Robert took them gruffly. I thought he was going to count them. One, two. He stabbed a finger towards the woman. 'I wonder what he's charging her.'

*Jaws of the Pacific*

When the road ran along the shore we could see the water whipped into a low spray, and the small water tornadoes we had glimpsed from the air came dancing towards us. Sheets of drops whirling like fifteen foot-high dervishes. Occasional shafts of thin sunlight shot them through with rainbows. Magellan, during his passage, must have looked at these water sprites and wondered what they portended.

He was one of a handful of great explorers who faced moments of pure discovery, an uncovering of something always there, but never seen by European eyes to make it part of their known world. Such moments of discovery are profound episodes in the history of human consciousness. A moment later the world is not the same, either for the invaders or the invaded. He lay off the eastern end of a strait which, if successfully navigated, would reshape the globe, his fortune and his country's fortune. His crew were tired, ill and scared. The average age of the men before the mast was just twenty-three.

Magellan and his crew saw what they were convinced were mountains appearing in the clouds above the straits. Below, the waters appeared to stream away as if over the rim of the world. He told them, 'I have seen a chart drawn by Martin of Bohemia, which is in the possession of the King of Portugal, and I know there is an outlet to the Pacific. If we have to eat the leather on the yards we will go on.' Once through they would not see land again until rats were selling at a ducat apiece, and they were dining on leather from the yards.

The phantoms they described in the air over the straits were not unique to them. George Anson, later Admiral of the Fleet, led a squadron here in 1741 and saw an obscure light turn the other ships into fantastic castles and palaces. John Byron, a midshipman on that voyage, returned in 1764 in *The Dolphin*, the first ship to be copper-bottomed against sea worms. Using the very charts Anson had produced, he plotted a course down the coast of Patagonia, aiming to be well out at sea. At four in the afternoon came the cry 'Land right ahead'. Officers were sent to the masthead. They reported land on both sides. In mid-ocean they were trapped in a bay. They watched waves break on lonely beaches, saw the wild line of hills. 'It was as plain as ever I saw Land in my Life. There is not a Man aboard but would have freely made Oath of the certainly of its being Land.' But it vanished in a moment, and was never seen again.

Nor has this New World feeling gone away. Magical-realism is the most important literary form to emerge from Latin America and its famous proponent, Gabriel García Márquez, is a great reader of early travellers' accounts. He has said that Columbus's diaries are the first works of magical realism. Mario Vargas Llosa said of Magellan's voyage, 'You are in a world in which there are no barriers between fantasy and reality.' At the same time, the accounts are real, because the journey happened, and they are fantastical, because the world they describe is not ours.

A rational Old World view could not banish the fantastic. Sometimes it could not even describe it effectively. Pumas were classified as lions which had failed to evolve, trapped in this half-formed Eden. But if you took a language derived from this New World, you would, conversely, lack words and concepts for everything that was familiar from the Old World. An obscure Peruvian priest called Pedro de Quiroga advised in 1555: 'Do not learn the language of this land. Nor even listen to it, for I tell you that if you do, one of two ends will befall you, for it will either drive you mad or you will wander restlessly for the rest of your life.'

Language floundered. In Márquez's *One Hundred Years of Solitude,* in the village of Macondo, 'the world was so recent that many things lacked names, and in order to indicate them, it was necessary to point.'

Magellan sailed on, and in less than six weeks he was through. On the way he found the topsy-turvy world predicted by Aristotle. Midwinter came in June, there were giants, and birds which couldn't fly but hunted fish underwater and nested in burrows in the ground. Naked Indians swimming in icy water. Castles in the air.

When his successor Del Cano took the only surviving ship back home, it was full of priceless cloves. The profit paid for the whole voyage, all the lost ships. The ship's log completed by the taciturn but careful pilot Francisco Albo was one day out. More strangely, everyone who had kept a personal diary had made the same mistake. They had lost a day. Horrified to think they had eaten meat on a Friday and observed the Sabbath on Monday, they marched penitentially to Mass.

In Milan the clear-eyed Peter Martyr, who had once laughed at Columbus's refusal to see that he had discovered a new world, was probably the first man to see why. They had revolved once less than the rest of mankind, taken one fewer turn than the earth itself, and were a day younger. There was no error.

## The Ritz 1

The airport minibus dropped me off at the Plaza de Armas, in the centre of Punta Arenas. The radio station had taken over the bandstand and was playing carols. The very first visitor stood in the middle; Magellan's foot was planted next to a cannon. Natives with spears cowered at his feet. A metaphor for much South American history.

I followed the barrel of Magellan's cannon towards the docks. The wind was relentless. Trees with trunks two feet across were only fifteen feet high. They stood like boxes, trimmed into topiary by the wind.

Half a dozen breezy blocks took me down to the dusty port. A group of very young men came down the steps of the Naval Officers' College and stood self-consciously pulling on peaked caps and adjusting shiny straps on chins they had only just begun to shave. The visors came down over their eyes and their age. Now they were just the mouth and nostrils of authority.

There were none of the cosy family hostels I had pictured. From a block away I sized up the only hotel in view, a white 1930s concrete building on a corner site. On the pavement outside, a squat tree lay torn out at the roots. The original corner doorway had been converted to a window veiled with dusty lace. Individual illuminated boxes sported the letters R-I-T-Z . They swarmed loosely around the vertical word Hotel, as though it had whistled, and they had come. A woman in a scarlet coat stopped me. 'Good hotel. Very cheap, very clean.'

'Do you work there?'

'Yes, I am the cleaner.'

A man approaching sixty materialised behind the yellow folding counter of the reception, like a panto magician propelled onto stage through a trapdoor. 'Can I help you?'

'Bed and breakfast, two nights please.'

'Certainly. Mama!' A woman with thin hair came forward pulling a brown cardigan around her body so tightly that the wooden toggles on one side, and the loops on the other, crossed over to snuggle under the opposite armpit. 'What a wind! More than a hundred kilometres an hour.' She huddled, suddenly cold in the windless room. The owner took my passport, put on his spectacles like a judge settling a long case, and registered me.

The large room had a sloping floor and gave a view of the yard below. Under a washing line, yellow newspaper scudded round a fine enamel bath standing on rusting claw feet. There was a tongue-and-groove ceiling and a pot-bellied stove. The wardrobe was stainless steel and opened with a noise like a sealed vault. The sun had faded the flowers on the wallpaper from red to gunmetal.

In the bathroom a bare light bulb shone down on the plastic yellow toilet-seat cover. It was brittle with age. Elastic tweaked the plastic into icing frills. The museum would come to seek it out, and its owners. See: this is how we used to live. In the street below, the road was unmended, the verges unkempt. The house was still and strong in the wind.

I went out for food. The owner said, 'Everywhere will be closed, because of the election.'

'Everywhere?'

'Most places.'

I walked the city. Every bar, café and restaurant was shut. At every other crossroads a bored carabinero flexed his olive uniform, automatic in his hand. I went into a petrol station and ate hot-dogs. The only other customers were young teenagers.

When I went back I asked, 'Are they forbidden to open?'

'No.'

'Are they frightened to open?'

'No. They just don't open.'

In the morning, the bells for eight o'clock Mass came weak and irregular down the street, bowled along by the wind. Around the Ritz, lorries churned mud into slurry, potholes pocked the tarmac. Starling colours oiled the puddles. I breakfasted at a brightly lit fast-food café. Slim girls ran round the tables and smoked in their minute's rest. The manageress sat like a statue at the till, her hands immobile with gold.

I walked west along the warehouses. Most of the buildings were from the beginning of the century. My grandfather could still have found his way around. An elaborate cast-iron clock marked the end of a boulevard. It had the air of a plastic mackintosh trying to look jaunty at the seaside. Fish warehouses stank out the street where old sluice water lay on the lorry park. On the docks road, a rough-cast concrete Parthenon housed the Naval Gymnasium. It was a huge building. I imagined the inside: springboards and trampolines, white-vested cadets ballooning through the grey air.

In the early days, this was a land where the police were either corrupt, incompetent or both. One man was convicted of murder after walking into a bar where a man had just been shot. He was still standing there gaping when the police came in and arrested him. He had gone out looking for a midwife; his wife was suffering contractions for the baby daughter which arrived before the morning. When he got out of Ushuaia jail the daughter was twenty-five years old.

But many of the men who fetched up here were sailors, and were used to worse things at sea. A local commissioner forcibly took one of three beautiful Tehuelche daughters as a mistress when he was in the country. Her father was humiliated and tried to flee. The ferryman on a river crossing tried to rape another daughter, and the boat capsized. Two girls were drowned. An ex-sailor told the commissioner to his face exactly who he thought was really responsible. The commissioner ordered him to be beaten with the flat of a sword. This would normally cripple a man for weeks. The sailor had a back used to the cat-o'-nine tails. He took the beating, politely thanked the commissioner and blew smoke in his face. The commissioner ordered a double beating. Afterwards, the sailor's thanks were doubly profuse. The commissioner had the sailor tied to a post. He seized the sword himself and beat the man until he was out of breath. When untied, the sailor was less distressed than the commissioner, but when a gun was produced he left.

If it was hard for the men, it was worse for the women. With fifty men to every woman they were stared at everywhere. One night a group of ladies having a piano lesson were interrupted by a man climbing in through the window. He hadn't known that some ordinary houses had pianos. They kindly explained where the whorehouse was.

The rigid gridiron imposed on the wild land couldn't impose sanity. One Punta Arenas doctor recalled respectable families whose well-brought-up daughters would slam the door and disappear into a brothel for days to get drunk and laid senseless. 'If they did go back home afterwards,' he remembered, 'they might act defiant, or unconcerned, but they were always saner and happier.' Others simply met a stranger and left town.

If it was purgatory in the towns, it was hell in the country. One farmer's wife in the interior only saw other women every two years when she came to town to have a baby. Then she went home again.

The writer Stan Hughill came here as a deck hand on sailing ships and wrote about the grog shops in the old sailortown here:

> Although it was only a small drinking shop, within its walls, when outside the snow was deep and the icy winds from Tierra del Fuego blew at full force, around the warm, inviting 'bogey', in an atmosphere one could cut with a sheath knife, would be ensconced some of the toughest sailormen in the world. I know, for I have sat drinking hot pisco with them more than once in days gone by.
>
> The pub's official name was Bar La Bolsa, but it was known to its seafaring clientele as the Seaman's Bar. To it would come, besides deepwater men from around the Horn, sealers and otter hunters, who actually worked the bays and inlets of the Horn itself, and carried out their tough trades all around the Land of Fire. They were mainly Scandihoovians of all kinds; tough, rugged men and heavy drinkers, and, when in their cups, brawlers and all-hands-in fighters. Added to these two types of seafarers were the Norwegian whalers who often made Punta Arenas a port o' call. These men too were heavy topers and awkward men in an argument. And to this real sailor community, which filled the cosy bar of this drinking place nightly, could be added the Welsh *capatazes* from the sheep stations, men who were not at a loss for sailor talk, since many of them had deserted sailing ships, such as the little *Merionethshire*, many years before becoming landlubbers.

The low-life bars now looked too tired to be threatening, or even tacky; they were slipping into dotage. The American Bar was made of corrugated iron painted in the same yellow and green as the Brazilian flag. It was midday. Four cadets came out, then I slipped in to join a handful of customers. The landlady had just arrived with her groceries. Her mother kept the grandchildren busy and helped unpack. The landlady gave me the kind of look that asks: Why are you in a bar at twelve o'clock? Encouraged by her, the son, aged seven, gave us a knowing look and took a bar stool. He began his homework on the Formica counter. I offered to help but he said no.

'A beer.'

'Crital or Ecudo?'

It took a minute. The southern accent misses out 's'.

'Crystal.'

All the beer was in an ordinary domestic fridge in the opposite corner to the bar. She fetched a bottle in slow motion. The wallpaper pattern was of bricks, actual size. A local radio station advertised bathrooms and used cars. A lamp made from a wooden sailing boat lit up a stuffed Magellanic penguin. Possibly to save the cost of stuffing, it had been preserved in sump oil. Decay would have been a kindness.

I sat in a chair with battered steel tube legs and a burst seat. The landlady was a handsome woman of middle weight with knowing, dark eyes that had seen all the men there were and how they misbehaved. Two, in their forties like her, drank pisco. One was a twist of sinew, hard. He flirted with her across the quiet bar, smiling with wet eyes and teeth. The other was very quiet, and nursed a glass in the fold of his arms, amazed at his friend's boldness. Each was saying *adios* to the final pretence of being sober. I watched. Her smile was cotton wool, her eyes flint. The talker waved at her to join them. She poured a whole bottle of brandy into a jug, took a glass for herself, and sat by his side.

A very thin black cat with long hair came through the bead curtain from the living room at the back. It had a small head, spindly legs and large grey paws. The boy took it by the end of the tail and dragged it across the room, smiling as it screamed.

After two beers I blinked in the sunshine flooding the street. A street vendor sold strings of smoked mussels, bolts of packed seaweed, and undercooked pork crackling. From another I bought a key-ring showing the extent of Chilean Antarctic territory. I took out my Argentinian one and compared them. Both claimed exactly the same area. [When I got home my own atlas said it was British Antarctic Territory.]

Some smart modern houses dotted the bay towards the Naval Dockyard. I took out my binoculars and focused on a rusted iron boat in the sea behind it. There seemed to be a pier with three clippers moored alongside, overlapping each other. The last one was something special – light and fast with a beautiful overhung stern. The larger hull next to it was tubby and graceless by comparison.

I asked the young sentry, 'Is it possible to look at the wreck?'

'No. I am sorry, it is not permitted.'

'I have a special interest in old sailing boats, I think it is a British boat. Is it possible to ask permission from an officer?'

'I regret, no one is permitted.'

'Do you know anything of the history of the ship?'

'No, nothing.'

'Its name?'

'No.'

'Thank you.'

'Thank you very much sir, enjoy your stay in Punta Arenas.'

Back at the Ritz I went downstairs to the desk to pay. Halfway down, by a trick of two mirrors, I could see the owner standing upright, smoothing down his silver hair with the palm of his hand, patting down time. His thin-haired mother came to say goodbye. They will grow old without knowing that standards of hotel comfort have passed them by. In time they will believe the area is declining and talk, over coffee, about how business is falling off. Guests leaving early. A house as old-fashioned as they are will keep guests dry but not warm, while the wind moves on.

While the bill was being prepared I felt someone looking over my right shoulder, although I had heard no footsteps on the bare boards. I turned to see two large staring eyes inches away from mine. They were Bruce Chatwin's. The photograph was a cutting from a German newspaper.

'Chatwin has a connection with this hotel?'

'Why yes!' The owner placed his spectacles on the register, straightened his blue cardigan, and stood to attention. 'He stayed here.' His strong finger stabbed down. 'There are three whole pages about this hotel.' He took out the hotel register for 1974. On 9 March in black ink was the entry Charles Bruce Chatwin, London. Someone had added above it, in heavily indented blue biro, ESCRITOR – writer. I had forgotten it. The Ritz Hotel was where the salesman of women's underwear had given lectures on the beach pebbles he had found that day. One morning he vanished. This silver-haired man was the one who had explained the salesman's sudden absence to Chatwin, '*Es loco*.' 'He is mad.'

## Institute of Patagonia

The Institute of Patagonia is on the edge of town near the duty-free shopping zone. It stands behind a large field exhibiting old tractors, caravans and machines from the turn of the century. Part of the University of the Magellans, it houses a collection of early maps, and I hoped to get contacts for two men who had helped create the recent Patagonia exhibition at the British Museum: the archaeologist and Selk'nam expert Alfredo Prieto, and the historian, founder and director of the Institute, Mateo Martinic. Low buildings stood around a small landscaped courtyard. It felt like a pavilion in a park. I stepped inside expecting to meet a row of lawnmowers.

I found myself in a narrow corridor without a reception desk. Round the corner I met a dome-headed man in his mid-fifties, in a green jacket that looked comfortable enough to belong to an academic. 'I am researching a book, and I would like to make contact with Alfredo Prieto. . . .' He interrupted me by putting out his hand, 'Come in come in, you've missed him, what a shame, sit down please. He's on a dig.' The man unrolled a map and showed me a remote location impossible to get to in less than two days without a four-wheel drive. 'He's doing work on native settlements, what a pity, he's certainly the man for you.'

'When is he back?'

'Oh, he has a family so he'll be back for Christmas, but not until late on Christmas Eve.'

'I can't stay in the Punta Arenas area that long. There's someone else I would very much like to meet, Mateo Martinic.' He stood up, and put out his hand again. 'I am Mateo Martinic!'

He took me to the Institute's library and map room and recommended books and maps. One of the two prize originals was a 1668

*The Magellanic Land and Islands,* by Guillermo, from the prolific Picardy family of mapmakers, the Sansons. His father Nicholas had been geography teacher to King Louis XIII of France. The other was the 1635 map magnificently titled *Freti Magellanici Ac Freti Vulgo Le Maire Exactissima Delineatio* – The Straits of Magellan and the Strait Commonly Called Le Maire Precisely Drawn. This was by one of the map-making greats, Iodocus Hondius, who was one of the first to print a map using the Mercator projection.

I walked round the framed prints in chronological order watching the persistence of Terra Australis Incognita. Drake suppressed and confused his most important discoveries, and so, long after his voyage and Fletcher's accurate 1578 sketch of Cape Horn, huge landmasses were drawn sprawling across the Southern Ocean. A Hondius of 1607 shows the south shore of the Magellan Strait as the tip of a nebulous unknown land. In 1616 Willem Schouten and Jacques Le Maire discovered and named the Le Maire Strait and publicised the existence of Cape Horn and open sea to the south. But an anonymous sketch map from that year still shows a huge peninsula coming north and terminating near Staten Island. Then, for thirty years, Terra Australis Incognita was erased until it surfaced once more, in the 1646 *A Geographical Map of the Kingdom of Chile,* taken from a book of the same year – the very same Alonso de Ovalle book I had found in Hay-on-Wye.

*Maps: True Lies*

The first travellers' maps were placed by the Egyptians in the coffins of the dead to guide souls to the afterlife. From the beginning maps did not just record what was known, they speculated about things unknown. Maps related fictions, but some of the stories turned out to be true.

Greek maps contained philosophical fictions. To reflect their belief in the symmetry of nature, another earth, Antichthon, was supposed to orbit the sun and balance the earth. A large southern continent must exist to balance the northern land masses, and its qualities had to provide a contrary balance to those of the known world. So it was uninhabited and uninhabitable. Snow was black and fell upwards. Such a world could not be attached to ours, so there must be a channel keeping the two natural orders apart.

In March 1493 Columbus had returned claiming he had found a new route to Cathay. Spain was opening up the world with voyages to the west, and Portugal with voyages to the east. To avoid a fight, Pope Alexander VI moved swiftly to divide the world between his Catholic sovereigns. On 4 May 1493, just two months after Columbus's return, he issued the Bull of Demarcation, later formalised as the Treaty of Tordesillas. A line was drawn north to south down the Atlantic, 300 miles west of the Azores. Later, to satisfy Portugal, it was moved to 1,110 miles west of the Cape Verde Islands. Everything to the east was Portugal's, to the west, Spain's.

Unfortunately no one knew where Spanish and Portuguese interests met up on the far side of the world. Indeed the Pope was head of a Church which burned people for suggesting they met up anywhere at all. Magellan had to speak his views quietly. 'The Church says the earth is flat but I know it is round, for I have seen its shadow on the moon, and I have more faith in a shadow, than in the Church.'

The men behind Magellan's navigation were Jorge and Pedro Reinel, the leading Portuguese cartographers of the time, serving the Crown. Jorge seems to have made a world globe for Magellan to use in arguing a case with the king.

Other navigators developed maps further, culminating in the Canerio chart, which embodied current knowledge, and set aside any part of Ptolemy which conflicted with it. The chart gained wide circulation through Martin Waldseemüller's twelve-sheet woodcut of it in 1507, from which one thousand copies were made. It included a channel separating South America from the supposed southern continent, Terra Australis Incognita. In 1519 Magellan had sailed to look for this channel. He voyaged into the unseen but not, he believed, into the unknown. He would also overthrow the reputation of the greatest of the Greek philosopers, whose work had underpinned Western science for nearly two thousand years.

## Killing Aristotle

In 1498 Admiral Christopher Columbus's ship lay in the Gulf of Paría, between Trinidad and Venezuela. Two mighty currents of water met around it so that 'both waters cause a great roar and thunder from east to west'. Pulling in the leather buckets they sometimes drew salt water, sometimes fresh. The weeds on the hull tumbled to and fro as the sea fought with a colossal current of fresh water. The greatest ocean in the known world was being driven back, all across the boundless bay, by the press of a huge river, later named the Orinoco. Columbus knew such a volume could not flow from a mere island. He momentarily confessed it seemed that he lay off 'a very great continent which until this day has been unknown'. Through the long warm night the coming together of the waters dinned his ears with a great and unwanted truth. The whole compass of his career was false. By the morning Columbus decided the continent must be done away with. Columbus was the last great navigator to deny the existence of two new continents, and the world's greatest ocean. He spent the rest of his life trying to prove he had not discovered America.

The discovery of the Americas threw science and philosophy into turmoil. Some said the new 'Indians' were not descendants of Adam, and Columbus had undermined the Biblical unity of the human race. After all, in AD 741 Pope Zacharias had excommunicated an Irish priest for preaching the existence of a Southern Continent, and thereby 'admitting the existence of souls who shared neither the sin of Adam nor the Redemption of Christ'.

Soon the great thinkers of Europe saw what Columbus had done to Aristotle. The Greek philosopher had been the hub of a medieval mindset which appealed to ancient authorities for the basis of all knowledge. It held their opinions to be above observation of the real world. The classics determined not just the *way* things were seen, but what *could* be seen. A new idea could be sneered out of the classroom if Aristotle had disagreed or simply remained silent on the matter. Eventually the scholarly weight of Aristotle became a drag on progress, hampering what medieval experimenters could say. Then Columbus came home, and later Magellan. Out of the fog of tradition appeared two huge landmasses and the world's greatest ocean, and Aristotle had nothing to say about either of them, the ancient authorities were dumb. In 1517 Erasmus asked, thinking of the New World, 'If the knowledge of the ancients had been so limited in geography, in what other undiscovered ways had it been in error?'

'Henceforth,' said Galileo, 'one thousand Demostheneses and one thousand Aristotles may be routed by an average man who brings Nature in.' In the words of modern scholar Anthony Pagden, discoverers were 'freed from the voices of the dead'. It was the start of an argument that led through Francis Bacon, and his essays on method in scientific inquiry, to the modern belief that facts, not faith, are the bedrock of knowledge.

## Puerto Williams

Punta Arenas, six am. Rain spat on the pavement. I was flying south to Puerto Williams looking for the last remnants of the Yámana people. The driver was late and I crouched in the shallow doorway of the airline office. A Korean man came down the street with a small holdall. He squeezed into the doorway with me and lit up a thin cigarette.

A minibus arrived. The driver wore black trousers and wind-cheater. His paunch stretched the buttons to make crowsfeet wrinkles in his white shirt. Slick grey hair came back round his head and crossed like wet clouts at the back. He smoked and coughed and braked late on the wet greasy roads.

I sat behind the pilot of our twin-engined Otter as he punched it into the clouds and climbed. Even at ten thousand feet it made only 140 knots. Coming out of cloud I saw a huge band of water beneath and thought we had quickly made the Beagle Channel. But when we crossed another the same size, I knew the first was the colossal Lake Fagnano, one of the eastward routes for the melting glacier water which did not quite cut deep or long enough to form a complete sea channel when the water finished rising at the end of the Ice Age. In winter the lakes froze, and Lucas Bridges would take out his long-blade speed skates on which he was never beaten. He could not always find time in the day, there was too much work to be done. But on moonlit nights he walked to the shore and skated alone in the steel blue vault of the cradling mountains, a solitary moving trace on a lake more than fifty miles long and seven miles wide.

The plane ran along the Beagle Channel. The islands to the south were free of cloud. Navarin Island is broadly rectangular and forty-five miles long, east to west. The lower slopes, facing north and the sun, are forested. The ground above quickly rises to bare rock. Even in midsummer the peaks are snow-capped. The rock is frost-shattered and absorbs light. Its blackness is not a colour but a hole in vision. The interior is bare. Further south is Nassau Bay and beyond it the stone theatre of the Wollaston Islands, then Cape Horn. We landed on a spit and in breezy sunshine I walked towards the town. A large hawk spilled from a nearby tree and glided to a black bare branch standing in the water of a creek. A big American pick-up truck stopped and gave me a lift into town.

Puerto Williams was founded in 1953 to consolidate Chile's claim to Antarctic territory. The navy built a tiny blue bungalow with a flagpole, lined up a brass band to face south, and saluted the future. Other bungalows followed, a dockyard, and a second-hand American frigate, renamed the *Yan Portales*. It is the most southerly town in the world (the Antarctic stations not being true towns, or part of any country). Puerto Williams now has a population of 1,800.

I asked the driver, 'Do you live here or just come over to work?'

'I live here now.'

'Do you like it?'

'It's fine, nice and quiet. We've got shops here now. You can't get everything, but Ushuaia's only a boat trip away. And in Punta Arenas you can get anything.'

He dropped me in the tiny town square. There were small single-storey shops, brightly painted in red, yellow and blue. English-style park benches faced inwards so you could sit and admire the gravel and the enormous puddle. The only vehicles were huge American station wagons. If the only thing to survive an earth holocaust were the town square of Puerto Williams, archaeologists would conclude that young earthlings were reared in little wooden houses, then, when they reached their full adult height of eight feet, moved to larger metal ones on wheels. I lifted my pack, a gust of wind spun me half around. It began to rain.

I found a room to rent in Mario's. Mario Ortiz Osorio is a councillor and ex-mayor of Puerto Williams. He owns the grocery CS Comercial, the only shop not in the square. The house is a two-storey chalet, the interior is finished only with hardboard. My bedroom had open shelves in an alcove, a small bedside chest, a chipped grey iron bed with a monstrous sag in it, and a nail above the headboard. The upstairs stove was not lit in summer, the window was single-glazed with net curtains only. There were other rooms for visitors, all empty. At the end of the corridor leading to the back of the house was a door with a lock on the outside. Behind it a child coughed painfully. I looked out of the window at the rain. Five years after first reading about them, I was going to walk along the coast to Villa Ukika and meet the last descendants of the Yámana, and the last Yahgan speakers. I stepped outside. The sun was now out and it was much warmer than inside the house. I walked down to the coast road. The water was tranquil, gulls and cormorants fed on the mud and gravel shore. Small cabins were strung out along the landward side of the dirt road. Chickens ran under the houses. Dogs lounged on the step. The Korean who had shared my Punta Arenas airport minibus kept appearing at every corner, bowing, smiling, talking in good English and bad Spanish.

The wind died to nothing. I took off two jackets and was still hot. Around a turn in the road was a white board with peeling paint, saying Villa Ukika. An orange pick-up truck with no wheels was engulfed by long grass, becalmed in a bank of gravelled time. A dozen bungalows and cabins were scattered between gardens and unpainted paling fences. In front of the first bungalow, jeans, T-shirts and vests were hung along the fence to dry. An old man in a smart grey cap sat talking on a boardwalk His gaunt face had full high cheekbones and was pure Yámana in appearance. He stood up and strode towards town.

I asked if they minded my joining them. A man in his thirties lay in the grass drinking thin red wine from a jug. I could smell it, sweet and fruity. It was eleven thirty in the morning. A thin woman with a blue baseball cap smoked Hilton cigarettes and said nothing. Camilla, a pretty five-year-old, came out of the house and showed me a pink and gold bauble from the Christmas tree. I admired it and carefully handed it back. She placed it on the boardwalk and kicked it. Two dogs gave chase.

I did not know how to sit down by strangers and ask them about their all-but-vanished language and life.

'I'm Pedro, you on holiday?' asked the man with the wine.

'Yes.'

'Where are you from?'

'Wales.'

'World Cup,' he said. 'Chile are in the World Cup, and England, maybe we play each other. Wales, I think, didn't make it.' We both laughed.

'I'm English, I don't mind.'

'Who's going to win? England won't win.'

'We've got a good team.'

'Chile will win!' Everyone cheered, the children stood up, 'Chile!'

I heard a strange noise beneath me, under the boardwalk. Another dog. Our cheering had woken it up.

Maria sat down close to me and asked me for a light.

She was sixteen, boyish with tight curly hair and ears that looked like Chinese wooden ear mushrooms. She asked me questions, about my job, how I had got here. I found her Spanish almost impossible to understand. They used unexpected words; when

I thought she was asking if I had a yacht, she was asking if I had come on the ferry. A boy went away and came back with a leather football with FIFA on it. Maria stood up and kicked it back and forth. She had very short bandy legs and her jeans were far too long. The ball flew round. Pedro caught the ball and signalled to me. I stood in the road with the last remnants of the race, and played head-tennis.

Pedro sliced a kick and the ball nearly broke a window. A woman came to the door. He put his hands behind his back, looked up in the air, and whistled. We sat down. The door opened and a man reeled out. He was tall, burly with very dark skin and hair. His face was strong-featured, there were no whites to his eyes. He looked half poisoned with chronic drinking. He stood staring at the jug in the grass. Pedro said, 'It's just juice.'

'It's not, is it?' said a little boy, and picked it up in both hands.

'Let me have some,' said the big man.

'It's just juice.' Pedro was laughing to himself.

The big man seemed to forget about it.

'Give him some.' The jug was handed up.

'I am looking for Yahgan speakers,' I said, 'I would like to hear the language and record it.'

Pedro turned to the woman in the baseball cap. 'He wants to know about Yahgan speakers. Are there any here?'

She jabbed the butt of her rollup down the road. 'He was one.'

'What about Ursula?'

'Christmas shopping.'

'Cristina?'

'Out.'

They ran through the entire village.

Pedro said, 'You see, they organised a launch to go Christmas shopping in Ushuaia, and all the older people, Yahgan speakers, went on that. They'll be back late tonight if you want to come back.'

'I'll call tomorrow.'

The sun went in. Pedro chewed a grass stalk. 'The forecast is rain early, rain later.'

On a hillock above the Naval Commandant's house, among grass

136

strewn with whale bones, I went into the Martin Gusinde Museum. Father Gusinde was an Austrian missionary and ethnographer, and from 1918 to 1924 he conducted the most complete study of the Indians of Tierra del Fuego. He published four huge volumes and took wonderful photographs.

He spent most of his time to the north, on the island of Tierra del Fuego, with the guanaco-hunting Selk'nam. Being nomadic, they could at least maintain an authentic way of life within their territory, even as their country shrunk and they dwindled in numbers. They are unique in being Stone Age-style hunter-gatherers, still living in their traditional lands. Other people who have been studied, such as the Bushmen of the Kalahari, lived in lands where they had been unwillingly pushed by the pressures of neighbouring people. The Selk'nam were where they wanted to be, where they had been since the end of the Ice Age.

They had no knowledge of the outside world. Most did not understand the camera itself, which froze them in time, living specimens. In the photographs it is common to see an expression which seems to ask, 'What do you want me to do?' Their eyes are variously questioning, uncomprehending, anxious, sometimes plainly frightened. They are looking into the future on short focus, and seeing nothing.

Some Selk'nam men, when wearing their own native clothes, displayed confidence and self-respect. Toiu, painted with white bars on his cheeks, indicating vengeance, was photographed in 1923, aged twenty-eight. He is handsome and unafraid. Normal dress was nearly naked. An unnamed teenager smiled broadly in innocent happiness as she held a young child. Kamanakar Kipa, photographed at Bahía Orange in 1882, looks fourteen or fifteen years old. She is naked, pretty and smiles a knowing smile.

In the furthest corner from the bright entrance was a rare picture of the Haush, a tiny cornered tribe related to the Selk'nam, living in between genocide from outsiders and the ocean's oblivion. They buried their dead shamans face down so they could talk to the spirits of the earth. It was their wailing which first greeted Charles Darwin from a desolate rock. He wrote:

A little after noon we doubled Cape St Diego, and entered the famous Strait of Le Maire. We kept close to the Fuegian shore, but the outline of the rugged, inhospitable Statenland was visible amidst the clouds. In the afternoon we anchored in the Bay of Good Success. While entering we were saluted in a manner becoming the inhabitants of this savage land. A group of Fuegians, partly concealed by the entangled forest, were perched on a wild point overhanging the sea; and as we passed by, they sprang up and, waving their tattered cloaks, sent forth a loud and sonorous shout. The savages followed the ship, and just before dark we saw their fire, and again heard their wild cry.

They were very dark, a family group. They shaded their eyes with long thick fingers.

Leaving the museum, I walked to the end of town, back towards the airport. In the creek was a workmanlike square rigger, called the *Contramaestre Micalvi*. A burly man in late middle age bounced out of a high four-wheel drive, and walked down to the jetty. 'Hi! I'm Charlie. Originally from Boston, Massachusetts, but I guess I'm now from Puerto Williams I spend so much time down here. Come on board and take a look round.' A notice described it as an 850-ton former Rhine cargo boat, brought here in 1928 and used to ferry munitions around the Magellans. In 1962, in the strange Spanish phrase of the notice, 'it was declared a pontoon' and later, in recognition of its work, declared a national monument. It was also holed and grounded.

As I left he pointed up at the mountain above. 'Cerro Bandera, good little walk. An hour to the top, max.'

Perceptions of time vary greatly.

### Cerro Bandera

On the boat to Antarctica I had sailed beneath these hills and promised to climb them. I had no food or water with me but the streams were clean, and even if Charlie's estimates were optimistic, I wouldn't be out more than two-and-a-half hours. I followed Charlie's directions, walking up a forest track in light rain.

North American beavers have been introduced here by a man called Schindler. Their dams created shallow lakes, making huge areas of land spongy. We can forgive him; he was also the man responsible for Schindler's list. The rain came in hard. I crouched under a twisted tree on the edge of one of these lakes, cloaked like a heron. Trees stood dying in the new water. Lichen furred every branch. When it eased I went on to the waterfalls where part of the stream goes into a pipe and becomes the town water supply. I ate berries and watched a muskrat climb on to the path, a sheaf of grass in his mouth, and walk towards me. At the last minute it stopped, saw me, did a cartoon double-take, and ran for a stream.

I knew what it was because I had seen one in the museum, where I had thought it was very badly stuffed. The body, about ten inches long, was baggy and unstructured. The tail was like a fat version of a rat's. In real life they also looked badly stuffed. It must be some consolation to know that after death, no matter how bad your embalmer may be, you will look no more foolish than you did in life.

The track became a faint path and rose steeply through woods which have not been cleared since the ice left here nine thousand years ago. On the ground the wind was still, but higher up it blew through the canopy like a distant sea breaking. Among decaying beech leaves the size of a child's fingernail, tiny delicate flowers coaxed a living. Star-shaped mosses made glistening green cushions at the foot of the trunks. Some of the trees had freshly drilled holes in them big enough to take my fist. This was the work of the spectacular black Magellanic woodpecker, a coal-black bird with scarlet whiskers round its beak.

I climbed without being able to see out and guess progress. An hour had gone by. Birdsong stopped. There was nothing to eat and I was above the running water. After an hour and a half I was thirsty and hungry. I made a note to buy Charlie a new watch. I rested in a partial clearing where something invisible talked in whispers. Goosepimples rose on my arms. I circled and located the source. Three trees had fallen on to their neighbours, and the dead wood rubbed against the live.

American researchers studied rates of tree growth in the virgin forests of the Chilean south. In one of their articles, a man is pictured holding two spindly trees at arm's length, like a father helping choose a Christmas tree. The one slightly taller than him had been dated at ninety-seven years old, the smaller at one hundred and eleven. This species averaged an increase in the diameter of its trunk of between a half and three quarters of a millimetre a year. The great beeches around me were at least one thousand years old, and growing. It is quite likely that the oldest trees uncoiled their first probing root from the seed when Alaric was sacking Rome sixteen hundred years ago. It is possible that the most ancient one of all reached towards the same sun that shone on Christ.

A grove of trees was festooned with brilliant orange spherical fungi, the biggest as large as walnuts. This was *Cytarria darwinii*, called yóken by the Yámana, who used it as emergency rations when hunting, but were not fond of it. I cut one open. Its flesh was halfway between pulp and jelly, and tasted of nothing in particular.

Fifty years ago the traveller Tschiffely, who once rode two horses from Patagonia to New York, had found an English hermit living in the forest. His tiny tent was made of sealskin. He trapped animals and lived on yóken. Every few months he called at a ranch to beg sugar and salt, which he was given. Further north, on the Argentine side of the Andes, in a remote valley, behind a barbed wire fence, lived an Austrian. Not in a house, but an astronomical observatory. The sign on the gate said 'Go! This is not an inn.' Tschiffely could find only one man who had got past the sign. The man found a splendid library, mostly on astronomy, and an educated man dedicated to his observations which he was convinced would prove that one day the moon will inevitably crash into the earth.

It is a good place to develop this obsession. The Yámana kept a legend of a flood. Bridges relates:

> Long ago the moon fell into the sea, which rose in consequence with great turmoil, just as water in a bucket will rise when a large stone is dropped into it. The only survivors of this flood were the fortunate inhabitants of Gable Island, which broke away from the ocean bed and floated on the sea. The mountains round about were

soon submerged, and the folk on Gable Island, looking in all directions, saw nothing but ocean to the far horizon. The island did not drift. It was anchored in some way; and when the moon rose out of the sea and the water subsided, it settled down again in the same place as before, with its burden of human beings, guanaco and foxes. From these, the world was peopled again.

Remarkably they guessed that the size of the moon was similar to that of the earth.

Through a thin break in the trees I could see out level to the next mountain: snow. For an hour I had been stepping up a slope as steep as a ladder. Abruptly there was light ahead. The trees I was standing among were of full height. Ten yards higher up, they were half size. Ten yards again, it was open ground. I hurried on to a rock garden of low alpine flowers. They formed low pillows of tiny leaves and delicate star flowers. But to the touch they were hard and tough. It started to snow. I climbed on to a gravel ledge, turned round to face the view.

In the wood I had not realised just how steep the ground was. If I took one step forward, I would fall twenty feet and, like the stones I dislodged, keep rolling. I sat down with a thump. I was still out of sight of the summit, and growing cautious about the deteriorating weather. To my left I could see four or five miles west. The wind drove white horses down the channel to the east, where Picton Island, in the very mouth of the Atlantic entrance, was burnished by a pool of thin sunshine. The town seemed not just below me, but almost underneath my boots, the blue rectangular roofs looking incongruously like swimming pools. The frigate seemed like an Airfix model I could reach out to and pick up. The snow was falling harder. After drinking in the view I knew it was time to go down.

I took two or three steps towards the trees. Stopping, I looked up. The shoulder of the mountain was curving away into a broad top. I had looked at these peaks from the boat and decided I would climb them to see this view. Tomorrow the weather might change for the worse. I turned and ran up the hill. Four hundred feet more brought me out on to a flat peak. A wooded valley ran inland towards the wastes of the interior, to the lakes, to the Horn. The wind fell, the sun came out. The views all around me had opened up hugely. I was trying to guess how far west I could see when sunlight caught a window. The first window in that direction was keeping the wind out in Ushuaia, twenty-five miles away. I could see east beyond Picton Island to Lennox, and Isla Nueva. Puerto Williams and the beaver lakes had vanished beneath the shoulder of the hill. This was exactly how the land had looked on the day the Haush saw the spars of the *Beagle* turn into the Bay of Good Success, and filled their throats with a cry from the dawn of human time.

I danced. I danced.

*Flowers in a Jam Jar*

The morning rain cut horizontally across Puerto Williams's empty streets, and gave way only to hail. Looking up above the town to Cerro Bandera, I saw heavy snow beginning below one thousand feet. Climbing it today would have been too dangerous to do alone. I walked to the cemetery where a wooden fence kept out a white horse. Knee-high grass soaked my jeans. Here was the grave. Rain bent the petals of small flowers in a glass jar.

'Rosa Yahgan de Milicic, born Tekenika 2 March 1903, died Puerto Williams 4 April 1983. The same epitaph is written in Yahgan and Spanish.

> Annu Halayala san skar
> Wathuineiwa annu katuti hiske.
> Ya los he dejado
> dios me llevó con el.

It means:

> I have already left them
> God took me with him.

Below it, in English: 'Probably the last full-blooded Yámana.' This was added when tourists started coming.

Born Tekenika. Even the name spelled out what was unbridge-able between the old and the new. Captain Fitzroy would sail with natives along the shores and ask what the various places were called. They had no common language. Early charts showed a land called Yaapooh. Fitzroy had pointed to a distant shore and asked what it was. The native, looking carefully with his hunter's eyes, had replied *iapooh* – otter. It wasn't always so easy to see what the strang-ers wanted. In a bay of Hoste Island the guide simply said *Teke uneka*, I don't understand. Down went the name, Tekenika. It's still there, I Don't Understand Bay.

When Thomas Bridges moved to Harberton the South American Missionary Society began planning a totally new mission, in even more inhospitable country. Ships failing to make the Horn often ran north into the bay between the Cape Horn and the Wollaston Isles to the south, and the large islands of Navarino and Hoste to the north. Here they could perish for want or, it was believed, be murdered by Yámana. The Missionary Society would go and live among the most southerly families on earth, and bring them to Christ.

Leonard and Nellie Burleigh had worked eleven years for the Society, in the Falkland Islands, where they had learned Yahgan. They had a young daughter, Kate. Leonard was a carpenter. He could, the Mission reasoned, build a home for his family, a mission, and other necessary buildings. On 14 October 1888 Captain Willis sailed the *Allen Gardiner* to Grevy Island. Reconnaissance had not extended to ensuring that the boat could approach the shore within two miles of the chosen base, or that the land had wood and fresh water within a mile and a half of it. The chosen spot was, they now noticed, fully open to winds arriving directly from Antarctica.

Next day they approached Bayly Island, where they had no per-mission to stay. But it was a better site. Burleigh took the risk and went ashore. Captain Willis and the crew stayed a while, to help fell a clearing for a house, and drop stones to start a jetty. They unloaded a wooden-framed cabin and assembled it. The *Allen Gardiner* sailed away. They were sixty miles of broken islands away from Cape Horn.

From Bayly Island Burleigh wrote, 'I should offend you if I were to picture their true condition; suffice it to say that I could not have believed that people could exist in such a state of loathsomeness and filth. One family, in particular, was in a dreadful state and one poor child was being literally eaten up with vermin. She had become a mere skeleton and life seemed a burden.'

In a short time, a hundred Yámana settled round the station. 'The frantic outbursts of savagery and passion have certainly subsided much since we came but we almost daily witness scenes of cruelty which make one shudder.' He tried to organise the Indians to work. Mrs Burleigh taught basic hygiene. Divining competition, the medicine men plotted.

They had planned to grow food, but the climate killed most things. The supply boat brought too little too late; they were always waiting, eking out, making do. The weather was often so bad that even the Yámana refused to venture out, staying huddled in their leaking huts. Poor Burleigh made appeals for more money from the Missionary Society, but they were going broke, and his southern outpost was not a priority. The Burleighs satisfied themselves that one old Yámana understood and believed the message, and they baptised him.

It was plain the mission could never be self-sufficient, and there was no money to support it from without. The Burleighs were told to leave. They packed everything and waited. A message came. They could not be taken away at present. They unpacked, and soldiered on. The order to evacuate came again. They packed. Word came, they unpacked. In April 1892, after more than three lonely years, the mission authorities took them a little way north, to the bleak but larger and less exposed mission on Hoste Island. At that Tekenika Bay Mission, eleven years later, a little Yámana girl was born, of two full-blooded Yámana parents. When she died there would be no full-blooded Yámana left to stand at her grave. She was named Rosa Yahgan de Milicic.

'Tekenika Bay,' wrote Bishop Stirling, 'is better than Bayly Island as to climate and soil but that is not saying much.' The Burleighs toiled. A year later the South American Missionary Society Office in England received a short letter:

I have, indeed, sad, sad news to tell you. My precious husband was drowned this afternoon in the Bay. I can say no more. He has been much worried about some miners who have just left, and today, Saturday, he wanted a little quiet and went in the boat there, and in some mysterious way he must have fallen overboard; I do not know. May God help me and my dear children. God's ways are so mysterious, but all He does is in love.

Nellie Burleigh.

Bishop Stirling said Burleigh had been hit by a sudden heavy squall, fallen overboard, become entangled in a bank of kelp, and sunk out of sight. Several Yámana canoes were nearby, the women dived in to look for him (swimming was women's work). They found no body.

Rosa Yahgan de Milicic remembered hearing the Yámana version. They said that he had been discovered with a Yámana woman by her daughter, and had drowned himself out of shame and remorse.

Rosa lies facing the north, on the next island to her native Hoste.

Rosa Yahgan de Milicic.

## Olga Hernandez

I walked out again along the coast road. My notebook is still blurred from the rain. Near Villa Ukika a young man and his mother appeared, walking towards me. From a distance they called, 'John! John!'

'You know who I am?'

'Yes, you are coming to talk to the Yámana, to Olga!'

He smacked his chest. 'Yámana!' He took my hand. 'Brothers. Come and visit us.' I could not tell when the men were drunk. His mother had a shaking tic, which flicked her head to one side when she talked. Continually about to open her thin lips, she bent into a word, then stopped, and her head went away. I took her hand and pressed it. She nodded. They walked on.

Olga's cabin was tiny. The fence and gate were chest high. I unhooked the string tie and let myself into the plot. In the long grass of her front garden was an old red chair, bowls full of creosote-brown water, a baby bath. There were two bare wooden steps up to a windowless door faced with two pieces of hardboard. I knocked quietly. The walls were flat metal sheets. A four-paned window to the right of the door had two glass quarters, one board and one cardboard. A face appeared in the lower pane, a woman in her late sixties, I guessed. Her brown face was well lined, her thick hair, grey on the head, was dark brown on her shoulders. I waved. I did not know if her neighbour had explained I was coming. She smiled and nodded. But the cabin went silent. There were noises like shoes being kicked on, stamped to fit. Long minutes passed. It started to hail.

She opened the door, I stood with mean pellets of ice bouncing off me, and explained who I was. She wore jeans and a long brown jumper with hooped patterns.

She nodded. 'I know, I was expecting you.' She took my hand and kissed my cheek. 'Come in.'

I stepped into a warm room; it was the whole house. She showed me to a tiny kitchen table behind the door and put a stool forward for me. She stood on the other side pulling more clothes from a small armchair and throwing them on the bed. She stopped twice and it seemed there was still no room on the chair. She pushed the rest back and cleared a ledge at the front. Before she could perch on it they rolled back again. She looked round frustrated, 'So untidy.'

I explained that I wanted to record our conversation. She pushed back the clutter on the table, cleaned the corner of the table top with the underside of her sleeve, and spread a blouse on it. She reached under her jumper and zipped up her jeans. Reaching down she rolled up the roughly cut denim hems. She wore sensible department store shoes and smelt like a woman who lived alone, with pets.

On the other side of the door was a small cooker and a wood-burning stove. In the further corner was an alcove with a lavatory. On the middle of the back wall was a sink; the far left corner was filled by a single bed heaped with clothes. The stove beat heat on to my back. I took off my jacket and hung it on a nail on the back of the door.

'How many Yahgan speakers are there?'

'Eight?'

At other times she would tell me three, or five.

'My mother was pure Yámana, my father a man of Spanish blood from Puerto Montt, in the north. When they married they mostly lived here. I was born here.'

'Can you speak some Yahgan for me?'

She began to recite names for knife and fork, child and house, repeating the Spanish afterwards.

'Can you remember a song from childhood?'

'Yes.' She said it confidently, and put one hand into the palm of the other, ready to begin. She chanted half a line then stopped. I waited for her to begin again. She frowned. 'I can't remember any more.' She smiled, but was surprised at something within herself. 'No more.' A smile and a frown, together. 'Do you smoke?'

'No,' I took out my asthma inhaler, 'I have a bad chest for free.'

She reached up to a shelf and brought down an identical inhaler. 'It's the smoking, you used to smoke?'

'No, I have had asthma since I was a baby.'

'Sometimes I have to go to the doctor, it costs a lot of money, once I was very bad.'

'Did you marry a local man?'

'Yes, he was pure Yámana. We lived here, in this house. He worked, doing what he could, cutting wood, working in the country. He worked hard, long hours.'

'Did you have children?'

'No, no children. One day he went out.' She looked out of the window at the rain and hail. The stove crackled. 'He had a heart attack, and died in the field where he was working. They came to tell me. I went out to the field. He was already dead. One day he went out, and he never came back.'

I switched off the recorder. 'Would you like to hear what we have been saying?'

A short pause. 'Yes.'

She listened, nodding approval at her own speech, as if confirming the machine had got it right.

Under the bed was a tool box, wellingtons and some more shoes. I realised that when I called she had been lying, undressed, under the pile of clothes. In among them was an opened packet of dry spaghetti, and packs of cigarettes called America, Hilton and Hollywood.

'Is it the first time you have heard the sound of your own voice?'

'Yes.'

'Many people don't like hearing their own voice, does it bother you?'

'No, it doesn't.' She found the question strange.

'How old are you?'

'Fifty-eight.'

'May I take a photograph?'

'Yes.'

She stood in the doorway, innocent. We said our goodbyes, kissing on the cheek. I walked out into the last of the light, flayed by the torrential rain.

Back in Mario's house, the big iron stove was roaring in the kitchen. He pulled me in. 'Come and meet my friends.'


*El Niño*

Two men, in their late forties, like him, sat at the dining table with two boxes of red wine. Wives and grown-up daughters sat at another table by the window, children sitting on knees to draw with crayons. I took off my Gore-Tex and hung it by the stove. The rain became torrential, battering at the window. 'El Niño,' said Mario. The other two nodded. The smaller man opposite me said, 'It's all wrong, this weather, all over the world. You know El Niño in Wales?'

I said we did.

'Wales,' said the man in a brass-buttoned blazer. 'Where is Wales? Is it part of Great Britain or the United Kingdom?'

I explained. Mario nodded at the television. Bronze-skinned children stood in the street, their fingers clutching the air. 'Mexico City,' he said, 'it's snowing.'

The little man said, 'El Niño.' We all nodded and Mario opened the second box and topped us up.

Brass Buttons leaned forward confidentially, 'So whereabouts in England is Wales?'

I explained again, with sketches. Mario's wife and daughter smiled, amused.

The rain attacked harder. We ate pasta and chorizo, the women joining us at the table, then retiring afterwards to the window. The second box emptied. I fetched a bottle of red from my room. When I came back down Mario's jacket was wet, and two more boxes of wine stood on the table in a paper bag. There is a gaucho saying, One drink is sufficient, two is too many, and three is not nearly enough. Near the end of the third box I felt Brass Buttons leaning forward again. He put the tip of his forefinger to the table. 'Wales is independent, right?'

'In part.'

He moved his finger left to make a line from a drop of wine. 'And it's in the west?'

'Yes.'

He poured a big glass for himself. 'In Scotland!'

I took a big one myself, downed it and went to bed.

The bedroom temperature was 42°F night and day. The sheets were so thin I thought I would put my feet through them. I poured a rum into my enamel mug. There were seven blankets on the bed and I used them all, and dreamt of golden children in Mexico, eating snow.

*The Ritz 2*

I flew back to Punta Arenas and to the Ritz. 'Is Chatwin's old room free?'

'Yes.'

'I'll have it.'

He took me up. It was small but well decorated. Señor
Fernandez left. There was a sign on the wall next to the mirror, no
doubt a note about Chatwin. I leaned closer, 'It is forbidden to
hang wet clothes in the rooms. If you have wet or damp clothes to
hang, please hand over them to the made.'

A Formica table with a gaudy viridian top rocked on crooked
legs. I folded a piece of card carefully to size. White swans swam
across green curtains. I sat on the bed, chromium steel with a
Formica headboard. There was a stainless steel wardrobe and what
looked like a nice veneer bedside table, a touch of quality among
the factory makeshift. I ran a finger across it: metal. There was no
sink. One of the lengths of wallpaper next to the door was hung
upside down. I opened a bottle of red wine and went to the bathroom. Then I nosed round the hotel. Chatwin's room was free. All
the rooms were free.

When I returned the room smelled of fruit. I stretched out on
the bed and drank from an enamel mug.

In the morning I stepped into the hotel breakfast room, a glacial
ballroom warmed only by the radio. Señor Fernandez came in
bowed, delivered the menu, and turned off the radio. A waitress in
middle age brought coffee, another in her mid twenties the food.
They wore black uniforms in cheap material, and hovered in the
hall as I ate. After a time the older one sat down with her hands
between her knees and her shoulders hunched. I ate eggs, beaten
and cooked in a little steel dish. Each time I put down a piece of
cutlery the young woman took a pace forward to check if I had
finished.

The woman with the cardigan came in and switched on the television. Señor Fernandez brought a teapot and a jug of milk. People
gave meaningless interviews in rainy Santiago. Then it was time for
the studio exercise work-out. Three girls with bodies from a new
century lined up behind a Brazilian who had thighs like the Nile
Delta. He directed the Lycra-filmed nymphets in a session of disco
dancing which they called aerobics. The woman with Señor
Fernandez pointed at a blonde girl whose hair was threaded with

beads. She looked knowingly at me, tapped the lid of the blue enamel teapot, and nodded, in disapproving knowledge.

The second evening I made telephone calls home from an agency. I gave the cashier the telephone numbers, she dialled them and sent me to a numbered booth. When I came out a respectable-looking middle-aged man was walking round talking very loudly to no one in particular. His walnut face was crossed by a white handlebar. He seized me by the arm and spoke at length to me in Spanish. Relieved they had escaped, everyone else stopped to watch the show. To cut it short I lied in English, 'I don't speak Spanish.'

He slapped his thigh in triumph, 'And I don't speak German!'

I walked around looking for a bar but not going in anywhere. Coming back I saw the young maid from the Ritz. I scarcely recognised her in a brown cowgirl leather jacket. We went for a beer.

She was Liz Dennys Ramón. 'It is the second time I have worked there. In between I worked as a cocktail waitress in Valparaiso in the north. It paid the same wage but the tips were much better. But I had a boyfriend down here and I felt I couldn't stay.'

'Was he working?'

'He was a bad man. He did nothing, didn't work, just hung around all day and scrounged my wages off me. But I had two children.'

'By this same boyfriend?'

She sat up and glared. 'Of course.'

I shrugged 'I don't know.'

'I loved the children. I worked hard for a little money and he did nothing. He was going to be an artist, but he didn't believe in himself. After a while he never drew or painted anything.'

'And when you came back?'

'It was okay for a while, and I had money saved. But soon I made my mind up. I left him.'

'And the children?'

'He had them, his mother looks after them.' Her eyes contracted. 'I have to work because my own family needs money, but his mother has a little pension.'

We sat silent. 'I miss the children so much. You have children?'
'No.'
'I didn't think so.'
'Why not?'
'I know some things about you, you don't smoke, you drink wine, you are untidy.'
'I don't unpack. Everything in the pack is in a smaller bag. I put all the bags I need on the floor, in order. I can repack in five minutes.'
'I couldn't believe how much you untidied your room.'
'You ruined my system, I'll never find anything.'
Now she shrugged.
'What is it like working at the Ritz?'
'It's okay. Do you mind me watching you eat?'
'?'
'At breakfast. We have to stand and watch in case you need anything. I wouldn't like it.'
'It doesn't bother me.'
'Do you notice us watching?'
'I've noticed you seem cold.'
'Oh! It's so cold in there.'
'I think the manager was wearing the same blue jumper last week.'
'And last year. Always the same one!'
'The woman is his mother, not his wife?'
She laughed. 'Of course!'
'Was he ever married?'
'No, never.'
'And he had always helped run the family hotel?'
'Yes.'
'And what will you do now?'
'I have a boyfriend, we have a flat together.'
'What does he do?'
'He's a writer. He's lovely,' her face lightened, 'so different from the other one.'
'Does he make money?'

'Not yet, he's just beginning, but he is very talented.'

'Does he have a job?'

'No, it would get in the way of being a real writer. It's okay, I make enough for both of us.'

The bar had gone quiet. There was a large man talking to the owner, no one else. They were both looking at us. She was a woman who attracted men. We left. The street outside was nearly dark. I wanted her but all I said was, 'Don't take the card away from under the table leg each day, I need it to write.'

'Another writer,' she said, and walked away up the hill.

At breakfast I asked the manager, 'Was there really a madman, like Chatwin said, who collected stones and said they were fish?'

'Oh sure.'

'And did he really sell ladies' underwear?'

'It's a long time ago.'

'Chatwin said he sold ladies' underwear.'

'No, that's not true. He sold certificates, copper plaques, qualifications.'

'For what?'

'For money.'

'I mean what were the certificates for?'

'Whatever you wanted.'

'They were fakes?'

'Yes, but good ones, you got a proper certificate for your money.'

'People bought them?'

'Yes.'

'Why, if they were fake?'

'To have something to put on the wall to say you are qualified in such and such a thing.'

'As a doctor?'

'No, nothing like that, small things, repairing cameras, installing cookers, an exam passed, a diploma. He was from up country, Santiago, I think, definitely a Chileno. You must understand, it was twenty-five years ago.'

I packed and looked out at the street from the window at the head of the stairs. I thought of Chatwin walking past the Naval

College. The cadets showing only their mouths and nostrils. I walked out into the wind.

## *The* County of Peebles

I walked to the Punta Arenas Naval Museum, which was also the home of the officers' Caleuche Club. At the top of the narrow stair, the museum was quite empty. There was a roll of purple tickets, but nobody to sell me one. I went in. There were exhibits of various, mostly unnecessary monuments erected at Cape Horn and Cabo Froward – the southernmost point of the South American mainland. The only one which didn't deserve pulling down was unveiled on 5 December 1992 and is dedicated to the seamen who died in the seas round the Horn. Two steel triangles mounted on their tips face each other to make a diamond shape, the space between them moulding the air into the silhouette of an albatross seven metres high.

Cape Froward had suffered more. A very nasty cross made of hoops and bars, like a Druid wicker man, marked the visit of Pope John Paul II. A twenty-one-metre-high concrete crucifix erected in 1956 lasted just twelve years. This is a pagan climate.

There were models of small Chilean Naval vessels including the *Yelcho* which rescued Shackleton's party. The Chilean caption emphasised that their vessel's work was the most daring part of the whole affair. Never designed for ice work, it was in the right place but it was the wrong ship. They had to use it, and she did the job.

I stopped at a picture of a very beautiful four-masted clipper. The *County of Peebles* was launched from Barclay Curle's Clyde shipyard on 25 July 1875, and was the world's first fully square-rigged four-masted ship. Strangely named after a landlocked Scottish county she was one of the County series, fast sailers designed especially for the Far East routes. Many of their voyages were out of South Wales, one of her fleetest passages being from Penarth to Mauritius in sixty-six days. A crewman's diary records the excitement of sailing a commercial racing machine, when it was in trim, the weather fair, with a captain prepared to drive her hard.

> On this voyage she seemed to be alive. Never shall I forget the thrill created by tearing through the mountainous 'grey beards' of the southern ocean at 15 and even 16 knots, the irresistible force driving her cutter through the boiling seas, the wake of white foam, the board-like stiffness of the sails, the roaring hissing rollers, lifting the stern, passing the ship, and surging ahead with sea and air filled with ozone-laden flying spume, every sail, spar and rope humming, roaring or whistling the song of the gale, increasing to a crescendo every time the ship rose on a crest and dying away as she slid into the comparative peace of a deep and broad trough.

This was the working life my great-grandfather had lived.

The basic wage for an ordinary skipper might be only £20 a month, but men who could drive boats like this were at a premium. Captain Anthony Enwright made a reputation for squeezing raw speed out of the English clipper *Chrysolite*, which had an evil reputation for trying to sail under when hard pressed, and drowning any man working on the bowsprit. He was paid an unbelievable £1,000 to change captaincy to the 1,462-ton American built *Lightning*. Captaining clippers was so stressful that officers would be good for a while, then burn out. Some tea-clipper captains screwed a chair to the deck and worked and slept there for the entire voyage. Ships were violent and cruel places, and many captains never went on deck without a loaded revolver. Special 'duck's foot' revolvers were made, with four barrels splayed in an arc to clear a mutinous deck. Forty was considered old to still have the bottle to do it.

The *County of Peebles* got good captains: John Wallace, James Blair and William Fordyce. She was also a lucky ship. Her sister ship, the *County of Roxburgh* was wrecked on the Pacific atoll of Tokarva in a typhoon. When she struck, half the crew took to the lifeboats and were drowned. The other half stayed on board and the wind and waves threw her over the reef and into the safety of the lagoon. They all survived. Another sister disappeared without trace homeward bound from Calcutta.

During her twenty-three-year working life with R. & J. Craig of Glasgow the *County of Peebles* made fifty-seven voyages, at a time when just a handful of successful voyages could repay the cost of the ship. Fully crewed, forty-five men handled 30,610 linear yards of canvas. A new suit of sails needed a roll of canvas eighteen miles long. As trade died away and owners economised, they might sail with a dozen men and a handful of boys. Ship designs adapted; they kept the same sail area but broke it into smaller sails but with more of them, so the reduced crew could still handle them. The last mention of the *County of Peebles* in Lloyd's Register is for 7 August 1898 when she sailed from Cardiff under Captain Dixon, sold to Chile. She arrived at Punta Arenas on 21 October 1898 and was renamed the *Muñoz Gamero*. She was used to transfer munitions, then for storage, lastly as a hulk.

I knew this vessel. I returned to the empty desk and shouted. A cadet came. I took him to the picture. 'Is this the last boat on the pier at the Naval Dockyard?'

'Yes it is! But,' he added strangely, 'there is no pier.'

I walked back along the dock road. Two men were planing new strakes for a fishing boat. A Rottweiler carried a puppy in its mouth. I arrived at the sentry post.

'I am the English writer John Harrison and I want an appointment with the Commandant to see the *County of Peebles*.' He stood to attention. 'Come right this way.'

I was shown into Captain Montaño's empty office on the first floor. It was lined with yellow hardwood in 1950s style. There were photographs of various vessels he had commanded, signed and framed as souvenirs by grateful fellow officers. From his window I could see the *County of Peebles*. Now I understood the cadet's comment: there was no pier. Three iron hulks, two of them great four-masted square riggers, were sunk end to end. The boats were the pier.

'I am so sorry to keep you.'

I turned round to shake hands with a smooth-jowled man with a round face. 'Captain Montaño.'

We walked across the yard, he shouted for keys. We climbed a wooden stair which rose through a hole in the stern of the first boat. A catwalk then wound its way round the inside wall of the hull. 'The *County of Peebles* is usually for VIPs.' The interior was open, the deck long gone. I wondered if VIP stood for something else in Chile, perhaps Vessel In Pieces. Captain Montaño pointed down, 'When they are finished as working boats, they are lined up, sunk, and anchored with stone ballast.' The catwalk went over the bow and on to the stern of the next boat, a colossal iron hull with the stumps of four steel tube masts. It dwarfed the *County of Peebles* and must once have been at least three thousand tons.

'Do you know the name of this one?' I asked.

'This is the –' he paused, seemed surprised at himself '– I forget now.'

It had probably been American. They built clippers up to the 4,555 tons of the *Great Republic*, whereas most British boats were much lighter. The *Cutty Sark* was only 963 tons. The *Taeping* and *Ariel*, which raced 14,000 miles to London with the season's first tea and arrived twenty minutes apart, were both under 900 tons. The American boats could be driven hard and maintain full sail in high winds. *The Republic*'s cloud of sail could generate 6,000 horse power, as much as ten Formula One cars. The Yankees' top speeds were greater; the 2,275-ton *James Baines* has the fastest speed ever logged for a sailing ship '21 knots with main skysail set' was the terse boast: 24 miles an hour without fuel. She sank, on fire, in Liverpool docks. As a child, I stood on her old timbers at the Pier Head. Her sister ship, the *Champion of the Seas*, once made an astonishing 465 miles in a day. While the lighter clippers like the *Cutty Sark* and the *County of Peebles* might only touch 17 knots flat out, they could find 14 knots in light winds which left the big vessels floundering. But the heavyweights were the ships for the long grain runs to Australia across the Southern Ocean where the lightweights, trembling under storm sails, might see a cloud of white canvas flying towards them and know a Yankee clipper was riding the wind.

We reached the *County of Peebles* herself. The clipper was in marginally better shape than the other two. Unlike them, she was creaking. Captain Montaño pointed down at her bow as we stepped on. 'Her back is broken, the bow is anchored but the stern is still afloat, and moves with the tide.' He smiled, 'She is still restless.' He was smiling at her, not me. He took out the keys and opened a mahogany door. 'This is locked because it is only for officers from the Caleuche Club, or visiting dignitaries.' We stepped inside.

It was dark and I listened to her great back groaning. The rich upholstery of her timbers creaked to adjust to each new lie. The figure of a woman dressed head to foot in white glowed in the dark. The captain groped for the brass dimples of the electric lights. The figurehead's face and arms were deadly white and she was eight feet tall. Her left hand shaded her eyes, her right scooped the hem of her cloak. Iron braces held her back to the foot of the mizzen mast where it plunged through the decks to its roots in the slowly writhing keel.

'The officers' quarters and captain's cabin have been knocked together.' He pointed the shiny toes of his black shoes at the stubs of the old partition. 'We are in the stern of the ship, here is a spare compass and wheel, so in emergency the ship could be controlled without going on deck. That is sometimes necessary in these waters.'

In a shadow on the wall was a grey print of *Fragata Peebles* taken about 1890. There were smudges of buildings in the background and she must have been in port as her long yards were drawn nearly parallel to the hull. Otherwise there was no clue to her whereabouts. Next to it was a list of her sailings from Liverpool, Barry, Cardiff, Penarth and Falmouth. Here, so far from home, were familiar names. They are places I have lived or worked in; I have walked round all those docks.

At the far end of the saloon was a curved sweep of glass bending outwards under the sloping, rounded stern. It was like looking out from a lantern. On a ledge below them lay an eighteenth-century brass telescope, its scratched lenses forever conjuring fog. A brass and mahogany wheel as tall as me caught the light and mellowed it into pools distilled from ancient summers.

## WCSA

The Welsh connection in many of the *County of Peebles'* voyages
was no coincidence. In the nineteenth century the economic
capital of Chile was Swansea. As early as the eighteenth century
Swansea was the world centre for smelting every metal except iron.
The biggest trade was in copper. Smelting copper took a lot of coal
and it was cheaper to bring the ore to Swansea's coal. English
copper ore could be 10 per cent pure, Cuban up to 20 per cent,
but Chilean up to 60 per cent. Ships sailed from Wales with coal,
coke, firebricks and fireclay, and returned with copper ore. The ore
was so heavy that only a small part of the hold could be used.
Special boxes had to be fitted within the hold to stop the cargo
shifting and sinking the boat in the return leg round Cape Horn.
A boat with a boxed hold was called 'Swansea fitted' and the trade
was called WCSA – West Coast South America.

Men apprenticed in the copper barques could get work in any
part of the Merchant Navy. They came from the beautiful Gower
peninsula near Swansea, they deserted the thin wet soils of
Cardigan farms further west. Joseph Conrad recalls visiting one of
the captains he served under, when the old man was sick at home,
a deep water sailor, marooned ashore, being nursed by his wife and
her spinster sister. The youngest son, twelve years old, chattered
about W. G. Grace's latest innings. Conrad said:

> I learned more of him in that interview than I did in the whole
> eighteen months we had sailed together. It appeared he had served
> his time in the copper-ore trade, the famous copper-ore trade of
> old days between Swansea and the Chilean coast, coal out and ore
> in, deep-loaded both ways, as if in wanton defiance of the great
> Cape Horn seas. A whole fleet of copper-bottomed barques, as
> strong in rib and planking, as well-found in gear, as ever was sent
> upon the seas, manned by hardy crews and commanded by young
> masters. 'That was the school I was trained in,' he said to me almost
> boastfully, lying back among his pillows, with a rug over his legs.

The bottleneck in the nitrate business was loading the ships. The
homewardbound cargoes were often manhandled aboard in ports

with no docks or cranes, in places like Iquique (pronounced Ee-kee-kay). Lighters ferried sacks of cargo to ships standing off the coast, exposed to the storms, earthquakes and tidal waves. It could take months to load two or three thousand tons. Since no steamer could afford to lie idle so long, it remained one of the last trades for square-riggers.

To keep it profitable, they innovated, and were among the first to employ iron in ship construction, first in the frames, then for the walls of the hull. The Swansea barque *La Serena*, built in 1848 by the Neath Abbey Company for the WCSA copper trade, was the first iron sailing vessel to round Cape Horn. The Swansea Iron Shipbuilding Company built the 81-ton iron screw steamer *Fire Fly* in 1849, which was the first steamer to pass through the Strait of Magellan. When Chile began to part-refine the ore, cargo volumes dropped, but there were always other homeward cargoes. Europe's farms were greedy for nitrate fertilisers. No one knew how to manufacture them artificially but in north Chile natural mineral deposits of nitrates lay in blinding sheets in the world's driest desert, the Atacama.

Its weather station used to report an average rainfall of 0.01 inches. But this was the result of averaging out, over all the years of its existence, a single heavy dew. Trains of donkeys and mules walked out through the desert, with no food and only a little water from artificial condensers. They were loaded with sacks and stumbled back, many dying. The inland nitrates lay in territory which once belonged mostly to Bolivia. The other major deposits of nitrates, the seabird guano, lay on islands which belonged to Peru. The islands stand in waters of the Humboldt Current, which runs right up the west coast of Chile and Peru, and are so rich that petrels come from Antarctica to feed here, albatrosses come from New Zealand, and skuas and gulls fly down from Alaska. Their dung built up hundreds of feet thick. It was mined by indentured Indian labourers, little better than slaves, and carried in sacks to the waiting windjammers.

But the majority of workers in both areas were Chilean, and in 1879 they seized the town of Antofagasta from Bolivia, and began the War of the Pacific, taking on both Bolivia and Peru. Chile won, Bolivia lost its only coastal territory and became landlocked. South

West Peru was seized by Chile. To this day, Peruvian army officers swear an oath to recover the lost town of Arica.

Europe was starved of fertiliser, especially for the large French and German sugar beet growers. There were fortunes to be made. Leading the way was Yorkshireman J. T. North, dubbed the Nitrate King. He created companies, talked up their shares and moved on. In 1887 he bought the Lagunas nitrate field for £110,000, divided it into three holdings, and seven years later floated just one of them for £850,000. When companies crashed he seldom still held shares in them.

Between the World Wars my grandfather Thomas Harrison sailed on tramp steamers carrying guano. He remembered the fine dust which dried and penetrated everywhere and everything. There was only one advantage; it killed all the rats and mice. This was just as well, as it also killed the ships' cats. Only fleas and lizards seemed immune. His father would have known another unpleasant trick. The dust caked to the shoe and rotted the footropes on which the men aloft stood to handle the sails.

At the end of the nineteenth century Chile provided 70 per cent of world demand for nitrogen fertiliser, and three-quarters of the country's income came from the nitrate tax. But in 1909 a German called Fritz Haber wrecked Chile's economy. He combined nitrogen from the air with hydrogen to form ammonia, and, as the Haber-Bosch process, it was taken further, allowing many nitrogen compounds to be synthesised. Before 1914 Germany had taken 200,000 tons a year of Chilean nitrates. The war crippled shipping, but the manufacture of munitions needed nitrates and Germany geared up to provided its farmers and its weapons-makers with artificial nitrates. After 1918 it would not need to import. Nor would the other industrial powers.

Haber had another claim to fame. In the First World War he masterminded German production of gas weapons. When Germany lost he feared being tried as a war criminal. Instead, in 1918, he won the Nobel Prize for Chemistry.

In August 1927 the British ship *William Mitchell* was finishing loading nitrate at Tocopilla. As the last bag was swung on board, the smallest apprentice jumped on to it with the Union Jack in his hand. He was raised up high to call for three cheers. The crew began the Homeward Bound shanty.

> O fare you well, I wish you well!
> Good-bye, fare you well; good-bye, fare you well!
> O, fare you well, my bonny young girls!
> Hoorah, my boys, we're homeward bound!

No vessel answered. The harbour was full of steamers. The *William Mitchell* began the last voyage of the nitrate clippers.


*John Rees Jones*

It was time to interview the living, then the dead. Some mountaineers had given me the name of John Rees Jones as the best man to meet in Punta Arenas. In an old-fashioned business block in the city centre was a large Renaissance-style archway and wrought iron gates. A small sign pinned aloft said British Honorary Consul. It was surely wrong. There was an airline office strewn with parcels and packaging. Boxes of cerise stewardess uniforms lay in polythene wraps. The secretaries admired two slim dark-haired women modelling the outfits.

I asked, 'Where is the Consul's office?'

'It is here.'

'I have an appointment.'

John Rees Jones's family had come from Wales. I had written a postcard from home asking to see him.

'Your name?' she asked.

'Harrison,' I said, 'John Harrison.'

'Señor Harrison John Harrison,' she repeated and left me there some time. Two men carrying a steel lintel walked through.

A stewardess escorted me to a chair deeper in the office. I heard John Rees Jones talking continuously in Spanish, moving from one plaintiff to another, directing and advising. He saw me and came up beaming, an arm outstretched; in English he said, 'John how good to see you,' in Spanish, 'Please show Mr Harrison to my office.' Back to English – 'I won't keep you one moment.' – and out of the door. I turned slowly in the revolving chair. The small office was homely with a hi-fi, a collection of classical CDs and tapes, and bookcases of art and architecture. A framed certificate announced his appointment as Honorary British Consul. Silver letter-knives and a hardwood inkstand. A den.

He came in with tea on a tray. 'You must forgive me. We are opening a new airline today, there is so much to do.' He reached behind him and pulled out my postcard, a satellite picture of Wales. 'You sent me this very interesting photograph. Remarkable – no cloud!'

He sat down and waited for the pot to brew. His fingers played a tiny accordion in the air.

'Our main job is shipping, we are shipping agents, seventy-six years old. After a very slack year in 1995 we have a very good year, these last six months have been very active, and now we are to become general agents for a new airline, which starts flying next Friday the 27th. It's a very very busy day. But Punta Arenas is a small city so there's always time for everything. Everything is ten minutes away, literally. It's a long day, lots of work, but you seem to have more time for the more pleasant things, not like a big city.'

'So what opportunities does the new airline see when the national airlines are in so much trouble?'

'We are talking about local travel. It's going to be a domestic airline for the time being. The domestic market has grown dramatically, it'll continue growing next year, the people who own this new airline are quite satisfied with 7 per cent of the market, it's a $24 million initial investment, we've got three airplanes and no debts at all. The important thing is we already belong to IATA which is the International Air Transport Association, which is quite a feat for a newcomer.'

I met him again a year later. They had just bought two more 737s.

'My great grandparents came from Swansea, I think the place was called Foxhole. They came in the late nineteenth century, they must have been extremely poor, because they changed the beauty of southern Wales for the ugliness of a desert in the north of Chile. My family established themselves in the area of Caldera, and Copiapó, which is about six hours north of Santiago, in the nitrate area. Later on my grandfather settled down in Valparaiso, the main port for Santiago. That's how the family got established in the capital.'

'Did they just go out looking for their fortune?'

'My great grandfather was what they called an assayer, and he was working for the nitrate companies, I guess he was some sort of an engineer or something, my father was an accountant. So we've been kind of a scientific family, architects and doctors and all that. I studied in the Grange School which is a very old well-established British school in Santiago. Later on, as a result of journalism, I got into sales, and started working for airlines in 1964. Then I got married to a local girl from Punta Arenas, and we left for Mexico. We lived in Mexico fifteen years. The last three years I was very fortunate to be private assistant to the Under Secretary of Finance of the Mexican Government, which was fascinating. As a result of my wife's father's death we came back to Punta Arenas.'

'You have been Honorary British Consul for – how long?'

'Five years.'

'How do you get to be offered a post like that?'

'Well the appointment is a complete mystery. They obviously check out people. They must have a list. Now first of all I must warn you that my father-in-law was Consul for over thirty years, so it was sort of in the family. One day the Consul General from Santiago phoned me from Punta Arenas, and he said, "John, I'd like to come and see you." After several hours of talking he suddenly sprang the question, Would you like to be Honorary Consul? I said Yes. He said, Well keep it highly confidential, I wouldn't even tell your wife, because you are being double-checked. So obviously something was going on, and about a month later I got a call from the Ambassador, he's gone now, he's retired. He said, Well you've been appointed now officially. So this is how it happened, I really don't know how it's done.'

'Was there any training or did you just read all the Graham Greene books you could?'

'Well I had read those before, in fact one of my very favourite books, having lived in Mexico so long, is Malcolm Lowry's *Under the Volcano*, which is about Geoffrey Firmin, an ex-Consul and his disgrace in twenty-four hours under the shadow of Popocatépetl, fascinating book. No, but there's no training, just common sense really. It's a busy Consulate, because of relations with the Falklands. There's a dwindling – I must say it's a sad story – a dwindling British community in Punta Arenas and in the surrounding areas.'

'But why does Britain need a presence here?'

'Shipping, first of all. Then tourism; the summer keeps me very busy with lost passports and pilfered wallets. The Royal Navy ships visit Punta Arenas from the Falklands at least four times a year. It's very active, and then there's commercial relations with the Falklands. Then there's one-offs; last week two men parachuted from a twin-engined Otter down on to the South Pole. One parachute didn't open and they can't understand it because parachutes just don't fail any more. There's a rather ridiculous theory that it was an elaborate suicide, but that's nonsense.'

I was curious to hear his take on the territorial disputes between Chile and Argentina. 'In Ushuaia, an earnest young man at the museum brought out a map showing twenty-three border disputes, and said, "Do you know, we have only won one of these." Is that true?'

'No that is not accurate at all, it is a historical fact that Chile has given up a lot of territory. The present government has a policy of appeasement, total appeasement, but yet there's a lot of opposition among important politicians and people in the street, who feel that enough is enough. So we are just waiting for the outcome of this last one, the ice cap north of Puerto Natales. It's being discussed by both parliaments, in Santiago and in Buenos Aires. The young man is wrong, we've lost a lot of territory.'

'But the ice caps are inaccessible. Are these real disputes about areas that matter, or just jingoism, a matter of popular feeling?'

'Well, we don't know. You see, this disputed land is a lot of high mountain terrain. There's always a question of oil, for example. We don't know which minerals might turn up, gold or silver or whatever. So there is a combination of jingoism and sincere hopes of keeping that territory. We've lost enough.'

I told him about finding Chatwin's entry in the Ritz. John rocked back in his chair fingertips touching, his hands tented. '*In Patagonia* is one of my favourite books. I've read it many, many times. And every time there's something new and thrilling in it. I think Bruce was a wonderful writer. I never met him, I was in Mexico when he came down. My father-in-law was very lucky, I think he was at the house for tea or something. And of course his early death was a very sad thing. I must tell you that both in Buenos Aires and in Punta Arenas Bruce Chatwin is not very well remembered by a lot of people, because he was writing a novel, really. The feeling they have here, some elderly Britishers, is that he sort of used them. He took out a lot of stories and distorted them. There's a famous story about a lady who lived up on the hill and he called her the duchess, which is sort of cruel, because she was extremely charming to him. But then of course he's dead, and he wrote a wonderful book.'

I stood up, leaving John to carry on opening an airline. 'One last thought, do you know a man called Tomas Daskam? I am hoping to meet him.'

'Chile's most famous painter – well, he's American but he lives part of the year here and his work is all about Chile.'

'What's he like?'

'Well.' He looked at the ceiling. 'No, he was fine.'

'But?'

'He can be charming, I found him charming.'

'But?'

'Well, let's say he doesn't suffer fools gladly.'


## Salesian Museum

The outside of the Salesian Mission Museum in Punta Arenas was so anonymous I walked past it twice. The dark glasses I wore against the dusty wind and the fitful sun left me blind in the sepulchral interior. They had an exhibition of goods made by natives from the San Rafael Mission on Dawson Island. There were throw rugs that would look good in Habitat, candlesticks, and a wooden box in the shape of a warped heart, and pictures of Selk'nam in guanaco fur, before they had been saved for Jesus and dressed in Lancashire cottons.

The Chilean government had given approval to Monseñor Fagnano of the Salesian Fathers to create a mission station for the Selk'nam, and granted him use of Dawson Island, a fifty-mile-long flint arrowhead pointing north into the Magellan Strait. Selk'nam were shipped here for the women to knit and make blankets, and the men to cut timber in a sawmill. Lucas Bridges was passing through on a steamer and went in. He spoke Selk'nam, which the fathers did not, and the natives stopped work and crowded round. He saw among the ones he knew, Hektliohlh, six foot three, broad and strong, wearing western clothes two sizes too small. The fathers frowned at the interruption to their work. Bridges returned at the end of the day. He learned that Hektliohlh had been captured in his homeland to the east and brought to Ushuaia, in Yámana territory. He escaped, was captured once more and brought further west to Dawson Island, the ancient land of the Kawéskar canoe Indians. He was a hunter working in a factory. He did not complain of his treatment. But he looked east, where his own mountains lay, out of sight. '*Shouwe t-maten ya*' – 'Longing is killing me'. He died soon after.

Between 1889 and 1898, one thousand natives entered San Rafael. When it closed in 1911, just twenty-five remained. A picture shows Juan Emilio Galindo Natales, a Kawéskar from the western channels, at his first communion on 21 July 1947. He wore a suit, and a sash tied to his arm, a medal in the lapel. Sabot shoes cased his feet, his hands held each other. In the day he would practise his copperplate on paper stamped Nº 3 Escuelas Publicas de la Republica de Chile.

> Acuerdate que tienes una sola alma,
> Con el sudor de tu rostro, comeras el pan.
>
> Remember that you possess just one soul,
> With the sweat of your brow you will eat bread.

Writing the lines out, again and again.

The museum was dark and brittle and smelled of dusty feathers. Tschiffely visited it just before the Second World War. He blinked at the curiosities which included a two-headed lamb. In the interests of taste this has now been replaced by the stillborn bodies of Siamese twin calves. The taxidermist was not favoured by his suppliers or, for that matter, with ability. Many animals look as if they had died from eating a rugby ball, or were waiting for knee surgery. The supply of brown animal eyes was very poor. Behind a door hid a beaver with black and white doll's eyes protruding on stalks. Originally placed in the centre of the wall, one moonless night he limped here out of shame.

Glass cases displayed crafted arrowheads in stone and flint and glass, and the delicate heads of fish-spears and harpoons. Preservation measures were basic: mothballs. Even though they were all displayed horizontally, each artefact was bound to a display card with fine cord. As I moved between cases, I had a vision of the natives spending their last days tying down small pieces of their past to grey card, as if gravity had been discovered too late to hold them here.

I left in melancholy mood and crossed the road to meet the most important person in Punta Arenas, who was waiting in the beautiful manicured avenues of the cemetery.

## The Last Repose of Don José Menéndez

My second interview in Punta Arenas was with the dead. Their bodies were whisked to the gridiron plots of the cemetery at the top of the hill, near the racecourse. High walls and proud gates. A neat map showed where each family was buried; all are grouped according to their nationality. Pairs of towering cypresses were trimmed into columns of dark green, which now almost touch each other. Damp from a sudden shower, I squeezed between them like a cloth through the wringer.

Some of the mausoleums, like those of the great Blanchard trading house, were temples built in red brick, and rendered with cement scored to imitate stonework. The Kusanovices contemplated eternity in a natty pastel polychrome number. The mausoleums were built with many empty shelves, planning for fertile dynasties. Some of the very newest had draught-proof aluminium windows and looked as if they were for sale: necropolis as garden centre.

At the east end, babies and young children were buried in glass-fronted sepulchres. The infant coffins were hidden, but each front was a window containing the memorabilia of short lives. There were favourite toys, dolls and model cars, crowding a picture of the child. It was December and some had new Christmas presents. Several had a silver clock stopped at the fatal hour, putting a finger to the heart.

Near them was the tomb of the unknown Indian. A lumpen bronze statue was the shallow apology for extermination. Its hands and lower legs were shiny from touching. Around it were plaques for favours granted: a heathen saint.

Here in the cemetery's central oval which, like the centre of the living city, admitted only the richest, was a neo-classical fantasy topped by an Annunciation angel. Its right hand held a straight trumpet, the left pointed up and beyond. Flaming urns marked the corners, eight stocky bronze posts led to the door. Once they were linked with chains, but these had gone and the posts remained only as a defence against ram-raiders. The bronze doors were girdled with shields, showing a wheel, a ship's rudder, and a sheep, faithful to the occupant, in bronze, for ever. In the boss of each shield was a round head with a wise stare, brisk moustache and a paternal face. He was bald as porcelain. It was the Hollywood biopic face of kindly enterprise. But the man inside was Don José Menéndez.

*The Holiday of Don José Menéndez*

In April 1899, as autumn slid into winter, the weather in Punta Arenas grew colder and the wind calmer, and servants scurried around the halls of the palace on the main square, folding clothes and pressing down trunk lids. Porters loaded cases into the line of carriages in front of the houses of the millionaires on Plaza Muñoz Gamero. These men controlled the southern livestock trade, when the south contained half of all Chilean livestock wealth. Handsome horses pawed the gravel, urchins stared and threw sly stones. The man whose family and business partners had built all these mansions was going north to enjoy the winter in Buenos Aires. In little more than a week, the modern steamers would land him in the balmy port where his usual suites at the Universal Hotel gleamed in polished anticipation.

A picture of him in middle age shows a different face to the benefactor and friend of sheep portrayed on his tomb. It is a face only his dog could love. A baron's head, more Prussian than Spanish, sits on a wrestler's neck bursting from a starched butterfly collar. A necktie with a stud below the knot clutches his throat. His head is smooth, his jowls round, the ears flat.

In June a respectful man from the newspaper *El Diario* was admitted to the study and office of Don José Menéndez in his suite at the Hotel Universal. The great man talked and the quiet man wrote. 'Mr José Menéndez is the prototype of the "self-made man of our time."' The journalist actually used the English phrase. 'The life of this man is a constant ascent towards the summit of fortune, achieved by the drive of constant determination and brute force in a wild and savage environment.' The city journalist conscientiously recorded all the triumphs and setbacks on Don José's road to success. Relaxed and always confident, Don José Menéndez felt himself far from the chill realities of the south. He even admitted to a fly in his opulent ointment.

'I could have 150,000 sheep in Estancia La Primavera alone if I did not have a large clientele in the form of the Selk'nam Indians who each year eat between 15 and 20,000 sheep. Those who are based a mile from Cabo Domingo on the Atlantic coast occupy a twelve-league plot of land which has come to be regarded as a refuge and a nest of thieves. Since being set up, the Salesian Mission has been surrounded by two estancias.' (Both his). 'The Indians continually go out, and from the huge dense thickets and woods which extend from Rio Grande to the south they cross the countryside and rob many head of sheep, then, if they are surprised, they say they are going to the Mission or returning from there and they play with a crafty smile and quietly make fools of us.

'So the Mission is a magnificent excuse to practise rustling without risk. Selk'nam Indians have incurable rapacity. They rob for pleasure and enjoy robbing other people's property.' He went on to recite the all-too-familiar charges. 'The Selk'nam rounded up hundreds of sheep and, if chased, cut off one hoof and left them, or slit their throats.'

'And the work of the missionaries?' prompted the quiet voice from *El Diario*.

The round glasses tilted back with the glowing head, catching the light of the tall windows in two mica discs. It was very pleasant to air his views to this agreeable man. Living here under the palms of Buenos Aires his interviewer must marvel at the problems which men of destiny and enterprise, such as himself, suffered at the cold frontier, to put lamb and beef on the tables of Buenos Aires and Europe. 'I consider them of relatively little consequence. The Indians who go to the mission probably present themselves contritely to the missionaries, but the majority have no other purpose than to rob sheep and return to their lairs in the woods. And the missionaries charge us one pound sterling each time they take a native into their care, then 30 centavos daily. We have to have a special budget for these singular pensioners.'

If the journalist asked what the government or the company had ever paid the Selk'nam for taking land they had lived in for ten thousand years, it is not recorded. The journalist's piece appeared on 13 June 1899.

Fourteen hundred miles south, Monseñor José Fagnano, Salesian missionary, builder of Punta Arenas Cathedral, founder of the Dawson Island Mission for Selk'nam, founder of the Candalaria Mission at Cabo Domingo, fixed the loop of his spectacles about his ears and sat at his desk at Candalaria, or, as it was now known in the world, 'a nest of thieves'. He set the copy of *El Diario* for 13 June 1899 a little to one side, and dipped his pen.

Señor Editor, knowing with certainty that you enjoy a code of impartiality which is the prerogative of serious journalists, there is no doubt that you would wish to give more space in your columns for me to place a reply to answer the charges made by your reporter against the Salesian Mission at Rio Grande, which are attributed to Don José Menéndez.

The letter continues in the lightly strained tone of a man wishing to sound reasonable while walking a cheese-wire tightrope wearing ice skates. He points out that Menéndez's agent McLennan had received extensive hospitality without charge for prolonged stays at the Mission. Then 'I come to the pound sterling which is paid to us for each Indian brought in. This business of the pound sterling awakes a certain memory, which tempts me to draw back the veil which covers it, but it is not a mystery to anyone, least of all to me – the gradual disappearance of the Indians – but I would never have done so without further provocation.' He declares he has never had a penny from the landowners and 'I await for Señor Menéndez to impose on me the pleasant obligation to state the contrary, to his credit.'

The south was Menéndez's fiefdom and Fagnano had called him a bully and a liar. But Menéndez had made the mistake of patronising Fagnano's life work, and he was the one man in the south who, in his own field, had achieved every bit as much as Menéndez, but done it altruistically. No one might care whether Menéndez had lost ten thousand or a hundred thousand sheep, but they would be very interested to find he had lied about giving money to the Church, and was hiring men to kill Indians.

*Indian Killers*

The ranchers recruited shepherds from other cold wet countries. Many Scots and Welsh came here. New contracts required them to bring a trained sheep dog. Within weeks there were no stray dogs on the streets of Punta Arenas. Some bought smallholdings.

The natives had no concept of owning land or animals. But they soon discovered the new white guanaco were easy killing. When the settlers' capital was annihilated by Selk'nam sheep raids, they became eager recruits to the new trade, of Indian killing.

A cyclone of rising violence began. When Selk'nam were shot, they began stealing whole flocks. To cross deep streams, they would break the legs of the leading animals until there were enough lying in the water for the rest to walk across them. If chased they would, as Menéndez had claimed, kill or maim the sheep.

The farmers organised killing raids. Bringing back a bow was as good as an ear because no Selk'nam would give up his bow while he was alive. Sometimes it had to be prised out of the dead man's fingers. The farmhands sold them to tourists on passing cruise ships.

The Selk'nam were handicapped by their codes of honour. They would not use poison on their arrow tips or shoot at a man once off his horse. McLennan was probably the man Lucas Bridges calls McInch. He was a red-faced Scot with a fondness for the bottle, and a glass tie-pin made from an arrowhead he had dug out of his own chest. He also had a code of honour, and would fly into a rage if he saw a horse spurred unnecessarily, or oxen being whipped. But he was proud of hunting, on horseback with rifles, naked men armed only with bows and arrows. John McRae boasted of killing sixty Indians. One ex-rancher had a full set of saddle gear and harness made from the skin of Indians he had shot. Another hunted canoe Indians from a steam launch.

El Jimmy knew two of the most notorious killers, Sam Hazelup and McDonald. Indian raids normally took place around the first quarter of the moon, and the gangs would be ready. They took supplies for twelve or fifteen days, and had one order: to kill as many people as possible.

If there were women for them, they hobbled them, like horses, outside their tents. When work finished, they took them to the river and scrubbed them. The women were docile, once captured. In their own society they were domestic property. Anthropologist Anne Chapman summarised a Selk'nam wife's role as follows: wife's obligations – serve the man; wife's rights – none. If the

Selk'nam women got pregnant by a white man, they killed the baby. If the women returned to their tribes after living with whites, their own men killed them.

McDonald rode a white horse and would not shoot old men and women, or children. That was a waste of ammunition. He dismounted and knifed them. If there was a young woman among them, he raped her then cut her throat. If she was pretty, he would rape her for days, then cut her throat.

Hazelup took an arrow in his wrist, and another in his hat. A tin matchbox dented when an arrow struck it, in his breast pocket, over his heart.

The killing was an open secret. The governments did not interfere until there were too few left to harm the ranchers. Some gang bosses and farm managers were taken to Punta Arenas, where they were given bail. No one was jailed. McLennan died of delirium tremens, raving that Selk'nam had come to kill him. Sam Hazelup left a saloon one night and was helped over the edge of the ravine behind it.

The Selk'nam had at least seven different words for the white men. An early one was *k'óloit* which means 'his cape is red' (the police used to be issued with red blankets). Two others were coined for bounty hunters. When hunters rode close together in dark clothes, the Selk'nam used a word meaning 'clumps of earth with roots pulled from black swamp water'. At other times hunters tied dummies to horses, as decoys. The dummies were made from hide stuffed with turf. The Selk'nam called these white men 'figures of earth covered with hairy hides'. That was how civilisation dressed to kill.

# 5

# *Last Hope Sound*

*Road to Rio Verde*

It was time to leave Punta Arenas and begin the long journey to Santiago, its grapes and smog fermenting in the sun two thousand miles north. But first I had a final piece of business. The Los Angeles film director Jo Menell had given me the telephone number of an artist he thought I would be interested to meet. Tomas Daskam, about whom I had quizzed the Honorary Consul, lived part of the year in a hamlet called Rio Verde, which even Tierra del Fuegians regard as small and out of the way. All I knew about him at that time was that he painted hyper-realist paintings, which sold all round the world, and had an interest in wildlife.

There was an estancia just outside Rio Verde which rented rooms, but there was no transport to get there. It looked as if I could catch a bus north on the Puerto Natales road, ask to stop at Cabeza del Mar, the head of a big sea inlet, and walk or try to hitch down a track which served a dozen or so big mainland estancias. If there was no traffic it was a two-day walk, but I had a bivouac bag. I packed a little food and some water.

The bus driver had a young assistant to stow luggage and collect the tickets. He was thin and eager in a maroon and grey jacket and did his job as if he had never wanted to be anything but a bus driver's assistant on the Puerto Natales run. The eight o'clock morning bus rolled along the shore of the Magellan Strait in blustery sunshine, past the Toro y Concha wine warehouse and the old wooden women's prison.

To the right was Cabo Negro; I recalled a story about El Jimmy's arrival. On his first Sunday Jimmy was invited to a picnic in the forest by James Louis, the owner of the saloon where he was lodging. A German named Sheaver owned a lemonade and ginger beer business, and offered to provide the drinks. With Mrs Louis and the picnic he went ahead on his cart. The rest of the men walked up to the agreed spot. No cart, no picnic, no Herr Sheaver, no wife. They did not show up until evening. She was carefree, Mr Louis rabid. He practically kept her under lock and key after that. But soon she left with Sheaver for good.

They opened a little bar and lodging house here on the Cabo Negro road but she fell ill straight away, and peered mournfully at visitors from the back of the shop. After some months she died. Sheaver took a shotgun and blew his brains out.

Twenty miles out of town was the last neck of land on the American continent, anchoring the bulge on which Punta Arenas lies. We stopped just once; on a flat straight road the bus turned down a winding track to the Hotel Cabeza del Mar. This wooden building stood on what seemed a lake shore but was in fact the sea (the channel that linked the lagoon to the sea was narrow and hidden). The water glittered and blinded. A huge pink and black pig with a domed back walked from the garden to the shore. The driver sat still for some time. Nothing stirred. A small boat called *Snows* lay in a drift of shingle. The driver knocked at the door and spoke to someone in the shadows of the hall. No one got off the bus and no one got on.

The bus driver drove back up to the main highway and almost immediately signalled to me that the dusty track on the left was the road to Rio Verde. I got out and the bus pulled away leaving con-trails of dust blowing across the open sky. When it cleared I saw a smart grey minibus standing on the gravel delta, at the junction where the Rio Verde track joined the main road. In it

The *Captain Leonidas* on the Cotopaxi Bank, English Narrows, in the Western Channels of Chile. 'How many people live here?' I asked. 'None'

The *County of Peebles*, Punta Arenas. Her heyday saw 'every sail, spar and rope humming, roaring or whistling the song of the gale'

Gonzalo's, Avenida San Martín, Ushuaia, from my room at the Hotel Alakaluf

Going ashore: unloading the Zodiacs from the *Sergey Vavilov*, South Shetland Islands

Punta Arenas, the palace of Sara Braun, widow of one of the founders of the Sociedad Explotadora del Tierra del Fuego. It was built in 1895, all the materials being imported from Europe

The owners of these palaces paid men on horseback to shoot with guns naked Indians armed with bows and arrows for a pound a head

Guarded by condors: Despard Bridges's home-made boat, Estancia Harberton, Beagle Channel

Antarctic Peninsula, Le Maire Channel, early morning. The mainland, which we did not make, is on the left, Booth Island is to the right

The road to Rio Verde: Nicolas and Violeta's estancia with Skyring Sound in the distance

The New Year Rodeo, Chonchi, island of Chiloé

Through Selkirk's eyes: the view from his lookout, Robinson Crusoe Island, Juan Fernández Islands

The dark artery through Tierra del Fuego, the Beagle Channel

was a scruffy driver and two men who looked like prosperous Sicilians who paid no tax. I walked up and they threw open the door.

'Can you take me anywhere near Rio Verde?'

'That's where we are going. Jump in.'

I asked, 'Did you know I was coming?'

'What?'

'Were you waiting for me?'

'No.'

'Why were you here?'

'In case there were any passengers.'

'You just wait on the off-chance?'

'Sure.'

'Do I pay?'

They all laughed. 'No.'

We drove west for an hour. The geography here is impossible. A quick look at the map suggests two huge rounded lakes coming in from the west, called Seno Otway, and, north of it, Seno Skyring. In fact it is one colossal bay, and slap in the middle and filling most of it is Riesco Island. Between the island and the mainland, linking the two long sea bays, forty and fifty miles long, is a channel five or six hundred yards wide, where the tides from each side of the island butt and snarl at each other.

They dropped me off at the estancia at Rio Verde. It stood alone, a long two-storey building overlooking the foment of the channel between the two bays. The walls were faced with vertical logs that still had the bark on. No one was in sight. At the back was a yard with four friendly dogs.

Violeta Drpic was in her early fifties with a strong handsome face and round, direct eyes. She said hello and waved me in. Nicolas Drpic came in, tall, quiet, his eyes shy and evasive. He showed me into a single lounge-diner which ran the length of the front of the building. Panoramic windows gave a view of the strait, divided in two by a stone fireplace you could park a car in. Trees tumbled into the embers. Two breakfasters streamed with sweat. After eating they paid and left.

In front of the estancia, at the water's edge, was a hard ramp for the ferry. There was a wooden paddle which could be fixed upright to call the ferry, white side for pedestrians, red side for vehicles. Pedestrians only paid if there were no vehicles and a crossing was made solely for them. On the other side, three houses nestled at the foot of a steep hill. Two were yellow with red roofs, the other was white with a green roof and a boat in the garden. The ferry left the far shore and headed up current and upwind to my right for a hundred metres to where two tides met head on, in lines of foam and low white waves. As the ferryman crossed them he turned the boat round and headed to my left, now sailing with the wind, but still against the reverse tide. The battered green ferry was carrying only one car but it was so low in the water that I made a note to go when there were no cars on it, even if I did have to pay. An old man with a cap over his face came to the raised square bow and turned a handcrank to lower the boarding ramp, revealing that the davits and the inside were painted buttercup yellow. Fifty yards away the pilot flung her round and just as the swinging bow was square with the shore she beached perfectly, and I could read the name, *Ponsonby*.

The car and two people came off. A minibus drove on. It looked too big. The man in the cap winched up the ramp. The boat reversed and turned its nose against the current again. The name on this side said *Pinguino II*. I took out my binoculars. I had been watching two boats. The minibus was on a motorless, floating metal box with a ramp at each end, called the *Ponsonby*. Lashed to its side, doing all the hard work, was a stubby fishing boat, the *Pinguino II*.

A voice at my shoulder said, 'Luis Aguila: the thirteen estancias on the island have a co-operative which pays him.' It was Nicolas. 'Every day the tides and the wind are a little different. He's never had an accident.'

'How long has he been doing it?'

'Thirty years.'

Last Hope Sound

## The Elusive Mr Daskam 1

I set out on foot for Rio Verde, to visit Tomas Daskam and buy food. Within five minutes the strait opened out into a funnel leading into Skyring Sound. I left the road and walked out along a sand and gravel headland with a bay cut into it. Below, on the storm tideline of the beach, was a graveyard of silver tree trunks coiled round one another like the drowned. Great bolts of kelp had been wound round and round on themselves, both corpse and winding sheet. Kelp gulls stood on the wind above my head.

Although it was named after a sailor, Skyring is also a perfect description of the sound on a sunny day. The roll of waves combed the caged sea, in a bowl of snow-wiped pyramids. Pied oystercatchers twittered along the shore. To my right a black blanket came away from the ground, flapping slowly through the moments when it was neither earthbound nor soaring, clambering up through the sluggish layers into the draught of energy flensing the earth. The condor gained the wind and tilted its wings. In seconds it was half a mile away over the next group of sheep. All were alive. It canted its wing against the world's motor and keened down the land, becoming a line, a dot, a memory.

I went back to the dirt road and tramped down the long shallow hill. The road turned away from the shore. The wind was in my face, nearly head on. Between me and the coast appeared a pond, two black-necked swans riding the waves. Behind wire, on the landward side was a grey Fuegian fox, stricken against the ground, pale forelegs stretched straight out in front. I wondered what had killed him. The wind brushed over him; only the health of the pelt told me the truth. As I approached he lifted his thin nose from the earth, danced to his feet, and turned to stare.

The road curved a little, then breasted a low hill revealing the whole scope and gulf of the next valley. The far side misted away in the distance. The name of Estancia Carmen was written on a red roof. Around it stood the only trees in the big landscape, dark and shadow-like.

I walked on and on, but the town seemed to come no nearer. A

179

hundred yards to my right a hawk ghosted through scrub. Three guanaco rose to their feet, which have soft pads like camels, making their gallop elegant and muted. Just before the foot of the valley was a dirt drive with an open gate and a cattle grid. I stood trying to see if this was the town. It looked no more than a big estancia, but if this was a farm, where was Rio Verde? It was not a landscape where a town could hide.

In the next field I saw a football pitch. So this was Rio Verde; six pretty houses, no shop.

A huge brown and white bull wandered across the road in front of me towards a fence on my left. Four big dogs, all different in colour and build, slunk away from a corral on the right, where hundreds of calves were penned, bellowing for their mothers' milk. The dogs walked towards me and began to fan out. I stood still, the hairs on my arms rose, and my palms prickled with sweat. The bull turned round to see what the noise was, which distracted their attention from me. I tried to slip between bull and dogs, but as if by command the dogs broke into a run, barking savagely. For a moment I was left imagining what being torn apart by cattle dogs was going to feel like, until they flew past me and set themselves at the bull's face and front legs, snapping and snarling. The bull looked uncomfortable and turned away but they followed him. I got the impression they wanted something to do. I kept going, walking backwards to keep an eye on them.

Across a dell, the sheep-shearing room had six stations, and six gates to turn out the naked sheep into the hollow of the paddock below. I walked the curve of the road, round and behind it. A white horse came to the fence, and neighed. I walked into the main street, which was also the only street. I passed the bungalow housing the municipal office, then a wooden school and a small first-aid station. A plot of grass had a low chain around it and a plaque saying the land had been bequeathed to build a church. At the end of the street I turned a blind corner under the spread of a large tree and came eyeball to eyeball with another bull. It was sitting down. The head was the size of an armchair. It got quickly to its feet and, before I could do the same myself, ran off.

One house stood out; it had a six-sided turret at the corner, and its verge was spiked with purple-blue and red salmon lupins. Two clouds of flowering gorse stood behind the white picket fence whose tops were sawn into arrowheads. There was a beautiful window latticed into small panes, some in gold-coloured glass. On the sill, and on two cleverly concealed shelves above, were small glass bottles of all shapes and colours. I knew Daskam was a collector. I lifted the knocker.

The raps fell in an empty house. I rang the bell, but only to postpone going away. The wind bent the lupins. I walked to the municipal office, rang the bell and heard a chair scrape, out of sight, in a room with an open window. A woman who could have been a town hall clerk anywhere welcomed me in to a room where she was packing Christmas presents into large cardboard boxes.

'Mr Daskam? I think he is in Santiago.'

'He doesn't live here all year?'

'No, he has two houses, at least two houses. He may have another in America.' She consulted a notebook with black board covers. 'Yes, no, he is in New York or Santiago'. She put a finger to a list of dates and telephone numbers next to his name. 'He's in Santiago . . .'

'For how long? I am going to Santiago soon.'

'. . . then he's going to New York for a sale. He's there until New Year. Do you want his telephone number?'

'Thank you.'

'You are welcome, Merry Christmas.'

'And to you.'

She never asked who I was. In the echoing hall I asked, 'What is he like, Mr Daskam?'

'He's an artist.'

'Yes, very famous. Do you know him?'

She shook her head. 'Not really.'

Only six houses in town but she didn't really know him. In an hour's visit I met four dogs, two bulls, one cat and one person. Walking back to the estancia, the wind behind me, took half an hour less.

That evening I found a book of Daskam's paintings in the study. It was a limited edition and inscribed 'For Nicolas and Violeta, with friendship, Tomas Daskam.'

I spent the evening with the book. He was best at buildings, which he painted as portraits. Usually there were no people but the houses themselves were personal, living the life of the people who had gone. And in the same vein, I had gone to his house when he wasn't there, and stared at it, and imagined him and his life. His home had become one of his own paintings.

Daskam came to Chile as a hippy. Aged forty, he bought a camera, all but stopped painting, and set about photographing wildlife and putting together two books, *The Birds of Chile*, and *Chile, the land and its fauna*. Some of the birds had never before been photographed in the wild. He went back to painting, but he still has eight large aviaries in his Santiago home.

Nicolas came in to the lounge where I was reading and sat on one of the soft armchairs in front of a wall of flame.

'I visited Mr Daskam's house, this afternoon. He was out.'

'He has another house in Santiago.'

'What's he like?'

'I don't know. I've never met him.'

I lifted up the book. 'But the inscription?'

'I think Violeta has met him.'

'What did she make of him?'

'She didn't say.'


*The Beagle Hills*

I was the only guest at the estancia. There was no menu; the cook just sat down by me and asked what I wanted to eat. I sat facing the Fitzroy Channel translating the correspondence between José Menéndez and José Fagnano. After the meal I walked round the garden. A lone lamb came to the fence and cried piteously. The wind got up a notch, grey sky darkened and I went inside.

The foreman came in and stacked the fire. He went to the

window and stared out impassively. Then he went to another. He had a flowerpot hat pulled down hard. He was like the peasant holding the sack of flour on his horse's withers in one of Daskam's paintings of central Chile. Both could have ridden out of a Bruegel canvas. When the windows were all done I asked him, 'Will the wind fall?'

'Yes.'

'When?'

'Tomorrow. Tonight, it will blow all night.'

A truck appeared with an orange steamroller on its back. The driver turned the paddle to red.

Nicolas came in. 'Bad weather.'

Together they moved round the room, doing sentry duty at the windows. After a while I felt churlish sitting down, and got up to help.

On Skyring Water white horses whipped up by the tide were running against the wind. I moved, to look after the window facing the ferry. The truck ground slowly on to the ferry which winced ever lower in the water, until there was just a foot or two of hull showing. The old man in the beret cranked up the ramp. Off they went, water breaking over the bows.

Nicolas turned to me. 'Do you want to go riding tomorrow?'

'Fine.'

'We need to round up 1,400 sheep from Riesco Island. The trucks will come up from Punta Arenas in the morning and take them back to the abattoir. The sheep have to be ready.'

At seven I was drinking coffee in the kitchen with Nicolas and the foreman, listening to the clock, a rain drip on a tin lid. In the old stable, now used as a garage, he picked up a sheepskin saddle and we waited for the ferry, next to an empty sheep truck. Three dogs came to Nicolas; they all had long hair and tongues, and never sat still.

'Is the hill on the island yours?'

'Yes, just a hill each side. It's a small estancia, two thousand acres; a big one is twenty-five thousand, but our grazing is better than most. Stocking can be as low as one sheep per ten acres.'

'In the Welsh uplands two per acre is considered pretty poor.'
He smiled.

The ferry beached and the sheep truck was loaded. It took up most of the ferry. A wooden wedge was kicked carelessly under one wheel. We fitted ourselves around it. The dogs ran excitedly from end to end. I chatted to the old man in the beret about the captain. Yes, he had been doing it thirty years. No, he had never had an accident.

'Would he speak to me?'

He smiled a gap-toothed smile.

We ploughed out into mid channel and spun around as we crossed tides. The truck shifted a little. The deck-hand found another wedge.

I asked Nicolas, 'Were you born here?'

'No, in a little village in Dalmatia. Violeta's grandfather came out here. She's third-generation Chilean, born in Punta Arenas. '

'And you?'

'I came here thirty years ago.'

'In Rio Verde I saw big brown and white cattle which looked just like an English breed – Herefords.'

'They *are* Herefords.'

'Locally bred?'

'There are local herds but we are always buying in to maintain and improve the bloodstock.'

'From England?'

'Certainly not! You have mad cow disease. From America.'

We closed on the shore. The dogs ran to the tip of the ramp, leaning forward, taking scent. As we beached, they leaped. Captain Aguila stayed in his cabin in the other boat. I tried to catch his eye to talk; but he stared out at the mill race in the centre of the channel.

In the first field was a stocky gelding, a pond skirted by nervous Fuegian geese, and a boat. It was *Pinguino 1*, the old ferry, a little sailing boat, still smartly painted in dove grey with maroon piping round the cabin and along the rubbing piece. Like a ladies' suit.

Nicolas saddled the horse.

Affecting a knowledgeable air I said, 'She looks strong.'

'She looks fat.'

The stirrups were carved wooden ones, like the front of a Dutch clog. I wore my walking boots and had to kick the toe of each boot to squeeze it in.

'You take the path over to the left and climb to the top field and bring them down. The dogs will collect the rest.'

The horse toiled willingly up the hill. Sheep were scattered in small groups. They were six-year-old ewes; in Wales they would be called brokers, their teeth broken on tough upland grass. Southern thrushes flitted between the bushes. At six hundred feet the ground began to level out and at eight hundred feet I reached a ridge and a fence, and turned along to start the sheep moving down.

From the hill's crest I looked back. The higher ridge of the Beagle Hills rose behind the estancia. To the east they formed dark high cliffs for nearly a mile. From their nests, above white-splashed rocks, condors fell on to the wind where it rose up the face of the bluffs, and spiralled upwards.

As I rode on, a lone condor rose from the ground and drifted a hundred yards to land and worry at something on the ground. It was upwind, and could not smell me. Like many animals it sees a man on a horse as another animal and is unafraid. The closer I got, the bigger it became.

Don't think of the wings, first think of the body. Think of a twenty-five-pound turkey, add a vulture's head and neck, because bare skin is easier to clean when it is caked in blood after plunging into a carcass. Add wing bones so slender and light they are used by Andean Indians to make flutes. Make the wings so big they are moved less than those of an albatross. Condors are eight years old before the plumage matures. One that was captured and kept as a pet lived a further fifty years. I edged the horse to within eighty yards but could not see what it was tearing at. I went back to work.

It was easy enough to move the sheep into small flocks. Then things got tricky. The lambs were three-quarters grown and no longer followed the ewes blindly. They were often the ones to loiter at the back of the flock, looking to double back the way they had come. After a while I found that simply stopping the horse for a minute steadied them. They streamed down the hill to the back of a shed where wooden rails funnelled them into pens. On the slope below me, without any instructions, the dogs flowed across the grass up to the heels of the last animal, then stopped in a low crouch. If the sheep slowed, the dogs ran a line across the back to keep them moving.

On the mainland the condors were beginning to peel away from the updraught above the cliffs and glide across the channel, coming directly towards Riesco Island. Once above it, they turned on to its thermals level with me and coursed higher and higher.

The horse did not enjoy walking downhill and picked its way with exaggerated care. We worked our way down in wide zigzags. In the pens, Nicolas and the foreman stood at a gate and separated ewes one way and lambs another. There was nothing for me to do. I rode back up to the ridge and watched the condors. There were now sixteen. They peeled away north tracing their shadows across the land that El Jimmy's friend, the Tehuelche Chief Mulato, had bought and lost. Apart from the Beagle Hills, I was on the highest land around. I could see the islands which appear to close the west end of Skyring Water thirty miles west. Eight miles south east the whole Fitzroy Channel could be seen winding into Otway Water at the Estancia Between the Winds. The snow on the furthest mountains was also thirty miles distant. Riesco Island, sixty miles long, rolled away till my view was eclipsed by the rising Cordillera.

The country round Rio Verde was named by the crew of the *Beagle*, in the later stages of her first surveying cruise. She had sailed under Captain Stokes, and spent the years 1826 to midwinter 1828 being beaten and mauled all round the coast of southern Chile and Argentina in a squadron under the overall command of Captain King in the *Adventure*. Stokes was an able and conscientious man with the kind of obsessive personality that makes good surveyors. But his work demanded control and precision in weather so vile that the ships and their boats, the platforms for his work, became uncontrollable. The task was a man-breaker, and progressively it wore him down. At the end of June 1828 his crew were exhausted and, despite a good diet, scurvy set in. Stokes took to his cabin, driven to depression and apathy by the endless impossibilities of his task. Lieutenant Skyring took tacit command and carried on surveying. When they rendezvoused with the *Adventure* a month later, Captain King was shocked by Stokes's physical deterioration but did not clearly see his mental condition. King planned to sail north to Chiloé to recover the fitness of both men and ships, but the thought of any further sailing was intolerable to Stokes's shattered mind. He shot himself in the head. But the torture went on. His shaking hand blundered and he took eleven days to die.

King gave command of the *Beagle* to Skyring. King opted for the simpler escape to Brazil, and the squadron anchored in Rio de Janeiro. Soon a grand visitor arrived; in sailed the *Ganges* bearing Admiral Otway who would not confirm King's promotion of the faithful, tactful Skyring, and instead installed the wealthy, well-connected Lieutenant Robert Fitzroy, aged twenty-three.

Fitzroy was eager to make his mark and justify his rapid promotion. He came south, leaving the *Beagle* in the main Magellan Strait. He then took two small open boats north into the unknown water of Jerónimo Channel. To make room for as many provisions as possible, he forbade anyone, including himself, to take a change of clothes. They laboured up the narrow channel which began northwest then bent back north-east. On 11 May 1829 they burst into an inland sea which Fitzroy, remembering his patron, named Otway Water. Quite abruptly, the shore changed from mountain to pampa, and they fell into the rain shadow of the mountains. As they went, they scattered the land with names of crew and loved ones until, anchoring at a convenient point to light a beach fire and spend the night, their affection and admiration were all but exhausted. The spot was named Donkin Cove: Mr Donkin's reputation was founded on supplying them with their favourite potted meat.

They dried their clothes in front of the fire, and looked around. They seemed to have reached the head of the bay; the north and south shores had closed in and a current of water came down what they assumed was a river to their north. Next morning the river was flowing back the other way. They sailed with the tide and found it was still salt water. In two topsy-turvy hours, they were through, past where Violeta and Nicolas's estancia now stands, into another inland sea, narrower but even more glorious in its wild beauty than the one they had left. Duty done to his patron, Fitzroy showed his sensitive side, and named it after the absent Skyring, whose opportunity for advancement had passed to him. The race of water in between, Fitzroy modestly reserved for himself, Fitzroy Channel.

After a few days they went back into the channel, landed on the mainland, and climbed the hills they named after the absent *Beagle*, the hills behind Nicolas's and Violeta's estancia. The condors which nest along the cliffs to the east would have shuffled off their ledges and loped into the air. At the top they looked east, hoping to see water. They gained breathtaking views to the west, of Otway and Skyring Waters, their deep blue scumbled with white horses, but to the east there was only rolling grassland. Stores were low, it was time to retrace. Another cul-de-sac in Tierra del Fuego's armoury of frustration.

From the shed we looked out of the door at the condors peeling away from the thermal and dispersing to hunt.

'Guanaco.' The foreman nodded at the other side. I could see nothing.

'On the ridge.'

I ran my eye slowly along it. One. Over a mile away, breaking its smoothness. The dot had a long neck.

'They like to stand on the skyline like that, watching.'

'I saw a fox yesterday, are there many round here?'

He looked at me. 'Not this year, we keep numbers down.'

'They are protected animals.'

'If you keep it quiet, no one minds too much. If you didn't kill them they would be all over the place.'

'And the condors?'

'Magnificent birds.'

'Do you shoot them?'

'No, they never take a live animal, only carrion.'

'They don't take lambs?' This is often given as a reason for killing them.

'They will wait around a dying animal, but they never kill. Once an animal is dead, it's a different matter. Four birds will eat a whole sheep. All they leave are the bones and the fleece. They eat the sinews, everything. The fleece is so clean you could wear it, and the skin is left whole, without a tear in it, except the first rip where they went in. Yes, they are very dainty eaters.'

It was now eleven o'clock, but the sheep trucks hadn't appeared. Nicolas was unperturbed. I unsaddled the horse and found a crate to sit on. A truck came to the far shore. In a while it was joined by a pick-up, and the ferry crossed to meet them. I stood up. Nicolas said, 'It's not ours.'

I walked round but there was little to look at. The ferry beached, Nicolas went down and talked to the family in the pick-up. One o'clock came, the trucks did not. All this time the foreman sat on a box and did nothing. He was very good at it. I fidgeted, and went back on the next ferry.

I finished translating the well-mannered vitriol of José Menéndez and José Fagnano. Two big trucks waited to go to Riesco Island. At half past four the patient sheep left for Punta Arenas. Farmhands and gauchos came in to the shop for cigarettes and biscuits, and took a beer standing at the counter.

I was still the only guest.

## Phil the Fireman

In the estancia shop, a thin man curved like a question mark and holding a bicycle was trying, in inadequate Spanish, to order drinks.

'American?' I asked.

'Yep, still getting a handle on this Spanish.'

'I'm John. Can I help?'

'Phil.'

Through me, he asked the price of many different drinks, then bought fruit juice.

Nicolas appeared. 'We are having friends round, you are welcome to join us for our grill.'

I jumped at it. He took us to an indoor barbecue with roast meat scattered over it. I picked a plate of lamb and ordered a bottle of red.

We sat down at a dining table. Phil was in his forties, with a thick black beard, wearing a baseball cap pulled down to the top of his bushy eyebrows. A neckerchief and shades obscured further parts. In fact only his cheekbones and temples were visible.

'I'm a fireman in Utah, not city stuff, big bush fires. It's stupid. The Feds fund most of it so the state spends lots of money containing small fires that would do less damage than it costs to put them out. In fact the caterpillars do more damage than the fire.'

'Wine?'

'Yes please.'

'So where are you going?'

'Utah.'

'How much of South America are you visiting?'

'Whatever it takes. I'm cycling all the way home to Utah.'

'How long will that take – two years?'

'Maybe. Food's good, you want some more?'

We got more.

'Isn't the Darien Gap impassable – just swamp?'

'I've been warned there's a – er – little trouble there.'

I looked down and noticed all the place mats had pictures of English coaching inns. Mine was of Jamaica Inn in Cornwall. 'You staying here tonight?'

'Oh no, I have to get to the hot springs.'

'More wine?'

'Yes please.'

'You're not married?'

'No, but I keep in touch with home. I live with my Dad.'

He picked up the last of the bottle of wine and poured me a little, and himself the rest. He pushed his empty plate aside. 'Real good. I got to go.' He regarded his empty plate. 'Do you think they want us to pay for any of this?'

'It's a restaurant.'

'They'll expect me to pay?'

'It's a regular custom down here.'

'Yeh, er, home, I send e-mails. My father worries about me all the time.'

With Tomas Daskam in Santiago I had no reason to stay in Rio Verde. I decided to try to reach Puerto Natales for Christmas. I asked Nicolas if next morning he would give me a lift to the bus stop on the main road. He said yes, but he'd have to charge. Late in the evening a middle-aged Viennese couple arrived, Peter and Martha. They were going to Puerto Natales in their hire car first thing in the morning and offered me a lift. Then they quizzed me about what I was paying and whispered that Nicolas was quoting rates much higher than their guide book said he charged. 'And so far,' said Martha, 'it has been so accurate', she waved the book in the air, 'I mean *exactly* right.'

*Puerto Natales*

As we drove away at speed down the dirt road Peter told me how expensive their hire car was. 'It's also totally unsuitable for the journey we are making.' My unasked question must have hung in the air. He went on, 'But the price they are asking for four-wheel drives is astronomical.' He looked at his watch. 'We don't really have much time if we are going to get there today.' The car grounded as we flew over the crest of a hill. 'Totally unsuitable.'

'Look!' cried Martha pointing at upland geese. 'Stop! I'll take a photo.'

She got out of the car and walked towards them. Peter studied his watch. The geese flew away. I said, 'It's okay, they are common, you will see more.'

In a few minutes 'Look! Sheep! So many sheep! Stop! I'll take a photo.'

A group of gauchos stopped work to stare at her.

When they dropped me off in Natales, Peter took off his watch and massaged his wrist.

The nineteenth-century founder of Puerto Natales, Von

Heinz, reached the spot on 24 December and named it Natales in honour of the birth of Christ. For many years there were only about ten houses, grouped where the square now lies in the centre of a town of 15,000 souls. Women did their washing on the river bank, hands blue, carp-scaled with chaps. In 1919 civilisation arrived: the first public lighting. It consisted of glass lamps with four sides and a little candle inside. They were ten feet high. There was tremendous excitement and an invitation to the opening, sent to the regional deputy to parliament, produced a letter of acceptance, from the aide to the sub-delegate. The candles were lit at seven in the evening, tended during the night, and snuffed out at seven in the morning. The system lasted only a few years. A steam electric power station was built in 1925, to spoil the fun.

I also arrived on Christmas Eve and went to a modern chalet with four guest bedrooms in a private house. The dining room was asphyxiating from good taste. From the artificial Christmas tree hung strings of golden pearls and cupids. Ceramic hand bells waited next to Santa and snowmen candles for the festivities to begin. On the television sat a large felt Donald Duck from whose ears shot the wires of the forked aerial.

On the seafront, and in the block behind, large new hotels were springing up, with government support. Young men and women in smart uniforms laid white linen and set out the cutlery with fingers made clumsy by the watching eyes of head waiters. Cups and glasses, salt cellars and plates, cruets and conserves were set with sacramental precision. Napkins were pulled open and refolded. The waiters retired to the walls like moths against bark, while the boss inspected, corrected. Then all went still.

No one came and no one went. In the glass-domed clock, twinkling brass waltzed. When it chimed ten o'clock in comfy drawing-room tones, the head waiter nodded, minutely. The waiters and waitresses left the chintz walls and put away the gleaming breakfast things. No one had marketed these new hotels in time for the season. No one knew they were here. No one came. Soon they would lay table for lunch.

*Puerto Bories*

The far south was only effectively colonised in the mid-nineteenth century. The earlier attempts are stories of poorly equipped garrisons suffering appalling hardship and ill-luck. Last Hope Sound, on which Puerto Natales sits, epitomises this. In the summer of 1557–58 Juan Ladrillero and Francisco Cortés Ojea came limping down the coast of Chile, leading the ramshackle expedition sent out by the country's new governor, Mendoza. His job was to rediscover the Strait of Magellan from the west side.

Spain's gold and ports were on the Pacific coast, and if it was to control the south and make this continent secure, their captains had to know how to find the western gateway to the Strait of Magellan. They were finding out that Magellan, coming from the Atlantic, had entered the Strait the easy way, but from the west it was a maze; there were thousands of islands, hundreds of bays and dead ends, and just a few long channels open at both ends. No one had charted it.

Ladrillero was an old war-horse of sixty. He suffered storms, and then separation from the companion boat, the *San Sebastián*. Its commander, Ojea, went on alone, reaching 52°30′ South before turning for home with his report: that the mouth of Magellan's Strait had disappeared and they had found only low cliffs and a great bay. In fact, 52° 30′ is the mouth of the Magellan Strait. They had simply not recognised it. In October Ojea returned to Valdivia with the news that their companion 'had died in his audacious enterprise'. But the cussed old Ladrillero was alive and doggedly heading south. Somewhere to the north of the true Strait, his pilot made a premature move into the labyrinth. The place names spell out their frustration, Obstruction Sound and Little Hope Bay.

At the site of modern Puerto Natales the channel narrowed. The crew and the ship were fit for just one more attempt, so they named it Last Hope Sound. They followed it mile after mile to the north west. Grass and rolling hills to the right were backed by strange olive and brown cliffs which dazzled in the swift bursts of sun. The mountains closed across their path and crushed their last hope.

They gave up and set out for home. On the way they stumbled by accident into a broad channel, and kept to it for a while, describing and naming islands on the way. They returned to the side channels, and home. They never knew the broad channel had been the Magellan Strait.

But the strategic importance of the elusive strait would soon be swept away and forgotten. Twenty years later Drake reported open water to the south and redrew the map. After Drake, the far south was left unclaimed by any nation. Since his discovery of open sea south of the Horn there was little strategic value in controlling the Straits. In 1837 the French navigator Dumont d'Urville reconnoitred the Straits and urged his government to take possession of them. At this time Bernardo O'Higgins, architect of Chile's independence was in exile in Peru. He busied himself firing off memoranda to keep everyone else on their toes. He suggested that Chile send someone south with a flag. Six years went by before anyone acted. In 1843 a bluff Bristol-born captain, John Williams, sailed south on a thirty-ton Chilean schooner named after its home port of Ancud in north Chiloé. They met the usual foul weather but four months later their battered boat crept up to the bare flagpole at Port Famine, south of modern Punta Arenas. Captain Williams formally possessed the southern peninsula of South American land for Chile. Soon a warship came into view, the *Phaeton*. After six years' procrastinating, the French had arrived just hours too late.

But the next day Williams saw the French raise first a new flagpole, then the tricolour. He sent over a reproving note and received an evasive reply: it was normal practice to raise the national flag above a temporary camp. Williams waited nervously. A few days later the *Phaeton* accepted failure. She sailed on, and claimed Tahiti as a French protectorate. Chile got half of Tierra del Fuego.

Gabriel Bustamente Barría was here in the early days. He was a workman born in 1893 in Ancud. Aged ninety-one he recalled, 'There were only a few houses here when I arrived, at least a few new houses, and there was also the oldest home, that of José Iglesias. Above Pedro Montt Street, down by the beach, they made a cemetery above it and the first dead person was brought there in someone's arms to be buried.'

The forces which shaped this area in the twentieth century were European capital and home-grown criminals. The region was put up at auction in 1906 and the franchise was won by the Sociedad Explotadora del Tierra del Fuego, a private company set up to make use of the natural resources of the area. Once established, it became the third largest sheep farming company in the world, behind two in Argentina. They brought in sheep and cattle, built factories, ports, towns and ships. The company took over, building not just the Bories freezer plant in 1913, but also a private railway along the shore to ferry workers to and from Puerto Natales. By the end of the First World War it was slaughtering more than 300,000 animals a year.

From the first, the workforce was tough, organised and radical. Entertainment other than drinking was limited. In short, the place was always Red and often drunk. The periodic clashes between owners and workers were political, deep-seated, personal and sometimes violent.

Workers were paid part in cash and part in kind. The goods in kind were overvalued but it hardly mattered; the only place to spend the cash was in company shops. They were so overpriced that one strike forced a tribunal to be set up, which actually found in the workers' favour. They made the company bring down prices, but at the end of the day the money still went round in circles and back into the same long pockets.

On Christmas morning I walked out along the shores of Last Hope Sound, heading for Puerto Bories. Black-necked swans rode the short steep waves. Although common on salt and brackish water throughout the middle and north of Tierra del Fuego, they never make the short additional hop south into the Beagle Channel. Ibises with red and gold throats delved in the turf for larvae, with curved-beak elegance. They and the swans are summer migrants. The collector Crawshay, in 1907, recorded that ibises required 'an extraordinary amount of killing, but [are] excellent eating'.

A boy rode bareback on a chestnut stallion with a wolfhound and a labrador at its heels. On a brilliant patch of grass he slowed and danced the great horse in dressage steps, an extended walk, a collected trot. The asphalt road turned to dirt. The land still belongs to huge estancias. The biggest holdings were broken up into more manageable units of 100,000 acres and a quarter of a million sheep.

Ten acres of poorer land fed only one sheep, although fleeces weighed in at nine or ten pounds and prize rams produced thirty pounds of wool. Herds and flocks from the remote farms walked for two or three weeks to get to the freezer plant. Much of the mutton went to Britain.

It was brutal and brutalising work. At a similar plant in Rio Gallegos, Chilean men worked a three-month contract away from home, killing sheep. Having nothing to do on Sundays they would go down to the beach and compete at cutting seals' throats as they lay on the beach. There was no use for the carcasses. The birds had them. Next morning the workers returned, rested and refreshed, to the abattoir.

From 1912 Puerto Natales enjoyed more congenial leisure with the formation of Last Hope Football Club, possibly the least optimistically named club in the history of soccer. A swimmming pool, gymnasium, shooting range, bowling alley, cinema and library followed.

As I walked I was full of the little tales I had read in Spanish in Jorge Díaz Bustamente's *Crónicas de Última Esperanza*, or Last Hope Chronicles. The best swimmer in town was Bernardo Glinka, known as the Mylodon Kid. The German would plunge into the waters in all weathers. In 1924, prompted by several large brandies, he swam the whole Señoret Channel, a mile or more wide. After that he swam it whenever the fancy took him. One day he fell overboard from his skiff and, too drunk to climb back in, drowned. It was several weeks before the corpse came home, washed up on Demestre Beach.

The Kawéskar Indian, El Chonqui, was a practised drinker who frightened the children with his growling accent. Now and again he worked. One day he turned up half-naked at the Bories freezer plant and saw men digging. He didn't know what they were doing, but he knew they got paid for it. He picked up a spade and joined them. The foreman told him to stop. He dug on. He told him again. El Chonqui grinned, pointed to the others, and dug on. The foreman fetched the manager who explained he could not be paid, and asked him to stop. He dug on until the job was finished. They paid him and he bought clothes and boots, and a lot of drink.

Later that year the fat-rendering plant caught fire and ignited other buildings. Fewer than 6,000 animals were killed that year, but a new fire service was established. In charge was Madman Reley.

Reley was a member of every club in town, and addicted to practical jokes. One morning he announced that Christ was not the only one who could walk on water. A day was mentioned. Word went round. A crowd gathered in the bay. Reley appeared with two huge floating shoes. He strapped them on and launched himself. One crossing, two. On the third his legs began to slide apart. Madman Reley went down into the freezing water. What was the second part of the practical joke going to be? The crowd watched. The water went very still. Someone shouted, 'It's not a joke' and fetched a boat. He was pulled out half drowned. The carabineros arrived and wanted to arrest him. But they were not sure what for. He was too tired to argue, but the crowd were having none of it. They compromised. The carabineros would not charge him. Reley would leave walking on water to Jesus.

About three miles out of town lay the skeleton of the company's wealth, the red-roofed wooden sheds of Puerto Bories. The jetty which received the great wool and hide ships now had missing sections. The huge complex of buildings was empty and shut. Plank walls had begun to tear away. A few cottages and the manager's house were still lived in. Rambling roses threaded the porch. The empty sound glittered steel blue. Bare gaunt mountains reared out of the water. Towards the sea the sun blazed on the channel. A fishing boat butted back into port. Oystercatchers cut low over the shore, black and white chevrons. A squall came down and the rain cut my face. Within minutes the sun blinded me again.

The distant markets became too tough for Tierra del Fuego to serve effectively. The company wound down the abattoir and freezer, then closed them in the 1960s. Now some people want it repaired. It risks becoming heritage.

*Mylodon*

The must-not-miss visit in Puerto Natales is the Mylodon Cave where Chatwin finished his journey, claiming a piece of mylodon hair to replace the one he had marvelled at as a child in his grand-mother's cupboard. I booked an organised trip, and got a taxi-driver called Henrique. I was the only passenger going to the cave, half a dozen miles north-west of town.

The mylodon was an Ice Age creature the shape of a sloth and the size of a large bear. In summer the cave lies in pleasant pasture land. In winter it is lined with ice and carpeted with driven snow. In 1896 a shepherd took shelter in the huge lens-shaped opening of the cave. In the ice he found a hank of reddish brown coarse hair. He ran to tell his boss Herman Eberhard, who took from the cave bones, skin and droppings, as well as the credit for discovery. Everything was in a remarkable state of preservation, and the skin and a skeleton were carefully pieced together. In neighbouring smaller caves they found the debris of human settlement later dated as 12,400 years old. In Europe this is equivalent to the last great thawing of the ice.

Speculation grew about the exceptional condition of the remains. After all the cave was ice-free and warm all summer. Perhaps this was not a freak of preservation, but of survival. Man and prehistoric monster seemed to have co-existed here: perhaps monster had survived.

In London, on the new century's first summer solstice, Professor Ray Lancaster addressed the Royal Zoological Society. 'It is quite possible – I don't want to say more – that he [the mylodon] still exists in some of the mountainous regions of Patagonia.' With this notion, H. Hesketh Prichard, armed with one of the strangest prose styles in academia, took himself to the end of the earth.

With Thomas Cook letters of credit he went to the Welsh colony in the Chubut Valley, which was then only thirty-five years old. The Welsh had come here looking for religious and cultural freedom – and land. They preserved their Welsh language but not their agricultural tools which, when they landed, were carelessly left below high tide mark, and lost.

Not long before a certain Lord Reed had arrived at Trelew. He was too rich to carry much cash with him, and for his immediate needs borrowed from the local community. He disappeared one day with all of it. *Burke's Peerage* revealed there was no such title. A posse eventually won security for the loans with the help of the live body of 'Lord' Reed in a lasso.

When another Englishman arrived, the locals asked Hesketh Prichard, 'Are you not *Lord* Prichard?' His letters of credit from Thomas Cook were looked upon as an amusing ruse, and he was forced to face five hundred miles of pampa travel with just thirty Argentine dollars. The horses they sold him were nothing but trouble from start to finish, fractious and wilful.

He saw the deep irony that, having come so far to save their Welsh language and culture from English, they might surrender them to Spanish. He blamed dark-eyed Argentinian maids, and inter-marrying. But in recent years concerted efforts from Wales have helped strengthen the language after it effectively missed a generation. Grandparents ask questions in nineteenth-century dialect Welsh. Children give answers in modern Welsh. In between, the parents wait for a Spanish translation.

Hesketh Prichard's party eventually left, kicking and bucking, for the south. His prose blossomed under the great skies. 'Up at sunrise, when the sun pokes its big bald lemon-coloured head out of the bedclothes of the sky.'

They met and talked to Tehuelche natives who had made the colossal space of the grassland their own. The pampa is so big and featureless that even gauchos kept the habit, on long journeys, of lying down for the night with their heads in the line of travel, so they could set off in the right direction the next day. From infancy they lived with and on their horses. 'We once asked a Tehuelche what he would do if he were left alone on the pampa without a horse.'

'Sit down,' he said.

Henrique drove us along the shore and past the Bories plant. 'Once, only big landowners. All the animals came here. Then we had the land reforms, many more landowners. Small farmers are different, they don't specialise. They do a little of this, a little of that. They do not want to kill animals every year. Factory close.'

'There were, what – six hundred workers there?'

'Yeah, more in high season. Very seasonal work.'

'Is it better to have the land reforms and no jobs?'

'Oh yeah. There's less work, but people have land. They aren't in the company's pocket.'

I stood in the mouth of the cave looking in, imagining the land in the Ice Age, before man came down here. The seasons coming and going, uncounted. The killing of animal by animal. The lost roar of beasts, now without breath. A cow bellowed behind me, and it reverberated in the cave, old as the wind.

The cave grew bigger and bigger as I walked into it. Excavations found that Ice Age hunters had lived, killed and cooked here. Bones showed the scraping of tools. Hesketh Prichard found no living mylodon. The specimen which triggered the excitement was exceptionally well preserved by the cold, but was it prehistoric? The mylodon remained stubbornly extinct. But since when? Had man and mylodon ever lived on this same land, side by side?

In the Mylodon Cave, the only radio-carbon dating was performed not on the animal bones themselves, but on skin and dung found next to them. Such dating is fraught: artefacts found together are not necessarily contemporary. It suggests that mylodons were using the cave up to about ten thousand years ago, which is about the same time as man arrived.

The last four or five million years have seen exceptionally rapid climatic change. Repeated glacial periods paralysed the earth, but in the warm inter-glacials hippos basked in the heat of the Thames Valley. The survival of each species often depended on its ability to follow its own climate and habitat, as it moved north and south. Islands were bad news. If you couldn't fly or swim to new land, you died. Tierra del Fuego and Patagonia were too small to support the diversity of mammals found in the equivalent northern latitudes. During the glacials, the region was populated only by a small group of hardy generalists, possibly ones with a greater tolerance of arid conditions. Mylodons and native horses could cope with low-grade vegetation if it was plentiful. Large cats made a living preying on them.

But the large animals that existed ten thousand years ago had survived everything climatic change had thrown at them. Why did they now die out? The loss of the megafauna is probably related to the arrival of human hunters at a time when animals were already struggling to cope with continual changes in their habitat. Even though early man only hunted big game as opportunity occurred, for animals under pressure it was one hazard too many. The Mylodon Cave shows other giant species, now extinct; a panther, two different camel-like animals, and two horse-like creatures. The evidence suggests that while these creatures were eventually squeezed into extinction, man did co-exist with the last of the megafauna. The slow, stubborn mylodon was one of the last to perish. It so nearly made it.

On the drive back Henrique stopped. 'We can climb here.'

We climbed a rocky crag which burst from the top of a small hillock by the roadside. He led me along a narrow ledge on to an apron of rock overlooking the Señoret Channel. It took my breath away. The whole lie of the land looked different from this pulpit. The middle distance was fifteen miles away, and the far distance was twenty five miles off in the sun's dazzle. Mountains cupped each shore. 'People drive past all the time, they don't know this place. See the cave, go home. I like this place, see the whole country, if you know where to look. You like it?'

I didn't have to answer.

'Where are you going when you leave here?'

'Up to Chiloé, then Santiago.'

'You are going to Chiloé? My wife is a Chilote, I give you some things you must ask about.' He wrote them down. I knew two of them, a measuring box and a sled which were peculiar to Chiloé.

He also gave me *curanto*, which I would remember with a vengeance.

'Are there any good fish restaurants in Puerto Natales?' I asked. 'I haven't seen any.'

'The Bahía.' He wrote an address. 'It's the best.'


## Bahía Restaurant

Henrique's note gave me directions to the street where I would find the Bahía restaurant. The commercial centre is at one end of the town, where the first streets were laid out. The hotels and more prosperous houses were there. The restaurant was at the other end. I had to cut a diagonal across the gridiron, walking a mechanical zigzag. Many of the smaller houses were freshly painted with neat bright gardens. The older ones had burly block-like trees outside them, squat, dark and impenetrable.

On my tourist map the town finished just beyond the main shopping street. The map and the asphalt ran out at the same point, but there was still plenty of town ahead. There was little traffic here, but many old car skeletons, and the occasional wooden fishing boat, beat up and dried up. A yellowing hull and a drunken wheelhouse. I crossed a long shopping street I hadn't seen before. It was poorer. The shops had less in them and stock was haphazard, piecemeal. One clothes shop had only knitted cardigans and cotton dresses, all of them white and powder blue. Another meagre window display was protected by a roll-down polythene blind the colour of Lucozade. I reached the corner of the block. From across the street, two thin dogs stared at the butcher sharpening his boning knife.

The front gardens became small and unkempt. Many houses now fronted straight on to the street and the wood or corrugated sheets had been mended with pieces which did not match. One whole gable wall consisted of oil tins, cut open, hammered flat and nailed tightly down. A woman in a telephone booth came out looking very respectable. She had an intelligent face, alert and thoughtful. At the corner of the block the wind caught her. She pulled her padded jacket around her. There were holes all through it.

Finally I turned right and walked a level road, staying near the middle to avoid the smell of the open roadside drains, which were stagnating. A plastic illuminated box sign was unlit. It said Bahía Café – well, Bah:a Ca:é. Dogs lapped at puddles.

In the house's courtyard stood a small tractor, the engine in pieces. The man who had been working on it was washing up in an outbuilding. A lamp in the window flashed on and off in the dusk. It wasn't a special effect, it was faulty wiring. I tried the red door under the sign. It was locked. I turned to walk back to town. The man at the tap sported a green shirt punched forward by a brown belly. He wore shorts and sandals, his legs were brown and strong. 'Can I help you?'

'The restaurant,' I pointed, 'I am looking for the restaurant.' He finished carefully drying his hands, 'Come in come in.' I made to follow him into the back. 'No! Customers round the front. Wait one minute.' He disappeared into the back and reappeared to open the front door and gracefully usher me in.

A very wide woman, about fifty years of age like him, squeezed past me in the dark hallway. The stone floor shone. 'Would you like a little drink? We are having a drink.' She took me into their own room, at the back. At a table were a younger couple. We all said hello. I asked for beer. The family drank demurely from small delicate glasses. I looked down the room and saw the huge cooking ranges, 'What a lovely kitchen.' The older woman beamed, the younger woman looked over her shoulder, 'That old thing.'

I went through to a small dining room where a local couple were eating Jurassic portions of fish, salad and fried potatoes. The menu was the day's catch. I had soup, crab, and fried congría steak. It was all cooked until scarcely done, no more. Most restaurants do not have confidence in their customers knowing this is how it tastes best.

When I was saying goodbye there was a hammering on the front door. The man in the green shirt answered it. Someone stumbled.

I went to see if they needed another pair of hands. A man in his late twenties was leaning forward while the owner pushed back against his weight to hold him up. The visitor was tall and thin and had to stoop to come under the door; his hair was shoulder-length and he wore a tired moustache. He was someone who drank heavily and regularly and knew how to take it, but was still very drunk.

A shorter plumper man appeared behind him, very unsteady, talking loudly, pushing against an unseen wind. The owner stood the first man up straight. He let go of him to shake hands with the second one. They came in. Two well-dressed women followed them in. They were sober and had two small children and a baby. The owner embraced them and petted the children. The men went straight through to the back room and shouted for beer. The woman with the baby called through. 'Hello Mum.'

*Milly's*

In Puerto Natales I ate lunch at Milly's, a 1950s American-style diner just behind the main street, with plate glass windows and Formica tables. It was plain, but it had style, and it was a place to go. Some natty dressers came here. A middle-aged woman in a fur coat and peeling make-up sat in a window seat with two men. Each wore a suit, one sported platform shoes. They looked round with a waft of distinction. She took out a long cigarette, both men both produced lights. At nine they would go home, hang up their clothes, align the creases, settle the shoulder pads squarely on the hangers.

Industrious seventeen-year-old waitresses in viridian green miniskirts whisked their beautiful legs between the shining tables. Between orders they whispered at the counter and gazed out of the windows. Their faces had two tomorrows pencilled on them.

One future was to leave, get right away. Then this would never be home again. It would be a town you used to live in. The people would be small and unchanging, and sit in the same seats at the same tables. You would come home with new friends and clothes. Your parents would disapprove of both. The new shopkeepers in town would take you for a tourist and try small, mean scams on you. They would laugh when you said you were local and look you up and down. On the bus ride back to the airport, tears would well up and you wouldn't know why. Your father would wave, your mother squeeze a handkerchief. You would leave feeling you had never talked to them.

The other future was staying here and taking the window seat. Marry a local boy and find a business. Complain about the waitresses in Milly's, their slowness, their mistakes. Most of all their legs. You would leave at dusk when your reflection appeared in the glass to remind you where you were.

When I left it was falling quiet. A plain waitress, her hair a long black curtain on her back, was leaning on the counter looking at the night street. The prettiest had linked arms with her, but facing the other way, staring into the cake display.

Soon one future would be inked in, indelibly.

# 6

## The Long Pacific Shore

*Navimag*

I woke up when the anchor groaned and the ship shuddered from the dock. I was heading north through Chile in the only way it can be done without flying. There are two hundred miles of southern Chile, centred on Wellington Island, which consist of mountains standing on the land or in the sea. There are no roads and may never be any. The roads of Chilean Tierra del Fuego link only to Argentina.

While people can fly quite cheaply on the very competitive network of internal airlines, the only way to move bulk materials and products up and down southern Chile is on the national institution known as the Navimag. It is a private company which runs a bright red 18,000-ton cargoship and ferry called the *Puerto Eden*. Each week it makes one journey north and another south, carrying lorries, livestock, cargo and, in marginally more comfortable accommodation, a few dozen passengers. For most of the trip it can stay in the channels between the islands and the mainland where, unless a strong gale blows, the narrowness of the channels and the height of the mountains prevent big seas building.

In the bunk above was Dieter, a small German man with the bearing and build of a shy clerk. His nose was split like a ripe fruit and his face was swollen and burnt. We began chatting. This slight figure had just climbed the volcano Aconcagua, the highest mountain in all the Americas.

On the other side of the cabin were a Swiss couple, a petite vivacious blonde and a friendly but bland six-footer, dressed in buffs and browns, looking like a stout scoutmaster, blinking through round glasses like an owl. The cabin window looked down on the cargo deck. Two double-decker wooden pens of silent sheep had been taken from lorry trailers, jacked on to stanchions, then lashed to the deck. The weather had changed, it was dull and cool with a stiff breeze.

I went out on to the cargo deck. We were sailing south-west across Admiral Montt Gulf. The sheep were packed in tight. Some had legs canted up on top of other animals. Every few minutes one would kick and buck for more space. Gradually the movement let other animals get all four feet on the boards. Drizzle blew in and stood in fine drops on the lanolin of their wool. A southern giant petrel swung in long lazy arcs across the stern.

Soon we turned into the two-mile-wide Valdes Channel, and by mid-morning we slowed and stood off a tiny side channel whose entrance was almost blocked by islets. Our twenty-metre-wide ship turned slowly towards the passage between the left-hand shore and an islet. This was the Kirke Narrows, the narrowest passage on the whole trip. The first mate remarked generally, 'The gap is one-hundred-and-forty metres but there's a rock in the middle, so we've got around fifty metres to aim for.'

Small trees on the island had small semi-circular tops and spindly branches and trunks. Two on the crest of a hummock looked like aerial jellyfish trailing their tentacles through the bushes. We were going with a slight following current. As we approached the narrowest pinch, the shore came closer and closer, faster and faster. Trees grew right down the tidal rocks. It was giddying. Sunshine lit a pocket of flat land on the right, highlighting the gloom of the dark forest all around. Two thousand feet above, the bare stone was dusted with icing sugar snow. We shot between the rocks. When I looked around at our wake, there seemed no way through.

The clouds came down, the wind picked up and we had turned

into the teeth of it. The bridge measured it as a steady 40–45 knots. The temperature was 5°C with 50°C of wind chill. I climbed to the small exposed top deck where I could see in all directions. Colour was draining from everything and the horizon had vanished in murk, all was grey and fury. It was midday and scarcely light.

Grey waves advanced like the armies of the dead, and were broken on the black rocks of endless low desolate islands. It was a corpse-cold hell where elements flung themselves on one another, tearing at throats. A fear lodged in my chest that everything around the ship was full of blind hate. Looking ahead I could see a wall of cloud lying across our path. A piece of it tore off and struck out at the ship. Its footprint as it stalked towards us was a raging ring of water. I walked towards the rail to have something to hold on to but the squall hit me when I was a yard short. The wind screamed, some piece of my own clothing hit me painfully in the face. I leaned into the wind and bent both legs. My boots began to slide backwards on the wet steel deck. For two minutes I kept my balance as it blew me slowly astern, hiding my face from the rain's hypodermics.

The land and the sea warred. This continued all afternoon until, at four o'clock, at the north end of Piazzi Island, we passed the last isolated rock, named the Islet of Madmen, and the storm abated. Later I read an account of Eric Shipton passing in a small boat through the channels just the other side of the mountain on the left. He wrote, 'I felt a sense of loneliness stronger than I have experienced in any other part of Tierra del Fuego. For all its haunting beauty, there was an atmosphere of hostility about this land, as though it resented our intrusion.'

The evening was fair. Black-browed albatrosses had joined the ship and were sailing the wind out a mile to one side, at the edge of the range of my binoculars, then turning and coming back to glide on the airwave punched up by our bow. As the sky lightened and the colour came back, I walked out on to the bow, where it was still bitterly cold. Seals came porpoising towards the ship as we approached the Guíd Narrows in a soft evening glow. A small band of Magellanic penguins played in the water, rolling over on their backs like otters. The albatrosses landed around one which had made a catch. Suddenly there were five, seven, ten, eventually thirteen bobbing like ducks. I stayed out until I could not feel my fingers.

When Captain Fitzroy came back from his small boat surveying around modern-day Rio Verde, he had clear orders to proceed direct to Chiloé, 650 miles north. However, having entered Skyring Water in its south-east corner, he now wanted to make use of the agile schooner *Adelaide* to look for a way in from the west, hoping to confirm a navigable route linking all the new waters. Disobeying orders could cost Fitzroy his new captaincy but the orders were written before the discovery of Otway Water and Skyring Water. He decided to be bold, delayed sailing, and sent Lieutenant Skyring himself to search for a way through.

Skyring went west along the Magellan Strait, then cut north through Canal Smyth which threads its way through these islands at the western entrance. In a clear spell he climbed a mountain and saw the Pacific, and, in the opposite direction, he could see along the channels we had just sailed and take a bearing which showed they were headed towards Skyring Water. Leaving the *Adelaide* in a safe bay, which he named Relief Harbour, he put a week's stores into a boat, and with the mate, J. Kirke, set out for the beautiful sea which was named after him, but he had not yet seen. They discovered and named Kirke Narrows.

When they passed through the narrows, they found, as they had hoped, more open water, but it was the tentacles of the gulf around modern Puerto Natales, not the broad bay of Skyring Water. They reluctantly turned round and battled back. Over-running their plans and provisions, they lived the last three days on shellfish. He and Fitzroy then sailed up to Chiloé where Captain King approved Fitzroy's departure from the plans.

In December that year the little fleet was heading south again. By April Skyring and Kirke were back at the entrance to Kirke Narrows. They separated and explored the bays, rowing and taking soundings. As the channels twisted, narrowed and opened again, apparently closed bays opened into fjords, seeming dead ends became islands with further channels behind. Hope was constantly teased and renewed. But one morning, at eleven o'clock, Skyring, like Ladrillero nearly three hundred years before, found himself at the head of the last channel, surrounded by high, enclosing land, rowing into a creek. 'All our suspense was removed and all our hopes destroyed.'

There is no way through these channels. At one point, a single mountain three miles wide blocks the way back into the Magellan Strait. At another point, had he climbed from Obstruction Fjord, up the flank of Mount Forgotten, he would have seen, just five miles away across a neck of land, Skyring Water. He did not. He never saw his own blue domain.

## Sinking a Continent

In the mid afternoon we passed a few islands north of the western end of the Magellan Strait. Our course took us away north, but Francis Drake, on 6 September 1578, had sailed clear of the islands and burst into the Pacific. He had not been blind to the wild beauty of the scene: 'The mountains rise with such spires and tops in the air, and of so rare a height, as they may well be accounted amongst the wonders of the world; environed, as it were, with many regions of congealed clouds and frozen meteors.'

Drake was ready to set about the real business of the expedition, to raise hell in the Pacific and plunder the almost undefended wealth of Spain for England's treasury, Drake's pockets, and the Queen's purse. A storm would sweep him off course into waters where he would remove from the charts and the maps not just the sea monsters, but the mythical continent of Terra Australis Incognita. They passed fifty-six days without the sight of sun, moon or stars. When the moon finally appeared through rags of cloud, it was in eclipse in Aries for two hours. They hoped it was a good omen. But the storm went on, then, incredibly, got worse. They were separated from sight of John Thomas's *Marigold* when, in the darkness, Drake and Trumpeter John Brewer heard fearful cries of men. That was the last of the *Marigold*.

The storm raged on. Come October they were still trying to claw themselves away from the Pacific coast and the safety of open water, but the now renamed *Golden Hinde* was steadily driven to the land. Francis Fletcher could see nothing but rocks and as they were swept on shore the waves were so high the ships surfed the crests and he could see the sea floor in the troughs. Suddenly 'we were driven as though through the eye of an needle into a great and large bay by a most narrow passage of rocks'. But in this haven, on 8 October, the two remaining ships were driven apart, when the *Elizabeth* lost her anchor. The *Elizabeth* sailed for two days on course to try to regain their rendezvous, but her crew had now had enough and turned for home, reaching Ilfracombe, Devon, on 2 July 1579.

The *Golden Hinde* went a month without seeing land, and was driven as far south as fifty-seven degrees, well below Cape Horn. Such prolonged soaking progressively undermines both vessel and men; the decks grow weed, the knuckles of the hand split, and the salt in the water rots and deepens the wounds. Calluses slough off leaving raw flesh to grasp the ropes. On 28 October the storm abated. November came.

But in the hardships, the sailors kept their wits and observed something which changed the way the world was drawn on maps. During their westward passage along the Magellan Strait, the south shore on their port bow was not the continuous coast of a Terra Australis Incognita, but in Fletcher's words 'broken islands dissevered by many passages and compassed about with the sea on every side, and therefore no strait'. The later account of Francis Drake, Sir Francis's nephew of the same name, is clear about what they had seen. 'The uttermost cape or headland of all these islands, stands near in 56 degrees without which there is no main nor island to be seen to the southwards, but that the Atlantic Ocean and the South Sea, meet in a most large and free scope.'

The mythical continent of Terra Australis Incognita was sunk.

Before they were finished with Tierra del Fuego, they visited a new island, which promptly disappeared.

## The Vanishing Island

Drake has often been credited with the discovery of Cape Horn. They had been blown south and fought their way back north to land on an island on 24 October 1578. The Drake account says they 'fell out most happily in his providence at the utmost island to the southward of America whereat we arriving made both the seas to be one and the same sea and that there was no further land (south) beyond the heights of that island'. They refreshed their water, collected wood and berries, there were 'herbs and trees flourishing'. He named it Elizabeth Island, and the harbour Port Francis Drake.

Fletcher drew the southernmost island as square, about thirty miles north to south, with a central lake. He and a boy climbed the most southerly point of the island and saw they were three parts of a degree further south than any other island. Later in life Drake yarned with Richard Hawkins, telling how he had 'cast himself down on the uttermost point, grovelling, and so reached out his body over it. Presently he embarked, and then told his people that he had been on the southernmost known land in the world.'

They were there three or four days, so their descriptions should be accurate. The problem is, Cape Horn Island is not like that. The island is not square and has no central lake. There are no trees to offer wood, no sweet herbs or berries. In 1926 the American historian Henry R Wagner settled on nearby Henderson Island as the best choice. But from Henderson Island other islands are visible to the south. There were enough islands for everyone to have a theory, too little information to prove anything. No island fits the bill completely. So where had they been?

The mystery is compounded by the fact that, to confuse the Spanish, Drake is known to have deliberately cooked the navigation books and spread misinformation about his course. The most critical geographical information of all, at that time, was that describing Tierra del Fuego, and in his lifetime Drake would not have allowed anyone to use his notes to publish accurate details of key episodes.

In 1908 in Mexico City an American named Zelia Nuttall made

a remarkable discovery. She was researching native beliefs by searching the archives of the Inquisition into Indian witchcraft. On the floor, in a dark, dusty corner, lay a disposition to that Inquisition by a captured Portuguese pilot Nuño da Silva who assisted Drake round South America. Curiosity took her on a paper trail to the General Archive of the Indias in Seville, where she found da Silva's original log, lost for centuries.

Da Silva's log was brief and factual, a navigator's record, not a narrative. 'October 24. Came to an anchor off an island in 57°S. October 25. This day we went ashore. October 26. We procured wood.' It had no helpful description of Elizabeth Island but it did enable historians to track the wanderings of the *Golden Hinde* during the seven or more weeks of the storm, and solve the mystery of the supposed landing at Cape Horn. But when they plotted the course described by da Silva, the result was a location for Elizabeth Island which was well out to the south-west of the Horn, in open ocean where there is no land. Over the years, the original chart entries for Elizabeth Island began to be marked PD, position doubtful, then ED, existence doubtful. Historians went back to taking Fletcher's account more or less at face value, and Drake was once again credited with the discovery of Cape Horn. Elizabeth Island and Cape Horn must be one and the same.

The historians' conclusions were strange as another account, published when Drake and da Silva were still alive, said of their departure from Elizabeth Island: 'the wind coming southward, they weighed anchor, holding their course northward for the space of two days, and then they espied a small uninhabited island.' To sail two days north from Cape Horn you need a land yacht but the London *Times* was repeating the story as newly proven, as recently as 1997.

Back in 1938, Felix Reisenberg, an American Master Mariner, under both sail and steam, made a study of the evidence. He looked at the courses they steered, the positions they estimated, and calculated their movements. Once again it put Elizabeth Island back in the empty ocean in 15,000 feet of water. Reisenberg had sailed those seas many times. He knew that in storms, a west to east surface drift often cut right across the more profound Humboldt Current coming north from Antarctica. In storms like the one Drake suffered, this drift would have been running strongly. Reisenberg added it to the equation and brought Elizabeth Island's supposed position back nearly a hundred miles east, which didn't seem to help because there was no island there either. He wrote to the US Navy Hydrographic Office which replied:

> Captain W D Burnham reports to this office that while running before a gale off Cape Horn in command of the American ship *Pactolus*, at 4 o'clock in the morning of 6 November 1885, the wind lulled and the sea fell, and noticing very highly discoloured water, he hove the ship to and sounded three times, obtaining each time from 67 to 70 fathoms, black sand and small rocks. Position of sounding, Latitude 56° 36′ S, Longitude 74° 20′ W. Then ran South for thirty miles before the water, which all the time was very thick and yellow, resumed its natural colour.

It is named after him: Burnham Bank.

It was in the right place, thirty miles north to south, like Fletcher's Island, and for the *Golden Hinde* two days' sailing from Tierra del Fuego, as Nuño da Silva had said. It was a rock soaring from colossal ocean depths of 15,000 feet, to just 200 feet below the waves.

Reisenberg had it. Small islands with a central lake are not common. They tend to be volcanoes with flooded craters. Elizabeth Island was no more, destroyed, he speculated, by volcanic eruption or perhaps sheared off by massive icebergs from Antarctica. He missed one decisive detail. The rocks and sand Captain Burnham found embedded in his sounding lead were black – they were volcanic. In a storm on the edge of the world Drake had found haven in an island which no man had ever landed on before. He had lain on its tip and declared it the southernmost known land in the world. He sailed away and it was torn apart by explosions in the empty theatre of the Southern Ocean. No one else would ever tread its sweet herbs.

Drake would have loved the name of the ship that found the island. It was in the River Pactolus that King Midas bathed to remove his curse. For ever after its sands ran rich with gold dust.

*Last Kawéskar*

In the remote heart of Chile's grey-green archipelago is Puerto Eden. It is so remote that the national visitor's guidebook misses out the whole zone. In Puerto Natales I had spoken to a local fishing boat captain who sails the southern part of the archipelago. Stabbing at the map, I asked, 'How many people live here?'

'None.'

'Very few?' I probed.

He looked blankly at my smile. 'No. None.'

And I still had not believed him. Now, Puerto Natales was about 275 miles behind us, the next town north worth the name, Puerto Aísen, about 425 miles further north. The rest was empty.

Puerto Eden. No running water, three shops, one café, one office. Population 180, five carabineros, twelve pure-blooded Kawéskar Indians living here all or part of the year, the last twelve in the world. The Navimag service runs here by government licence, and as a condition of that licence they must stop at Puerto Eden and provide trade and transport links to north and south. The town, and the last Kawéskar, could not survive without it.

After the end of the last glacial period, the ancient Kawéskar, like the Yámana, migrated south by boat, along the Chilean coast, and the two cultures are very similar. Even early explorers seldom met native groups in the western channels. Either they were always scarce, or they always knew how to make themselves scarce. More often the natives' first contact with the outside world was with the crews of sealers, forced into ever more remote locations to wipe out the animals, and move on. These sailors were usually the dregs, contact was brief and savage. When the area began to be settled in the middle of the last century, Mateo Martinic, whom I had met at the Insitute of Patagonia, estimated there were 3,000 Kawéskar.

In all, from Eden to the Horn, ten thousand native people occupied a domain the size of Italy.

Most of the later contact took place in the south where Kawéskar attacked passing ships. A vicious cycle of reprisals followed. From the 1870s missionaries arrived, and trading and survey vessels bartered trinkets for expensive otter skins. There is an engraving in the British Museum, after a drawing by Brassey in 1880, showing naked canoe Indians, probably Kawéskar, alongside a passing boat, below the shrouds. Notes and coins are handed down to two men, skins are passed up, a woman bails with a pot.

Jacques Cousteau came here in the late 1960s to look for the last Kawéskar. The Navimag's steward played a video of the programme he made. He found just five families of pure-blooded natives. A young girl was filmed outside the village school, singing a song and reciting a verse in Kawéskar. The interviewer asked what she thought would happen to her race. She replied promptly, 'They will die out.' Then she thought about what she had said, and cried.

The video then reported five families still fishing, collecting mussels, and trading with passing boats. Two tiny canoes came alongside a passenger ship and blond heads leaned over the smooth steel cliff. Two men and an old woman held up lidded baskets the size of oranges, woven from grass, and models of their own bark canoes. They wore crudely cut western dress. Hands above pointed, handicraft was held up, blond heads nodded. The Kawéskar stood straining, stretching up with their small goods. Rolled bank notes were lowered on string, trinkets were pulled up, a neat reversal of the first exchanges where Victorians gave trinkets for skins and furs. The passengers lost interest and the men in the canoes, who had sold most of their goods, picked up the paddles. The old woman held up a model boat. No one had bought from her, she cried out. Even as the canoe bore away, she raised her model hopelessly towards the steamer, repeating the price. A sailor threw a cigarette in the water. She held up her canoe long after anyone was looking.

The only difference over the gulf of nearly ninety years is that in the smaller Victorian boat, by stretching arms, the two cultures physically touched.

The audience broke up. Some went to the bar, which was playing party music. The Swiss blonde danced twice with her husband who moved like a man trying to free his feet from chewing gum without attracting attention. Duty done, his wife danced with a boyish, black man from Johannesburg. He was younger than her, with a cheeky smile and fast nimble feet. She came alive and they danced until late, including the slow numbers. Her husband sat miserably on a sofa, blinking at his own feet, nodding his head, out of time with the music. I went to bed when I could no longer bear to look at him.

At 5:30 in the morning I went out on deck and saw we were making a slow turn in the bay within the channel which marks the village of Puerto Eden. Air and water were quite still. Snow dusted the high mountains. The sun, still hidden from us, had found a high corner of a hill and lit the thin vegetation with a light like golden moss. The town was mostly single-storey cabins and bungalows, built of timber studding, but some were no more than huts. The common colour scheme was blue walls with a red roof.

A small yellow motor boat with a white cabin cut an arc to our stern. The cabin met the bow deck in a gentle slope. Leaning sideways on it, feet secured by blue cord, was a strapping lamb. It moved its head around, looking, but did not kick or struggle. Three Kawéskar stood modestly waiting. They were short and dark with broad faces, wide cheekbones, and the narrow eyes of a life spent out of doors. Both men and the woman had thick hair cut to collar length, very black. Their age might have been fifty. They wore bright red buoyancy aids and carried cardboard boxes which they brought on deck.

They took out models of traditional canoes they no longer used. They had beautiful small baskets woven in a spiral still smelling of grass. Each was the same as in the Cousteau programme, the same as in the museums. The baskets are made by the hitch coil method. The weaver works a stout stem in a spiral out from the centre of the base. A separate line of finer grass spirals loosely round this and weaves in and out of the spiral on the coil below, locking them together. In the whole of South America, this method is typical only of the Kawéskar, Yámana and Selk'nam. The grass is *Juncus magellanicus*, which is coarse and round-stemmed. The Kawéskar chew it flat to make it more pliable. The autumn baskets are bright red, but fade in weeks.

All three spoke quietly, courteously, in short sentences.

'What are these called?' asked a passenger, reverently examining a basket.

'Baskets.' The man replied, without irony.

I picked two small baskets from the box of one of the men. 'How much?'

'Three thousand.'

A few pounds. They smelt fresh and sweet. I hung them over my bunk.

There is no obligation to let the Kawéskar on board to trade; this is done on the initiative of the officers, to make a little income for the Kawéskar, and provide some interest for the passengers. But travel here is governed by the tides and on this occasion they were hurried on and off in fifteen minutes to make sure the Navimag made the next difficult narrows at slack water. I walked away muttering under my breath. A member of the crew came up behind me and caught my elbow (I'll call him Victor). 'Did I hear you saying you did not think much of the company?'

I blushed. 'I was annoyed at the speed the Kawéskar were hustled from the boat.'

'Let me tell you,' he pulled me close. 'I think the company is no good.' He looked around. 'I will get sacked if they found out I said this. Do you know about the Selk'nam, the way they were hunted down? Do you know who paid to shoot those Indians like animals and bring back their ears?'

'The ranchers.'

'One company more than any other, owned by Braun and Menéndez. That company still exists. Now someone published a book about the extermination. The same company bought the rights, bought up all the copies they could, to hush it up. The same company, my friend, owns the Navimag.'

'Navimag is owned by the heirs of José Menéndez? The one who quarrelled with the Salesian Missionaries?'

'The very same.'

With the help of Victor, who had the trust of the Kawéskar, I later obtained interviews with eight of the twelve pure-blooded survivors. The conversations with the Kawéskar were in Spanish, and recorded, but despite playing and replaying the discs I struggled to complete my transcripts. In the end I enlisted the help of a friend, Roser Gaitano, a native Spanish-speaker. She said, 'I think all the older Kawéskar are still thinking entirely in Kawéskar and translating it into this strange hybrid. Some of it must be in the structure of their native language with the words changed to Spanish. For instance, one has used 'When I was in process' when he means 'When my mother was pregnant with me.'

After meeting the Yámana I had thought carefully how to ask the Kawéskar to talk of the past and the future when both were equally painful. Most talked hesitantly, unsure what I was looking for when I began by asking 'What are your first memories?'

## Eden

'My first memories are of smoking mussels over the fire, and playing with the empty shells.' Gabriela Patirito said she was 'about 50 years old. Yes completely, totally natural one hundred per cent Kawéskar.'

'What did your grandparents do?'

'I didn't know them. No one, no family, no one older, not even my mother. The only ones I remember are my brother and sister. The rest are all dead.'

I asked, 'Do any children speak Kawéskar?'

'Not one.' She thought for a moment. 'Well just one, Juan Carlos Tonco, who's a student in Santiago now, he got married there. There are no children, now there's nobody. No young women. It's a result of the young ones marrying Chileans until they are no more, no natural.'

'How do you feel about the loss of your people?'

'More or less, there's no more, we're so few. My son, my daughter, very far away, in Temuco.'

Each Kawéskar had a different idea of how many pure-blooded natives were left, and how many spoke their language. There are more than Gabriela thought, but it does not matter. The numbers are so low, around a dozen, that the outcome will be the same.

Juan Carlos Tonco was the youngest person interviewed. He was born here, in midsummer, thirty-one years ago.

'What are your first memories?'

'In Puerto Eden, many years ago. We played at making small journeys, making model boats, copying the big ones. I also remember when I went out sailing with my father. We navigated practically the whole of Isla Wellington, hunting for otters and seals. Practically all the time I was off navigating through the islands of Madre de Dios, to the Island of Santero, and further through the Fallos and Covadonga Channels, Brazo Norte, Horno Sur, Playa Solitario, Cueva de Lobos.

'It was a very important period for me, discovering what it was to be a Kawéskar and receiving a little of the teaching of my people. Getting to know things from my father, like sailing a boat, how to navigate at night, steer by the stars. How to look at the sky to see if tomorrow there would be rain or wind, or if the next day would be stormy. All this passing on of the culture was, to me, very strong. The feeling of being a Kawéskar was much stronger in me than in my two brothers.

'Later, the time for lessons, school began. When I spent time with Chilote children, from the island of Chiloé in the civilised north, there was a lot of discrimination because we were different. In those times, it wasn't thought important to be Kawéskar. At first it made me feel small. But changes were coming, a significant change of feeling, recognising the culture, a different way of thinking.'

'What did your parents do?'

'My mother has worked making crafts until the present day. My dad was a hunter of otters and mussels, and worked at the drying of mussels.'

'Do you remember your grandparents?'

'My grandfather I never knew because he died when my mother was carrying me. I would have liked to have known that generation of my family, to get another vision in the sense of an older perspective, another point of view of the culture. So it's a thing which for me makes me a little sad in my soul. I might have been able to compensate for the loss of other things, by hearing our myths, the legends that have been told from generation to generation.'

'How do you earn a living?'

'I work in Santiago, I am in the third year of studying journalism, but that's frozen, because of problems with money. But at the end of my personal journey, I will finish it if at all possible. Meanwhile, I am in charge of a printing house.'

'Is it a good living?'

'Coming as I do from the area of Puerto Eden, it's very hard work, it demands sacrifices, going to the city is a big change, the hours are long, in some way it has its rewards, but I don't know that it's the best way of living.'

'Do you speak Kawéskar?'

'Yes, perfectly, my father and mother are Kawéskar, I spent a lot of time with them. Language is where the heart of a culture lies. Those who go to the city lose their sense of being Kawéskar, it's another way of life, more sedentary, they don't have a boat to go out and make voyages. They work at other things. In my opinion the Kawéskar way of life is being extinguished, it's finishing. It's impossible to recover it. Because we are going to be descended from the islanders, the Chilotes, not authentically Kawéskar.'

'Will the Kawéskar stay here in Puerto Eden?'

'Yes, I was talking with my mother on this voyage and she said she would never go back to the city. Her thoughts are always going back to Puerto Eden, it's her land, it's her world, where she moves, where someday she will die and go to the cemetery of Puerto Eden.'

'How do you feel about the loss of your people?'

'I regard it with a great sense of responsibility. It's a personal loss, very, very, very deep-seated in my emotions. My mother is sixty, sixty-five years old. In five or seven years time, if she dies, there won't be any reason for me to come back to Puerto Eden. At the moment my mother is practically the only anchor holding me to Puerto Eden and when that tie goes, the life of Juan Carlos Tonco will be in Santiago. I think the Tonco family will be in the city and they will never come back to the Puerto Eden area.'

Another of the younger men, José Tomo, talked quickly, interrupting himself. 'I'm thirty-four years old, born in Puerto Eden a long time ago. Look, it's really too long ago to say about my childhood. Moreover the house of the ancestors at the time when I became aware of things was already civilised, we didn't used to hunt, we were sedentary, so I lost that childhood. I don't know how to hunt. They collected mussels, from the sea, they dried them and then they sold them to ships passing through the channels.' I realised José Tomo would have known the old woman in Cousteau's programme, holding up her unsold model canoe.

'Do they teach Kawéskar at the school in Puerto Eden?'

'The truth is they do not. A few months ago the University of the Magellans asked me to advise on how to teach bilingual education in Puerto Eden. In fact I've been trying to make this proposition work for all my thirty-four years, but we'll see what effect it will have, if it will simply fail for lack of support. Chile has forgotten us for a long time. There are a few hundred per cent pure-blood Kawéskar and five or six hundred *mestizos*. There is no proper census but I know the 1991 census of four hundred was an underestimate.'

'Will the Kawéskar stay here in Puerto Eden?'

'The older people here in Puerto Eden will always stay here. They will die in this place. But for the young ones who are growing up, I think Puerto Eden is a small place and they will look for other horizons. I think the best place for young Kawéskar to improve themselves is in the city. Puerto Eden doesn't offer these opportunities, they can only get a basic education. Older ones will die here, working like labourers. I think that shouldn't be, they should keep studying. Loss of peoples is a reality which you have to accept. It's a fact that Kawéskar people are going to disappear from here in fifty years.

'It's very sad that the Kawéskar language will disappear. It's already disappearing, the language is a big thing to lose. The politicians have not created a special programme to rescue the native culture of the southern zone and the Kawéskar people. It's nearly lost, but not completely. For instance, they're making a Spanish-Kawéskar dictionary and grammar, but to date it's not been edited. But even that is a personal project with local money and not with any central government support.'

The last words come from Juan Carlos Tonco. 'The Kawéskar once had a vision which was self-contained in nature, a people who could live from nature. Everything is there, there are no bad spirits who can spoil a healthy life in the natural environment. But if someone is not capable of the cultural rescue that is required, they will save a few aspects of the culture, pick some people, like museum specimens, just a few, but we will lose the whole story. But my mum told me not to be so sad, these things happen because we are now a people who don't have any religious feeling, who do not believe in God, who don't believe in the great spirits.'

*Wager Island*

In the morning the weather stayed clear and calm. There was a Tannoy announcement advising passengers to take sea-sickness pills now in preparation for the Golfo de Penas, which we would enter that afternoon and spend twelve hours being hit from the side by Pacific rollers. When the wind is due west, or a little south of it, these waves have come right around the world, not seeing land for twenty thousand miles since they left the other side of South America, heading east.

Dawn clouds like honeyed oatmeal spilled light on to the high snows. The captain came up to the bridge as we entered the English Narrows. It is essential to arrive here during the slack water when the tide changes; in between, the tidal race is faster than most vessels plying the route. A captain cannot go through without a pilot until he has made ten supervised passes in each direction.

We wound through Disraeli and Cavour Islands, ferns reaching down to touch the water. Our stern left a graceful wash though the morning. On the smallest islet was a shrine and a small statue of the Virgin. The first mate, a burly uncommunicative man, came outside on the bridge by me and threw a few coins in the water. He crossed himself and his lips moved in brief prayer.

'There was a shipwreck here?'

'Yes.'

Another coin into the long low ripples.

'What was the ship?'

'I don't know the name, but sailors died, it's enough.'

Soon I could see a rusting boat in the waters to port. It was listed towards us. The third mate saw me training the binoculars on it. 'She's not going anywhere. Greek, the *Leonidas*. It's on the Cotopaxi Bank, has been since 1968. Went aground at nine-thirty in the morning. I was on a boat which came through on the second day. The crew all got off, the boat didn't.'

'What was the weather like?'

'Good weather.'

'Navigation error?'

'Maybe.' He gave a shrug, his eyes smiling.

I mimed drinking from a bottle.

He laughed. 'Who knows?'

The weather slowly began to worsen, colours paled again. The Messier Channel was opening slowly out into the Golfo de Penas. The ship took on a slight pitching motion. A headwind sprang up and black-browed albatrosses picked up the stern, while tiny Wilson's storm petrels flitted across the face of the waves in ceaseless effort. All around were mountains of wild grim beauty. We sailed down the flooded valley until there in the murk was Wager Island, and beyond it, fading in and out of vision, Byron Island. Wager Island was capped by the block of Mount Anson, a flat-topped brute of a rock towering above everything else. The poor light flattened each part of the panorama. It receded, interleaved, tricksy, falling away west, fainter and fainter like watercolour washes. The cloud above mimicked the process in colossal stage backdrops. Mountains stumbled down into islands, low islands skirted with vicious rocks and shallows. The land kept coming up again, re-emerging in rock teeth, as if it would not give up the struggle to deny the water. The land died screaming in the rocks called The Mice, the long ridge of a drowning mountain riding a mile or more out to sea, the waves tearing and worrying at the stone, foaming the water, flaying the air above with water hard as shot pellets. It was a shore you would not wish on your enemy.

I went forward to the bridge until the clinometer showed we were rolling from 25° to port though to 25° to starboard. It was now hard physical work not to get thrown and hurt. The third mate saw me looking and said, 'One time she rolled 36°.'

'What happened?'

'I fell out of my bunk.'

I went to my cabin; my rucksack burst out of its locker. I wedged myself in the bunk and read.


*Poverty, Vermin, Famine and Destruction*

In 1743, at the sign of the Golden Lion on Ludgate Hill in the City of London, a small book appeared, price three shillings and sixpence. It was written by boatbuilder John Cummins and ship's gunner John Bulkeley, and was the history of a shipwreck. All good travel books have a purpose; theirs was to save them from being hanged by the neck as mutineers.

It had begun in 1740 when two squadrons set sail from England to harry the Spanish on both sides of their empire. The strategy was for one squadron to go east and plunder Manila, a poorly defended port receiving more than three million dollars of silver from Acapulco each year, while the other would go west round Cape Horn, and seize the treasure of the Americas directly from the Pacific ports. Commander George Anson's Cape Horn mission was far more taxing, but he was junior to the Commander of the

Manila fleet, so he got second best of everything, from masts to food.

Ten months before the squadron sailed, the thoughtful Anson was already petitioning the Admiralty not to foist on him 'the Pease and Oatemeal put on board his Majesty's Ships [which] have generally decayed and become not fit to issue'. The Admiralty sanctioned the changes but through corruption the same old goods were loaded. On the *Gloucester*, forty-two out of seventy-two barrels of beef were rotting before they sailed.

If the goods were shoddy the men were worse. At first Anson was allocated Colonel Bland's regiment and three hundred other men. This became five hundred pensioners, but only those who were too ill or old to march. Sir Charles Wager, First Lord of the Admiralty, joined Anson's complaints but was advised that 'persons who were supposed to be better judges of soldiers than he or Mr Anson, thought them the properest men that could be employed'. They were fitter than they looked. As soon as they learned of their proposed employment round Cape Horn, 241 of the 500 walked clean out of Portsmouth, leaving only broken men, some over seventy years old.

The *Centurion* set about its own cruel recruitment, sending out boats to incoming merchantmen to seize trained sailors returning from two-year voyages, unpaid, and impressing them for six years at one third of the pay. Although desertion was a hanging offence, nineteen of the seventy-three they got this way absconded. When the five boats limped into the Atlantic in September 1740, enemy spies decided the departure was a feint. No one would take such wretchedly equipped ships to the worst seas in the world.

In charge of the *Pearl* was Captain Dandy Kidd, a man with a depressive turn of mind, who forecast 'Poverty, Vermin, Famine and Destruction'. He was right. He would be spared three of these torments, but only by experiencing personal destruction almost immediately. He was succeeded by George Murray of the *Wager*. Lieutenant David Cheap was promoted to Captain of the *Wager*. He was young, and immature in his use of authority.

On 7 March the squadron entered the Le Maire Strait. On their right were the islands of Cape Horn. On their left, Staten Island. There was a clear sky and a brisk gale. The men were filled with dreams of Chile's silver, Peru's gold. The fleet would never unite again. It was the last day of hope most would ever know.

A storm hit, and they were bludgeoned backwards. The *Wager* did not clear the twenty-mile gate of Le Maire before the sky darkened; the tide turned against her, and the wind veered south, into their teeth. When they fired distress signals they were close enough to see Staten Island's grim glory. The highly experienced Anson admitted:

> Some amongst us had lately treated the difficulties which former voyagers were said to have met with in this undertaking as little better than chimerical, and had supposed them to arise rather from timidity and unskilfulness than from the real embarrassments of the winds and seas: but we were now severely convinced that these censures were rash and ill-grounded, for the distresses with which we struggled, during the three succeeding months, will not easily be paralleled in the relation of any former naval expedition.

The squadron steered south-west and was blown twenty miles east. The sea rose up in steep high waves, hitting the ships so hard that men were thrown off and lost. One broke his neck, another his thigh, and the bosun fractured his collar bone twice. Canvas was reduced to a single sail, and then to the bare poles. When the wind eased, they raised sails, but sleet and snow cased the rigging and froze the canvas. The rotten cordage snapped. Working barefoot was common. Toes and fingers fell off. On 3 April another storm began. It was worse than all the rest and lasted a terrifying three weeks.

On the *Centurion* the mainstays began to tear away They took down the sails. Still the cheating ropes broke so they took down the yards. Men started to fall ill with scurvy. The *Centurion* recorded one of the sickest voyages ever. Perhaps because so many men were old and had been eating poor hospital food before they left. The squadron set out with 1,872 men. When they reached the green shores of Brazil, before any storm or shipwreck was suffered,

160 were dead and 450 ill. The Royal Observatory at Greenwich keeps the brown-covered ledger of deaths. A steady script rolls over page after page.

In April, forty-three died on the *Centurion* alone, in May, double. When they reached shore only six men were fit for each watch. Without vitamin C the body rots. Flesh blemishes, limbs swell, gums fester until teeth fall out. On the *Centurion* men became too weak to rise or even protect themselves. Scurvy killed and killed. They fell out of hammocks and rolled around the deck like logs. Pascoe Thomas wrote, 'I have seen 4 or 5 dead Bodies at a time, some sewn up in their Hammocks and others not, washing about the Decks, for Want of Help to bury them in the Sea.'

In its last stages, flesh rotted on the body – 'such a luxuriancy of fungous flesh as yielded to no remedy'. Scurvy also causes depression; black minds surveyed green bodies. The final horrors were reserved for battle veterans. One invalid on the *Centurion* had been wounded at the Battle of the Boyne, fifty years before. The scars of half a century ago reopened as if they were fresh wounds, and his mended fractures dissolved into broken bones.

On 22 May the *Centurion,* now sailing alone, was struck by a tempest so violent that 'the fury of all the storms which we had hitherto encountered seemed to be combined, and to have conspired our destruction'. Nearly all the sails were split, its rigging half destroyed. Supposing the other much smaller vessels sunk, they sailed for Juan Fernández, the semi-tropical island used as a watering hole and repair base for vessels escaping the Southern Ocean. On 28 May in the right latitude, 33° south, longitude uncertain, Anson looked west and called 'Land!' His officers persuaded him that they lay too far to the west and it was a cloud. They turned east. Two days later the snow-capped Andes broke the horizon. Their desolation was complete. It took nine days and eighty deaths to claw their way upwind to Juan Fernández. This was the cost of guessing longitude.

They had to help one another ashore, carry others, bring food back for the prostrate. Despite wild celery bursting with vitamin C, fresh water and meat, they buried six more before the disease was arrested. They found goats with split ears crippled and marked more than thirty years before by Alexander Selkirk. The tiny *Anna* followed the *Centurion* there, the *Tryal* and *Gloucester* retreated to Brazil. One ship was unaccounted for: the *Wager*.

## The Wreck of the Wager

At eight o'clock on the morning of 13 May 1741 the *Wager*, the converted East Indiaman now under the command of Captain David Cheap, was sailing blind through a gale in the uncharted waters of the Golfo de Penas, or Gulf of Afflictions, on the west coast of Chile. Its course would have crossed ours, on the *Puerto Eden*. The *Wager* had already been battered and half broken in the storms further south. Defective iron plates holding the mizzen mast's main supporting rigging had torn off with a noise like gunshots, and the mast had crashed down.

The night before, Captain Cheap had summoned his experienced gunner John Bulkeley and discussed their position. They agreed that at best they were 180 miles offshore, at worst 60. Then carpenter John Cummins went up to the forecastle to inspect the damage, and saw land. Cummins went to Lieutenant Robert Baynes, the second in command. Baynes said, 'It bears NNW. It cannot be land, it is impossible.' He refused to tell Captain Cheap that land had been sighted.

In the middle of the day, blocks holding the foremast broke and one of the largest yards fell to deck. Then the ship threw Captain Cheap, badly dislocating his shoulder. Only twelve men were fit for work. John Bulkeley, officer of the watch, went aloft to help. 'I saw the land very plain, on the larboard-beam, with hillocks and one remarkable hommacoe like a sugar-loaf, very high. I came off the foreyard and acquainted the Captain.'

That fateful 13 May, the *Wager* was sailing into one of the most treacherous bays in the world. On her deck was a seventeen-year-old midshipman from an aristocratic family. The hardships would be so severe that he would not bring himself to write a memoir of the voyage until he was safely in middle age. But his grandson would trawl the memoir for details for a colossal and innovative poem, a novel in verse, *Don Juan*. The young officer was John Byron, grandfather of the poet.

According to John Byron, Captain Cheap stayed calm, despite being in great pain from his shoulder, and relayed orders to deck. They were in a large rectangular bay. Having seen land to the NNW they sailed a clockwise turn, going east, then south, and finally tried to beat back westwards into the wind and escape past the southern lip of the bay. At half past four on the morning of 14 May 1741 a shudder passed down the ship. The seas had been hitting the ruined ship so hard they did not immediately realise they had struck a rock. The ship rolled off it but struck another rock so hard she keeled over on her side. As the few crewmen still able to move rushed on deck, a wave broke over them, while men too sick to move drowned in their hammocks. Everywhere the living looked were rock and foam. Another huge wave lifted them off, but when they struck again the tiller broke.

> . . . and ere she could lift
> Herself from out her present jeopardy
> The rudder tore away: 'twas time to sound
> The pumps, and there were four feet water found.
>
> Don Juan, Canto II, verse 27

One of the bravest men aboard looked at the hopelessness all around him and dashed to the rail to hurl himself into the sea. Others stopped him. The sick, worn out, were knocked down and washed into the scuppers. One seaman appeared on deck with a cutlass and strutted about brandishing it over his head and shouting, 'I am king of this country' and struck out at anyone who came near him, till someone knocked him down.

At the helm was John Jones the mate, who called out serene and calm, 'My friends, let us not be discouraged, did you never see a ship amongst breakers before? Let us endeavour to push her through them. Come lend a hand, here is a sheet, and here is a brace, lay hold, I don't doubt but we may stick her yet near enough to the land to save our lives.' In fact, as he often said afterwards, 'I did this purely to keep up the spirits of the people as long as possible. I thought there was not the least chance of a single man's life being saved.'

But it worked. Byron said, 'Many who before were half dead seemed active again, and now went to work in earnest.'

The boat came free a third time, and using only the sails to steer they got nearer the shore and wedged her between two rocks, out of the worst of the weather. They struggled to free the ship's boats from the confusion of fallen rig. When one was floated, so many men jumped in that she nearly sank before they reached the shore. Some of those still on board rose from their knees, where they had been settling spiritual matters, and set to breaking open chests of fine clothes, casks of wine and brandy. Bosun John King, a quarrelsome bully of a man, swore, 'I will never leave this vessel while she has a drop of liquor left on her.' Since the *Wager* carried most of the fleet's supply, this was the bravest cry of all. He dressed up and got drunk.

> There's nought, no doubt, so much the spirit calms
> As rum and true religion; thus it was,
> Some plunder'd, some drank spirits, some sung psalms . . .
> Strange sounds of wailing, blasphemy, devotion,
> Kept still aloof the crew, who, ere they sunk,
> Thought it would be becoming to die drunk.
>
> Don Juan, Canto II, verse 34

On the shore, in a wood, the officers found a single Indian hut. The men lit a bonfire under a large tree and huddled together, but through cold and exhaustion a lieutenant and two men died during the night.

All next day the storm raged, and the rabble on the ship drank and fought and strangled each other over plunder. The day after, John King lined up a four-pounder and sent two shots whistling low over the captain's hut. It was two more days before the bosun came ashore. Cheap beat him to the ground with his cane and cocked his pistol. King tore his shirt open and bared his chest.

Cheap swore he was not worth it, and stormed away. One hundred and forty made it to the shore.

## Hunger is Void of All Compassion

The survivors continued to strip the wreck, hampered by the flooding below decks, and the bump of floating bodies. Some meat, flour and much drink were saved. Behind them was the flat-topped hill now called Mount Anson. They climbed it, saw where they were, and gave it its first name, Mount Misery. Gathering shellfish they had to endure seeing the mangled bodies of their comrades broken on the rocks. One boy was found next to the torn body of a sailor whose liver was exposed. The boy had the liver in his hands and had to be stopped from eating it.

As best they could, the survivors put up tents and built huts. Outside, the shelters were miserable affairs, but inside they were lined with precious fabrics intended for trade goods. Byron found a puppy left behind by an Indian dog, and kept it as a pet. From Cheap's library he took George Shelvocke's account, *A Voyage Round the World*, published just fifteen years before, which described how he escaped from the shipwreck in the *Speedwell* on Juan Fernández, by building a new boat out of the timbers.

On Cheap's orders John Cummins was adding twelve feet to the midsection of their largest boat to prepare it for escape. Cheap was set on continuing three hundred miles north, to the weakly defended Spanish island of Chiloé. He planned to seize a Spanish ship and rendezvous with Anson. But Bulkeley wanted to sail two thousand miles back through the Magellan Strait and north to a friendly port in neutral Brazil.

Meanwhile winter wore on, into August, and they starved. A deputation of fellow-officers arrived at Byron's hut with a proposition: they wanted to eat his dog. He was still arguing with them when they took it off and killed it. Reflecting he had more right to a feed from it than any of them, he joined the feast. 'We thought no English mutton preferable to it.' Three weeks later Byron was so hungry he went back to the place where they had killed his dog and ate the rotting paws and skin.

The men launched the rebuilt boat, and christened her *Speedwell*, oddly choosing the name of the wrecked Shelvocke vessel, not his getaway, the *Recovery*. The *Speedwell* and a little cutter left for good, heading south on 8 October 1741. They had been five months and four days on Wager Island. The men rapidly proved they were no more governable under their own rule. Bulkeley complained they were 'ripe for mutiny and destruction'. The weak froze and starved to death. Bulkeley noted how in their last hours they became light-hearted, started 'joking and laughing; and in this humour, they expire'. On 19 November young Thomas Caple tried to buy extra flour. He had a watch, a silver cup, and more than twenty guineas. No one would sell. His guardian was on board and tried to console him: 'I will use the money to buy clothes for you in the Brazil!'

Thomas cried, 'I shall never live to see the Brazil; I am starving now, almost starved to death; therefore, for God's sake give me my silver cup to get me some victuals, or buy some for me yourself.' He died. He was twelve years old.

Bulkeley recorded, 'Persons will wonder how people can see their fellow-creatures starving before their faces, and afford 'em no relief: but hunger is void of all compassion.' Not until January 1742 did they slip over a sandbar near the River Plate, into a friendly Portuguese port.

Back on Wager Island, all attempts to sail out of the Golfo de Penas, against the wind and seas, ended in exhausting failure. Exposure, starvation and accident whittled away their numbers until only a handful remained, including Byron and Cheap. One morning an Indian arrived bearing the silver-topped cane the Spanish gave to trusted *caciques*, or chiefs. They learned he was from the Chonos tribe, from Chiloé. News of the wreck had travelled from group to group, tribe to tribe, and Martin the Cacique had come to see for himself.

They told him they wanted to get to a Spanish settlement, and he said he would guide them if he could keep the boat. This was agreed. There was little to eat and the Indians would only provide food in exchange for goods, and they had no more goods. Cheap was treated as a chief and given food, which he did not share, even when his men died of starvation lying in the bilge-water swirling around his feet.

Cheap, despite better treatment, soon needed help to walk. The vermin on their bodies were so bad that Byron would lie naked in the snow to sleep, since most of the vermin stayed in the clothes. Cheap was an anthill. He no longer tried to keep clean. His beard was down his chest, his upper body a skeleton, his legs bloated. At last they fell on to another shore and saw, across the sound, the island of Chiloé. The local Indians, although very poor, went out and killed a sheep and baked bread. Each succeeding day peasants arrived with gifts of food. They ate and ate.

It was not until October 1746 that Byron saw Dover. The different stragglers made it home. They told their own stories. Bulkeley and Cummins wrote their book and sweated on the return of the officers. Had it been left to Cheap they might have hanged, but it wasn't. Anson had sailed with 1,972 men: four died in combat, and 1,300 of disease. He was sick of death. He had also come home with treasure to fill thirty-two carts in procession to the Tower of London and he wanted to enjoy it. A court martial was held into the loss of the *Wager* in which Cheap disposed a single charge, against Lieutenant Baynes, who was reprimanded.

John Byron became Vice Admiral in 1778. His wild, handsome Guards Officer son 'Mad Jack' Byron fathered the poet, who seemed to have a soft spot for his grandfather. 'He had no peace by sea nor I on shore,' he remarked ruefully, in *Epistle to Augusta*.

Anson put much energy into reforming naval yards and became First Lord of the Admiralty. The publicity given to the *Centurion's* losses from scurvy led James Lind in 1747 to begin the first scientific investigation into the disease. In 1753 he dedicated his *Treatise of the Scurvy* to Anson, but it was fifty more years before the establishment would listen, and act.

Caleta Angelmó

We docked in the late evening. The sheep, without water for three days, were motionless, silent, licking the rain from their neighbour's fleece. Puerto Montt crouched under grey cool rain. I walked two miles along the sea front to try to book a flight to Juan Fernández. I wanted to stand where my eight-year-old self had, in imagination, stood. I had imagined these places, they must exist.

I tried a travel agency, knowing the planes were small and the midsummer service was usually full. The assistant was young, calm, uniformed and polite. She said, 'There are no flights to Juan Fernández. I can get you a flight to Easter Island.'

'Three companies fly to Juan Fernández.'

'Do you have their telephone numbers?'

I resisted the temptation to lead her outside by the arm and point to the sign above the window saying 'Travel Agent' and suggest that they might know a telephone number or two themselves. We worked at it together, brochures, phone book. Three hours later I had a booking added to my rising credit card bill.

She handed me a paper. 'The tickets will be in Santiago. You are very lucky to get a flight.'

One hour later, in Cardiff, my phone recorded a message from Barclaycard. Someone was spending my money like water. Had my card had been stolen? Unfortunately not.

I took a bus back along the bay to Caleta Angelmó, a fishing port where the beach consists of old shells thrown from the back of the cafés. The market sold fresh seafood taken one hundred yards from family boats to the covered market. Great sea-fish a yard long lay pink-gilled on the slabs, lantern-jawed monsters hauled up and up from the hydraulic pressures of the depths until, near the surface, their eyes prolapsed on condoms of tissue. I saw one wooden case full of blocks of stone. Barnacles an inch and a half long studded them. I bent to look closer; the largest barnacle changed into a claw and lunged at me, snapping. The stallholder, a fat woman in black, flapped a dishcloth at it, 'Agh! Stop it, you nuisance.' The claw retreated.

'What is that?'

'They are pico rocas.'

'Is it a crab?'

'No, it's a different animal, tastes very nice, in soups, in *curanto*. How much do you want?'

'Do I have to buy the whole rock?'

'No! I'll break it open, you don't need a wheelbarrow. This much?' She picked up the biggest rock. The claw came out again.

'I'm not cooking.'

The market looked medieval. There was a warren of stalls all run by wide women dressed in black who ran out, caught my arm and tried to wrestle me down behind one of their trestle tables. Drums of seafood steamed, the rolling broth brought a procession of beasts to the surface. This was the *curanto* stew the taxi driver Henrique had told me about after my visit to the Mylodon Cave. When I met a woman too wide to wrestle, I sat down and ordered. I ate a cold starter of pico rocas; they were delicate and soft, like tissuey crab-meat. A bowl of *curanto* arrived. Every creature in *Genesis* was belly-up somewhere in it.

Before going on to Santiago, to Mr Daskam and my plane tickets, I had some local business. In a hire car I drove south west to Pargua and took the ferry to the Island of Chiloé. The west coast of Chiloé is in line with the rest of the Chilean Pacific coast, but the sea runs in behind it forming the Bay of Ancud. To the south is a twenty-mile gulf through which the tides wash with a force that nearly drowned Byron and Cheap. To the north, the same tides tear through a gap only two miles wide. A car ferry crosses the narrow Chacao Channel and spins about in the currents. Like all car ferries it seemed to need a sign painted on the hull saying, 'Launch other way up.'

It was a beautiful summer morning. Magellanic penguins hunted in the eddies and slow whirlpools where the tides spin fish up to the surface – the same versatile penguins which fight the waters of the Horn. Seals made their way purposefully across the channel and two dolphins blew lazily across our wake. This was the gateway to the island of myths. This magical passage took me to Chiloé, the home of witches and one of the world's great ghost-ship stories.


*Castro*

The island is shaped like a brick, with one long broken edge facing the mainland. It is a hundred-and-twenty-five miles north to south. Darwin wrote, 'In winter the climate is detestable, and in summer it is only a little better.' Today was sunny and warm and the landscape was soft and domestic. Gorse flowered in the scrub, Dracaena palms, familiar to me from Cornwall, prospered in the gardens. There was plenty of time to observe since every road was dug up. A huge machine mixed and spread concrete; behind it men sprayed a mist of water and erected polythene tents to keep the sun from drying it too quickly.

There were many hitchhikers, their banana-republic clothes betraying they had come from the furnace of the far north. They carried high-rise backpacks fetished with zips, straps and Velcro. Each pocket bulged, every strap strained, the Velcro cried itself open. Local drivers with flat-backed trucks gave them lifts, and carabineros with sniffer dogs pulled them over every five miles and made them unpack everything to search for drugs.

The main town is now Castro, on the centre of the east side. Founded in 1567, it is Chile's third oldest town. I pulled up and urchins ran round the car pointing at it because it was new, and asking if I would like to stay at their house for US$2 a night. Wooden-walled stilt houses stood along the shore, their front doors on the road, their backs above the water. They were originally built in all the east coast fishing towns but remain only here.

I chose the Blue Unicorn hotel on looks alone. It was an old house with a glass-sided covered passageway rising up the steep hill behind, and a line of chalets following the contour. Everything was painted pink and blue. I booked in at the mahogany desk and looked at the modern artwork on the walls, some very good. 'The owner's daughter,' said the receptionist. 'She's at art college in Santiago.'

A short man, thin as fuse wire, appeared at my side. 'He'll take your luggage.'

He lit a cigarette, coughed, spat on his hands and picked up my backpack by slipping the shoulder straps over one arm. He walked towards the stairs, contorted into a human paper clip, with the bag banging against his legs. I followed. After three long flights he stopped, sweating unhealthily, and pinched his cigarette out between finger and thumb, popping the stub in his shirt pocket. He moved the pack to his other forearm. Halfway up he cried out, threw down the bag, reached into his pocket and took out the smouldering stub. As he bent down I took one strap and indicated the other to him.

The room was simple but stylish and its veranda gave views over the harbour. A tall cypress growing on the sea front below rose up high above me. At my eye level, in the upper branches, stood a duck.

In the corner of the dining room was a bar. Dark hardwood boards of ecclesiastical solemnity shone in the low light. In the dark shadows, a white shirt with knife creases made pisco sour in a stainless steel shaker. Silver links on double cuffs drew lines in the air like sparklers. Behind them a brown-voiced barman told me, 'It was a house, the home of a timber merchant. For years he kept back the very best of all the woods he traded in to build his own house. As soon as he finished it business went bad. After he died in 1986 it lay empty for years, the business closed, the family had no money to keep it going. It's only been a hotel a couple of years; Chiloé's most famous architect, Edward Rojas, did the conversion.'

The hill up to the town was vertical. In a turn in the road, near the top, was a dusty blue house growing among shadowy pines and cypresses, with tipsy extensions added uphill and down. The eyes of its windows were misted with starry cataracts of lace. I recognised it as the house in Tomas Daskam's painting 'Almirante Thompson'.

In the square, my thoughts lost in the singing coming from the church of San Francisco, I took a picture. The island is famous for its churches and chapels, most of them built in the eighteenth century by Jesuits from Bavaria to Scandinavia who all brought their own methods of constructing wooden churches. No two are the same. They do not have a nail in them. Iron was so scarce they were pegged and jointed. San Francisco at Castro is the most photographed. This is not just because it was the biggest and one of the last to be built – designed by Eduardo Provasoli in 1906 – or because it was constructed by local craftsmen using local woods, since much of it was then clad in corrugated iron. It photographs well in the evening and morning when low sidelighting picks out its folds. But the reason its picture is on the cover of the national guidebook for southern Chile is that the church is painted orange with a pale purple roof.


## La Posada Antigua

I drove out to the west coast along gravel roads with log bridges. Between two rocky headlands drenched in cloud and spray a colossal bay took the Pacific's rollers. At the southern tip of the island's road, Quellón was drab, municipal. Half of its roads had been dug up and laid on top of the other half.

I went back north to Chonchi. I left the tarmac road and crossed the valley on a dirt road with kerbstones and lampposts. Another road was on its way. The streets were empty, the town strangely quiet.

There is an inn, La Posada Antigua, famous for its cooking, and I pulled into the drive which wound through an acre of gardens overlooking the harbour. There was no other vehicle. The wind breathed in the pines, a pergola wrapped in grape vines led to the steps of a bungalow with a central eye-shaped dormer window curved into the roof tiles over the portico. The horizontal boards of the walls were painted deep red. Cows lowed in a small meadow.

I heard footsteps in the gravel. A round-faced man in grey trousers and a grey jersey came shuffling along the edge of the drive, his back too bowed for his age, one shoulder hunched up to his ear. He smiled nervously and went into the house. I followed him. The first two columns of the pergola were carved in a meticulous spiral thread. I wondered why anyone would go to such trouble, until I realised they were wooden screws salvaged from an old cider press. A bright sun lounge ran the width of the house, a bell tinkled in a far room. The man went through the house, hugging the sides of every space he crossed.

A thin woman in her sixties held out her hand. 'I am Teresa Vera Alvarez, you must call me Teresa.' She twined an orange cardigan about her ribs and mixed some English in with the Spanish and apologised for her mistakes. She showed me up a broad staircase past corn-dollies of Chilote mythological figures. A wooden-floored gallery strewn with cream woollen rugs ran the length of the building to the eye-shaped dormer at the front. In the middle was a huge stone and iron pot-bellied stove. She left, gesturing at the house like a dancer leaving a stage '*Mi casa es tu casa*, do you understand? My house is your house.'

I poked around the room. A soft-mattressed brass bed with a home-made quilt. The shower had a small electric bell push outside it. The wires led out of the room and downstairs. There was a knock at the door. Teresa wrung her hands. 'My daughter is not here, I cannot cook meals.'

'I cannot eat dinner here?'

'No, not now.'

'Breakfast?'

'Breakfast I will cook you myself.'

'The town is very quiet, where can I eat?'

'You can't. Everyone is at the rodeo. There will be food there.'

Down country lanes the bus bounced, dropping me at a field where there was a permanent arena and a big hall. The whole town was here, except for Teresa and the shuffling man. It was the last day of a three-day New Year rodeo. An accordion and guitar band was setting up on stage in the hall. To one side down a few steps was a long men-only bar. I ordered a beer. Families sat round the edges of the hall at turquoise Formica tables spread with tablecloths patterned with red roses.

The riding gear was boots and loose trousers; an ordinary collared shirt was topped by a large woollen poncho whose simple geometrical patterns were woven in earth colours. The felt hat had a flat six-inch brim encircled by a leather or plaited rope band. A man at a stall had a form, which could be adjusted for head size, on which he ironed the hats into sharp perfection. The gauchos are marked for style, as well as horsemanship.

I ate a lamb roast. The band began to play and most of the room got up to dance. Every head of hair in the room was black or grey. After an hour, a lot of men in the room looked to be in the limbo that drink manufactures between sensible and insensible. I stopped drinking and took a seat in the arena. A circular ring had smooth wooden walls round three quarters of it; the rest was a holding pen for waiting horsemen and bulls which had already been run. Riders waited in pairs until a young bull was released. C. J. Lambert, in his memoir of running a Chilean farm between the wars, recalls the power of these animals. Several of his largest had been put together in a corral. They would charge any other bull which let its attention drop. He heard a bellow and turned to see one victim sailing sideways through the air, clearing the six-foot fence with ease.

The waiting bulls were penned up under the stand. One at a time they were released into the arena and the two competitors had to run it round the wall under control, turn it, and bring it back. At some point they also had to stop it still, and pin it against the wall. A plump father and his teenage son walked their horses to the gate. They wore wooden clog stirrups to stop their feet being crushed against the boards. The pen beneath the stand banged open and the first bull sprinted out. The father picked him up and rode in a prancing, slightly sideways motion keeping his horse's chest to the bull's shoulder. His son rode a little behind to stop it turning. They held it steady at a canter to the end of the ring wall. The father then kicked and cut across the front of the bull and at the same moment the son spun round. Bull and horses pulled up and turned in an explosion of sand. In two seconds, two and a half tons of animals were running back along the wall at the same speed.

The competition went on another hour. The sun was falling. The Chilean flag cracked at the tall pole. It was the first one I had seen which was not torn and frayed at the edge by the Fuegian winds. The winners dismounted and a small boy rode in and collected their great silver-rowelled spurs. The prizes were donated by a local fish-farmer. A flat-backed truck with his name all over it drove into the ring, and the queen and princess of the rodeo walked unsteadily across the sand in high-heeled shoes and white dresses to dispense packs of smoked salmon. The public address played music and they danced the national dance, the *cueca*. The queen and the princess climbed up behind the winners and rode out.

I bused back. Distressed at watching so many other people drink for so long, I found one shop open in town and bought a bottle of *licor d'oro* to drink in my room, and some chocolate. Crossing the hall a door opened and Teresa shot out. 'What are you doing now?'

She looked as if she might disapprove of solo drinking. 'I am very tired. I was just going to have some chocolate and go to bed.'

'Why don't you come into the kitchen and have a drink with me? I have some *licor d'oro*.'

In the kitchen were a local couple, and a middle-aged Frenchman called Thierry writing something out from pages of notes. Teresa poured a small glass of gold-coloured syrupy liquid. The bottle label had a picture of the Posada Antigua on it. 'I make it myself, from the milk of my own cows.'

'Milk?'

'From our own cows, which Pancho my son hand-milks, blended with sugar, vanilla, lemon, and pure alcohol.'

It tasted syrupy with a tang of milk.

'I see you are interested in my work,' said Thierry, although I had been day-dreaming about the rodeo. 'Every year I go on holiday somewhere special and write articles for *Le Monde*. It pays for most of the holiday. Teresa is helping me with local detail. Before I was in Chile I was in the Philippines. You know about the cult of the injured?'

'No.'

'They believe that if a person has an accident and they survive, they are empowered. The more serious the accident, the narrower the margin by which they have cheated death, the more empowered they become. Children are especially valued. They act as fortune-tellers, sages. I met a number of these *animistas*. One boy had been in a car accident and suffered a fractured skull. He was fourteen days in a coma so he was very powerful. People brought him a lot of money, he made a good living. His uncle managed the business side.'

We all spoke a little English, French and Spanish, and wandered from one to another. The couple left. Teresa gazed lovingly on the kitchen soirée. I stood up. 'I have to go to bed.'

'One last drink,' said Teresa.

I sat down. I had one more question. 'The roads, are they always like this?'

'Like what?'

'Dug up.'

'Our local member of parliament is a rising star. He has been made Minister of Transport. He is spending as much money in Chiloé as possible.'

At breakfast I was alone. On each table was a stone sculpture of Trauco, a Chilote mythological creature, a three-foot-tall woodsman with a magical hold over young women. He lures them into the woods and shags them senseless. On each grey statuette, the coat was parting at the front under the pressure of a large erection. The walls were covered with certificates for cookery courses, local competitions, district finals for hospitality or regional cuisine. They were all in Teresa's name, none in the name of any daughter.

In the evening we sat in the kitchen again. Thierry had gone. I wanted to know about her family so I asked about the house.

'My grandfather built it, he was a dealer in timber and other products. All the house is made from the wonderful woods of Chiloé and the mainland, Alerce pine, cypress, roblé, the best. Come and look round.'

She took me on a tour of the whole house. There were no personal memorabilia, no wedding picture, no photograph of a man who might have been her husband, father or grandfather. No young woman who might have been a daughter. We sat down again at the kitchen table.

'Have you always lived here?'

243

'I was born here in this house which my grandfather built. Salvador Allende!' She banged her glass down and golden liquid spilled in sticky droplets on the scrubbed pine.

'My grandfather employed four hundred men. This was his. He had built it up from nothing. What had Allende done? What did he want with it? Jealousy! Mean jealousy!'

'He seized the house?'

'We were away, staying in our house in Santiago.'

'Why pick on your grandfather?'

'Because he was big, because it was a prosperous business.'

'What did he want to do with it, nationalise it?'

'He didn't know what he wanted. They didn't even understand what the business did. It employed four hundred men in a town with no other big companies. That was all they knew. You've been to Rio Verde.' She pointed a thin finger at the centre of my chest. 'Kenneth Maclean, who had just bought into the Ponsonby Ranch at Rio Verde, was sitting in his own kitchen listening to the radio when he found the ranch was being seized, and that by the end of the month he had to quit the ranch he had worked on for thirty-five years. The shearing wasn't even finished. Yes! Señor Allende now had control of the means of production, but he couldn't shear sheep. They had to hire back Kenneth Maclean to finish the job.'

She looked up at the slumbering shadows on the ceiling. 'Allende fell in 1973, we got this house back in 1974, but it was in rack and ruin. The business had fallen apart. They hadn't had a clue what to do. It never recovered.'

She had lost that feeling that the house we grow up in is untouchable, inviolate, but she had nowhere else to go. The house was physically sound and well maintained, but emotionally she lived in the ruins of her family, its fallen reputation and lost security. She did not go out. Her visitors were her society. The house was desensitised, no portraits. The keys to her past had been removed from the locks.

'Is Pancho married?'

'No! Pancho is a good boy, a good son. He has a little boy, who is also very good, with no problems.'

That morning I had gone to the Museum of Chonchi Life, a typical old wooden house preserved as it was, respectable, lace-curtained, middle class. Most exhibits had been donated as they fell out of fashion or their owners died in the manner they had lived, in the style of a generation or more before. The rooms spoke of the stubborn acquisition of goods. The walls were a rare touch of life, bold reds and blues, bursts of parrot colours escaping from a cage of respectability. There were also pictures of the town after an earthquake. I could not orientate myself until I realised the whole harbour front and quayside street vanished underwater for ever. The shock sent a wave halfway round the world, and knocked down the Tongariki statues on Easter Island over two thousand miles away.

On one wall were two photo-portraits. The first showed a buxom, heavy-jawed woman with a look of peasant stolidity about her. You would guess she had native blood. A rosary lay on her black Victorian dress. The other was dated 1909 and Cyriaco was thirty-six years old when it was taken. His eyes were soft, his cheek-bones handsome, the jaw strong. He was known as the King of Cypresses, and as well as trading in the high-class timber which abounded on the island, he had made money in fishing, then in transport when the fishing was slack, and had become the biggest shipper of potatoes and of fish. He had sat on every committee and board in town and had even taken time off to give lessons at the school of which he was a governor. Despite this he always dressed modestly, in a grey poncho of local material, a shirt and jacket, and waistcoat and trousers of cow leather.

He was Cyriaco Alvarez Vera, she was Transita Vera. They were Teresa's grandparents. None of the museum's donations was credited to Teresa Vera Alvarez.

When I left the Posada Antigua, Teresa cried and asked for a picture of me. She held Pancho close so he had to bend his head to her thin bosom. She ran her fingers through his hair and stroked him.

Caleuche

Europeans have suggested that the Chilote legend of the haunted ship *Caleuche* originated in the disappearance of Vicente Van Eucht's Dutch vessel *El Calanche* in the Southern Ocean. But it is a native legend; the story was old when the Spanish came. It is a native word; *caleuche* means people-changer.

Schools of dolphin tell you the boat is near, and if you hear them crying, someone will die. The rattling of chains announces its arrival. It can make itself invisible and travel at great speed. Sometimes it is a phantasm and it can change itself into animals or objects. At times it is solid, and mortal men and women can join in the parties. They may take place on land where women can be had, the bored daughters of merchants who were repaid with free provisions from the ship. This explains the rapid rise of some merchants, like Cyriaco Alvarez Vera.

Such legends are ancient and eerily persistent. In AD 1161 monks recorded, 'Demon ships seen on Galway Bay, and they sailed against the wind.' Dithmar Blefkins records that mariners off Iceland saw a great wonder, 'namely that a ship of certaine strangers departing from Island, under full saile, a most swift pace, met with another ship sailing against winde and weather'.

Stories like these had equivalents in the English West Country, which would have come back to Coleridge when one of his spirits looked down on the Ancient Mariner and wondered how the ship sailed on without wind:

> 'What makes that ship drive on so fast?
> What is the ocean doing?'

and

> 'But why drives on that ship so fast,
> Without or wave or wind?'

The reply:

> 'The air is cut away before,
> And closes from behind.'

The elements part and reclose to create supernatural motion.

*Santiago Express*

It was time to move north to Santiago and catch up with the elusive Mr D. The railway station at Puerto Montt was on the sea front at the far end of the sweep of the bay. Outside it, in the bright sunshine, stood an old steam engine. On the first platform were three carriages converted to a pizza restaurant. The ticket office was on the plaza in front of the main entrance; above it, across the entire frontage of the building, a sign boasted 'This is a Pepsi Cola Station' and below it 'This is the Most Southerly Railway Station in the World.'

I queued to book a ticket for the sleeper to Santiago, which my guidebook said was a journey of 999 kilometres, taking twenty hours. The cashier dripped long red fingernails, three dazzling rings on her wedding finger made a bonfire in the sun. I reserved a bunk for six o'clock the following evening, then asked, 'What time is it best to arrive? Does the train leave promptly?'

'Yes, come here for the bus at five o'clock. The bus will take you to Puerto Varras.'

Puerto Varras was just a few miles away. The conversation had obviously gone astray somewhere.

'I am sorry, I wanted a train ticket to Santiago.'

'Yes, that's right.' She said cheerfully, 'The bus will take you from right here to the train station at Puerto Varras.'

I looked more carefully into the shadow beneath the station roof. Rows of rusty rails led out of the station. Grass grew between them. The station doors were chained shut. The only rolling stock in the station was the pizza restaurant.

She smiled. 'The track needs repair. The trains don't run from here any more. Just tickets.'

Next morning the minibus toiled up the hill lined with dusty wood and shingle houses, and out of town. I had taken an early bus to spend the afternoon at the lake resort of Puerto Varras. The bus dropped me in the centre of town and I carried my pack to the pier. A youth tried to sell me cookery books. The weather was hot, allowing for wind chill, 80°C hotter than in the western channels a week before. My body was bewildered.

Across the blue sheet of Lake Llanique was Osorno, forty miles away, its summer snow cap rising to over 8,000 feet, but the body of mountain below it had dissolved in the heat haze. Mount Osorno is the Chilean Mount Fuji, a perfect cone-shaped volcano. Teenagers larked about in a hire boat; their laughter came across the flat water undiminished, tinkling, careless. A toy siren went off, sounding exactly like the whizzer on a ghost train. A patrol launch puttered up to the teenagers and, when the captain was close enough to whisper to them, he lectured them through a loudhailer on the dangers of being young and happy.

Outside a modern lake-front hotel, the flags of Chile and Germany hung in fraternal limpness on white poles. Behind a long veranda was a cool dining-room where elderly burghers transplanted from Munich tea-houses dabbed napkins at invisible morsels of propriety. I suddenly felt travel-worn. A maître d'hôtel bore down on me, jaw first, with the walk of a dancer and the body and bearing of a light heavyweight boxer. 'We are closing for lunch very soon.'

'Is there a simple meal I could have?'

He looked at his watch, perhaps waiting for the bell which would begin three more minutes of hitting undesirable customers. He looked up beaming. If anything this was even more frightening. 'If you have the three-course set menu, we can fit you in!'

As soon as I sat, iced water and a beer arrived in a limousine whisper. One sip and a plate of clams arrived. When I squeezed lemon juice on them they tried to get out of the way. They were fresh, raw and alive. Lemon, salt and pepper stopped them moving long enough to eat them. I thought of them dying in my mouth. Or later. The main course was a kind of wiener schnitzel in dingy brown batter.

A young man came into the foyer and the maître d'hôtel fixed him eyeball to eyeball before he left the welcome mat. It was the boy selling cook books. Raging Bull took the pile of books out of the youth's hands and called into the kitchen for the sous chef. I assumed it was because he was personally too important to cleaver tradesmen into small pieces. The chef leafed through them and

Raging Bull spent some time pointing out the finer points. The chef took his cue and bought one. I couldn't wait for the dessert.

Tinned peaches and cream.

The train station was at the top of a steep hill and, reassuringly, had a train with an engine running. I had a Fifties-style compartment to myself. It was 31°C. I bought half a gallon of cold water in bottles, and drank, looking forward to the train starting and getting the air moving. The train lurched. It moved out of the shade of the station. The thermometer moved upwards. I stripped off to my shorts. We reached a top speed of about forty miles an hour. The temperature reached 34°C. I cracked open a beer.

Plane journeys are interruptions in a trip. Train journeys are part of it. I watched the villages journey through the hot evening with me. Children played football on a dusty pitch with a rock the size of a truck in the centre circle. A woman hanging washing on a line blew me a kiss. A boy on a tiny bike pedalled down a road trying to keep pace. The bike wobbled back and forth between his knees.

Looking for toilets I found a shower, and returned to it with soap and towel. I turned the stopcocks on the hot and cold water pipes. They had very long threads. When they reached the end, they fell off in my hands. No shower. Back in the compartment I began to wash. The water in the sink leaked away. When I was covered in suds from wrists to waist I turned the tap: out of water. We pulled into Osorno Station. Passengers generally averted their gaze. We stayed there as long as I can ever remember staying in a railway station. But when we restarted, the water tanks had been filled.

Outside, in rivers and ponds, screaming boys jumped from bridges, fat men floated in lorry inner tubes, mothers in conservative bathing suits calmed babies, cut sandwiches and wiped mops of hair back over their ears. A lake came into view and on it floated two black-necked swans, each twelve feet high. They were carved wooden boats. In the heat of Chile some lonely devotee of Wagner had dreamed of distant Germany and built Lohengrin's swan to sail back to the Castle of the Holy Grail.

At sunset the train stopped. We stayed there all night, just 150 miles into a 625-mile journey. At six in the morning we rumbled away. The first station I remember was Temuco, the same town where the children of the Kawéskar, Gabriela Patirito, had come to live, far from their lonely mother. When Chile was being carved out of native territories, this was the toughest frontier, where settlers pursued genocide against the Araucanian Indians and the natives fought back with skill and ferocity. The poet Pablo Neruda was brought up here; his father was a conductor on a ballast train, dumping stone over the sleepers to anchor the railway. 'I have travelled a lot,' he said in his memoirs, 'and it seems to me that the art of raining, practised with a terrible but subtle power in my native Araucania, has now been lost.' But the sun rose as high and fierce as the day before.

Cattle country came, and stayed. The Andes came in and out of vision on the right, just the white tips of the giant volcanoes floating far away as if unattached to the earth. The engine changed from diesel to electric, the track became straight and fast. We had been due in at noon. The journey went on through the day. Lunch, unplanned for, was free. An Australian in long shorts and walking sandals sat reading *The Brothers Karamazov*. He talked almost continuously under his breath. 'No, no. That's not right! Damn you, damn you!'

Back in the compartment I finished the last of my half gallon of water. The thermometer read 27°C.

At ten in the evening, eight hours late, the skyscrapers of downtown Santiago came into view.

*The Elusive Mr Daskam 2*

I walked into 32°C of humid night. The street teemed. Men with microphones preached the gospel below the station's Parthenon front. In the seedy side-streets pairs of poor prostitutes darted out of the shadows, touching my sleeve with a finger, whispering, offering me nameless bliss behind the wheelybins. Their clothes were cheap and soiled, their eyes wild and desperate. I thought how little business they would get accosting western tourists.

I walked up Avenida Libertador Bernardo O'Higgins, which Santiaginos call the Alameda, an Arab word meaning a tree-lined avenue with gardens. Santiago's is four lanes of mayhem in each direction for twenty hours a day; before the capital was modernised and improved, it was the River Mapocho.

Nearly a mile up I came to the great church of San Francisco, part of whose red walls include the old bridge of Cal y Canto, built with slave labour and half a million eggs to bind the cement. I turned right to the Hotel Vegas, a small 1920s colonial-style house. One of the buildings on the opposite corner of the crossroads seemed to be staging a political rally, another was bricked up. Outside on a bench on the pavement, a plump, conservatively dressed couple in their twenties canoodled.

In my room was a huge picture of tulip-filled woodland, ghoulishly picturesque. It looked just like the German island of Mainau in Lake Constance, a short trip from a friend's house. I checked the title: *Primavera sul Bodensee:* Spring on Lake Constance.

I rang Mr Daskam.

'Hello, may I speak to Tomas Daskam.'

'Speaking.'

'My name is John Harrison, Jo Menell has given me your telephone number and said you would be interesting to talk to. I am an English writer researching a book on Patagonia. I have been to your house in Rio Verde.'

'I think you want my father. Wait a minute.'

I heard footsteps retreating, a conversation, larger footsteps coming. I rehearsed my prompt notes.

'Hello?' A woman's voice.

'Hello.' I repeated the speech.

'Can you call back in half an hour?'

'Yes.'

'He has had to go out unexpectedly.'

'Half an hour?'

'Yes.'

I switched on the television. It was live coverage of Manchester United versus Chelsea.

Take two.

'Hello, Tomas Daskam?'

'Speaking.'

'My name is John Harrison, I am a writer, Joe Menell gave me your name and said you would be interesting to talk to about Patagonia, the wildlife – and painting, of course.'

'Well, we've got something happening here. It's not really convenient right now. Family problem.'

'Okay, I have to go to Juan Fernández, then I have thirty-six hours when I get back, before I have to fly home.'

'Well, I don't mean to sound awkward, but if you could ring when you get back . . .'

'That will be Sunday.'

'Yeah, right.'

His voice sounded hesitant, weak; a slowish drawl with a fuzzy edge.


## The House of Brick Windows

Fifty years ago Santiago was a small city where everyone complained about the noise and the traffic. Now, a third of Chile's thirteen million people live in this city. Most swelter in their stationary cars, blowing their horns at the thirty thousand unregulated buses which rip the air to turbulent, hot fuming shreds. I went to the agency to pick up my plane tickets to Juan Fernández. The pavement cooked my feet, and the threadbare whores came out again, following behind my elbow, persuading, promising. I wondered sadly if they persisted because enough western tourists said yes. In a tall modern office block a young woman introduced herself. 'Señora Solange, it's pronounced as if it were French.'

'Is it a French name?'

'I don't know.'

'The tickets for tomorrow?'

'Yes, they will be ready at lunchtime.'

'I'll call in at twelve thirty?'

'Fine!'

I walked to the grand central square, a museum of retailing from every decade of the twentieth century, from fusty family store to glass-walled mall. Jugglers and country musicians played among shoeshine men and artists. One man sold 'Immortal Phrases'. I went to an exhibition of Nazca Art at the Pre-Columbian Museum. This was the civilisation which flourished in Peru before the Incas, and constructed huge pictures in the desert from lines of stones, which can only be seen from the air. But I spent longer mulling over the fragments of bone and horn and ivory that had made a living for Selk'nam and Yámana in the cold lands far to the south.

Back at the agency at twelve thirty, I asked for Señora Solange.

'She is at lunch, you have just missed her.'

'My tickets?'

'They will be ready at two o'clock.'

At two o'clock Señora Solange said, 'There is no problem but the tickets are not ready yet. Where are you staying?'

'Hotel Vegas.'

'So close! We will deliver them.'

'What time?'

'Luis passes it on his way home, seven o'clock.'

I walked back through the shopping streets. A digital display said 38°C. There was no wind. My shirt was a nice warm one I had bought for Patagonia. As I approached the Alameda a group of office workers formed a rough line and chanted and clapped, falling apart after a few lines, as if it were a joke. At the next corner I was on the Alameda. A big crowd was on the far side. I was wondering why a water-cannon packed with carabineros was drawn up on the central reservation when another one joined it and they opened fire.

At first they aimed at the crowd across the road. I was still looking to run, working out whether it would be safer to be thrown against a low wall on the central reservation or into the railings along the kerb, when I was dowsed. They were aiming over our heads. My shirt was soaked, but I was unhurt. In fact it was the only time I had been cool all day. I asked the man next to me what it was about. He looked unimpressed. 'It's the hunger strikers, the authorities don't mind the supporters chanting, but when they run out in the road they arrest them for blocking the traffic.' I wondered how you could prove someone had made traffic on the Alameda any worse.

A bus stopped on the other side. Out stepped a woman in her seventies, very respectable. Her husband was older, very frail. He bent over his walking stick and they began to cross the road when the water cannon hit him and he tottered. A carabinero officer next to the truck shouted at him to go back. The woman stood in front of her husband. He had taken off his glasses and was trying to dry them with a white handkerchief. He could not go on until he could see. In the middle of the road his wife harangued the officer, 'What do you think you are doing, he's an old man.' 'Just get back,' he shouted. His visored helmet made his voice indistinct, metallic.

The crowd taunted the carabineros and, chanting, edged away up the Alameda. It was now impossible to fire the hoses at them without also soaking the Rolexed guests coming and going through the smoked-glass doors of the five-star San Francisco Hotel. But the carabineros fired anyway. Doormen in swallow-tailed coats and top hats sheltered their rich guests from the forces of law and order. I ran over the road just as a group of youths took off their wet T-shirts and swung them in circles over their heads, jeering. An officer shouted. The doors of one wagon opened and carabineros streamed out and ran at the crowd which dispersed into the side streets. I went back to the hotel and found a station wagon outside. Two carabineros watched the building opposite from behind mirror shades. I stopped to read the banners, hid my sound recorder in a bag, and went over.

It was a round-nosed building on a corner plot, built as a town mansion on land sold off by San Francisco Church when it needed money in the 1920s. The first floor was double height. On its corner Greek columns framed a large balcony. At ground floor, ashlar masonry around the doors and windows was cut in swaggering keystone blocks. An eye-shaped window glared from the corner; to either side of it iron-gated arched doorways were padlocked shut. A small group of people were talking through the bars to others inside. Letters and messages were pasted to the stonework.

I asked a tall pale young woman on the inside what was going on. 'These are the offices of the coalition which governs Chile, the Liberal-centrists of Eduardo Frei. We have taken it over, we are pensions workers. All the public pensions were privatised in 1981, leaving just a superintendent as a kind of regulator. Now they are changing the terms of employment of twenty-two thousand workers for the worse, without any consultation. There was an accord that they would not alter the terms but they did it anyway. Nine weeks of negotiation produced nothing, so fifteen of us went on hunger strike, nothing but water for seven days. This is the eighth day.'

'How do you feel?'

'I am okay, a little weak.'

'And the others?'

'Some are not so good.'

'What is your name?'

'Maria Angelica Crisostomos.'

I smiled. It was a good name for someone acting as a mouth-piece. 'You know it means golden-mouthed, in Greek?'

'What does?'

'Crisostomos.'

'I didn't know.'

We had spoken in Spanish. I opened my bag a little. 'I am record-ing some programmes. If someone can do an interview in English I will see if I can give it some publicity in Britain.'

She called 'Miguel!' and went to make a call from a wall phone in the foyer. Above it was sellotaped a piece of paper: 'Thank you Señor Bustamente', the minister responsible.

From the other side of the street a man in a dark suit with a car-nation in the lapel came over. He poked a large finger at me. 'Who's this guy?'

Maria said, 'He's English, got a recorder, can you do an inter-view?'

'And who are you?'

I explained. 'But officially I am on holiday, not working. I don't want the police to see the recording gear.'

'Got any ID?'

I showed what I had. 'Okay. There are fifteen people here who are eight days without anything but water, you understand what I mean? No food at all. They spent Christmas here, and they'll spend New Year here. There are twenty-two thousand workers affected, with their families that's a hundred thousand people maybe. Today's a nice day, you think there are no problems. It isn't always this pretty, pensions, education, health: all privatised.' He looked up at the sky. 'The goddam weather is the one thing they haven't privatised yet. You need bread, you know, money. If you haven't got money in Chile, there's nothing. The pensions superintendent says the value of the pension – say it pays 100,000 pesos today – well, next year it's only going to pay 80,000 pesos. When you look at the fund, there's 1,500 million gone missing. We held strikes. Every demo day the workers had to sign in at their office. If you didn't, they assumed you were at the demo and you got sacked.'

A hunger striker in his mid fifties spoke to me through the bars. 'I am Eugenio Madrid. I am doing this to protect my family's rights and my pension. I have had no food for eight days.'

'How long will you keep this up if the government does nothing?'

'As long as it takes?'

'Would you die for it?'

He looked tired and grey. 'Yes, if that's what it takes.'

'It is that important?'

'Yes certainly.'

One of the banners hanging above us read, 'We refuse to be the aborted children of the new economic model.'

A thin man stayed by me. He pointed at the building opposite. 'One of Pinochet's houses.'

It was a slightly less grand building than the one the hunger strikers occupied. The corner piece was a round tower, on the second and top floors were airy balconies, still open, designed to seize the small cooling currents on stifling summer days like this. The doorways were closed by cheap security doors, padlocked shut. The first-floor windows were crudely sealed with bricks and breeze blocks behind the original wrought iron grilles.

'He lived there?'

'No. One of his torture houses. The security forces just had freedom to do as they liked, no questions asked.'

In this and other houses torturers trained by the American CIA went about the business of hurting people until they were no longer in control of their mind or will. Tortured them until they talked or died or passed out or became mentally ill and their answers made too little sense to continue. The enemies of Pinochet and Richard Nixon and Henry Kissinger were human rights workers, trade union leaders, militant politicians, popular leaders, students, journalists, musicians. Protest singer Victor Jara was arrested, starved and tortured. After one session the guard taunted him, 'Let's see you sing now.' Jara sang *Venceremos*, We Will Win. They broke his hands and shot him.

Their heads were plunged into buckets of water, electric cattle prods or mice were put in their mouths and anuses, they were blindfolded and subjected to mock execution or Russian roulette, then taken back to be strapped to wet bed frames and given electric shocks. Those responsible admit that at least 3,000 died or vanished. A piece of graffiti from the time said *Podrán cortar todas las flores, pero no podrán detener la primavera*: They may cut down all the flowers, but they cannot hold back the spring.

'How long has it been empty?'

'Ever since elections were held and we had a civilian president. But Pinochet is still senator for life. He controls the army, the army gets ten per cent off the top from all the copper income. The foreign companies just pay it direct to the army.'

'I suppose no one wants to use a building that people were tortured in.'

'It's more out of respect for the victims. He had houses like this all over the city. No one knows what to do with them.'

Just weeks before Salvador Allende died, he confronted an opposition member. He warned what would happen if they used the

257

military to overthrow him. 'It won't cost you much to get them in. But by heaven it will cost you something to get them out.'

Soon after I got home I watched the television as an old man wiped away a tear from the corner of his eye. It was Augusto Pinochet, sentimental about formally stepping down as head of the army. Pinochet's voice broke, his brow creased, and he wept as he thanked his wife, Lucia Hiriart, for being 'the true soldier's wife. I do not want to look back because that anchors the country in the past. But the armed forces can now proudly say: mission accomplished.' The army will still crush any government that tries to punish individuals who electrocuted and drowned their fellow citizens in stylish town houses for the sake of national unity.

At the far end of the street chanting began; people were marching towards us from the Alameda. I got up to go. As soon as I moved, a young man with short hair and a green suit moved purposefully towards me, stopping nearby. He looked me up and down, his face hidden by large, impenetrably dark sunglasses and a moustache. I took him for plainclothes police and started to walk down the only empty side street to test if he was following me. He followed. I did not like this. I stopped half way along the block. He walked past me, reached the corner. His sunglasses must have been very dark; right on the corner he missed the low step and tripped over. I headed in the opposite direction.

I went to San Francisco cathedral to calm myself in the cloisters, contemplating an olive tree, a cloud of bougainvillaea. A grass-green parrot with an overgrown top beak landed close by, and chided me. Pedro Valdivia, the conquistador who was given the south, founded a chapel on this site. He rode with an Italian wood carving of the Virgin of Succour tied to his saddle. When Indians attacked she threw dirt in their eyes.

Across the cloisters was the Cathedral gallery. In the late seventeenth century Cuzco in Peru was home to a school of painters trained in the European style. They produced the greatest series of paintings of early South American art, showing the life of San Francisco, and here they were, all fifty-four of them. The sense of composition is Renaissance, but the style is highly decorative late medieval. The perspective hovers between the two eras; in each part of the painting it makes sense, but the parts don't fit.

When the noise of sirens and more chanting drifted in over the high roof, I went outside. It was late afternoon, blind white light, the heat high again. An ambulance was parked outside the hunger-strikers' building. A gurney came through gates briefly opened by nervous men. One of the hunger strikers, a woman with frizzy hair and frightened eyes, lay on it. Maria Angelica Crisostomos told me she was Roxana Leyan, and was suffering from kidney problems. They locked the gates.

I returned to the hotel, but my tickets had not come. A carabinero was using the phone and inspecting the register. I wondered if the plainclothes man had accused me of tripping him up. Luis from the travel agency walked in and asked for me at reception. Nervous of identifying myself in front of the police, I took the documents and went up to my room to open them. I checked the departure time; leaving tomorrow at seven am. I checked the return; coming back yesterday.

*Island Beneath the Cloud*

Next morning the taxi driver arrived when the newly watered hanging baskets were still streaming cool water on to the pavement. He was a small round man with a postage stamp moustache. He took me to the military airport of Los Cerillos, where flights leave to Juan Fernández. 'My birthday,' he said. I tipped him.

In the departure lounge only one desk was staffed. There were four other passengers. I could hear the whine of a distant engine, although the propeller on the plane outside was still. I put my bag on the scales. 'Where are you going?' she asked.

'Juan Fernández.'

'You are at the wrong desk. Aerolineas Isla Robinson Crusoe are over there.'

I surveyed the empty hall. All I could see was a cleaner, hoovering.

'The señora isn't here yet.'

The cleaner bent and touched the hoover. The sound of a distant engine stopped.

A tousle-haired woman appeared at the desk of Aerolineas Isla Robinson Crusoe. I walked over. She said 'Señor Harrison.' How did she know? I looked at her printed passenger list. Three words: Señor John Harrison. I was the only passenger.

'Would you like to look at a picture book of the island?' She handed me an album of photographs and postcards. 'You know the flight is dependent on the weather?'

I looked outside. It was dull, grey, calm, warm.

She pointed up and moved a finger back and forth. 'Right now there is a lot more weather on the island than here. Big windies.'

I sat down with the book. The dirt airstrip on Juan Fernández looked like a ski-jump which had been half-heartedly hammered flat and laid between two cliff-tops. There was a picture of man, some distance inshore, playing with a seal. I made a note to close the door last thing at night. The transfer from airport to town was by small boat. I took sea-sickness tablets.

Soon after she came over. 'Now we are ready.' She led me to a six-seater Cessna. A middle-aged man and a brash thirty-year-old dressed like a US airforce pilot chatted under the wing. The younger man took off his round steel-rimmed sunglasses. 'Hi, John, I'm Imanuel, you're English, right? I spent my first ten years in Dallas then I lived in London for five years. The English teachers hated my drawl.'

I climbed in and he followed me for a chat. 'You flown in small planes before?'

'Yes.'

'Your pack can go right here. You need to sit on the other side of the plane, for balance.'

The older man passed me a lunch pack. 'Help yourself to our flask if you want a coffee.'

After taxiing we took twenty seconds to reach take-off, at ninety miles an hour. Even at eight thousand feet we only made 155 miles an hour. Behind us the Andes slowly rolled away behind the horizon until the last sight of them was a line of peaks, only the snow visible, merging with the broken cloud. I sat alone, facing the open Pacific, flying into imagination, flying back to childhood, flying at Crusoe's Isle.

When Richard Henry Dana approached Juan Fernández on a square rigger in the 1830s, he wrote, in *Two Years Before the Mast*,

> November 25th rising like a deep blue cloud out of the sea. We were probably nearly seventy miles from it. So high and blue did it appear that I mistook it for a cloud resting over the island, and looked for the island underneath it.

The same cloud had induced Anson to think the island was a phantom and sail away from it, consigning eighty more men to death from disease.

After three hours Juan Fernández came out of the calm blue ocean. The island is high, nearly six thousand feet, topped by the triangular volcanic mountain of El Yunque, the Anvil. Steep hills cloaked in vegetation dived into green vertical cliffs. As the sailors said, it was capped in a cloud almost big enough to hide it. I could see woods and sand, a godsend for mariners exhausted by the grey and white clamp of the cold south. Here was sweet water, the vertiginous green, tender goats and cats.

The furthest island of the three looked sandy, bare and sunny, but the plane turned away to the long westerly arm of the main island. There was a dirt runway, which ran not along it but across that arm. We headed towards the flatter end, came in ten feet above the lip of the cliff, and touched down. The plane shot up the dirt towards the skyline. We were still doing forty miles an hour when we reached the tiny patch of flat land on the cliff top on the other side of the island. I had a brief glimpse of the sea, the plane swivelled and I leaned into the turn.

Imanuel taxied back to the bottom where a battered Land Rover drew up. I wiped my palms on my jeans. It was a calm day, good weather. The flight, I reasoned, was obviously routine to the pilot. 'Is it a technically difficult landing?'

Imanuel grinned. 'Well, Chile has a lot of difficult landing strips.

But this! This is madness! There's two hundred metres not fit to use any more, so you have to land and stop the plane in six hundred metres. Madness!'

A man from the Land Rover carried screw-top plastic flagons to the wings, and refuelled. His son, Gened, fourteen years old, transferred baggage and parcels to the back of the Land Rover. His father pulled out one parcel and gave it to him. 'Here's yours. Happy Christmas.'

He opened it on the spot. A computer game with a gear-stick. 'Thanks.' He looked embarrassed to hug his father in front of a stranger.

We drove down a rough track to the head of a cliff-bound cove. The broken orange soil was colonised by pink poppies, whose colour was chemically intense. It was the only place on the island I saw them. Their seeds had probably come in on aircraft tyres. We zig-zagged down the cliff to a wooden jetty. Luggage and parcels were taken out to the end of it in an ancient wheelbarrow. Seals lay on their backs, front flippers touched in prayer. After twenty minutes a launch pulled in returning an elderly, very white American and an equally white English couple. The wife waved a limp blue-veined hand. 'We're from – ah – London.'

We motored out of the cove and into the open Pacific. I could have saved my sea-sickness pills; it was glassy smooth. Gened talked me along the coast, naming the headlands and coves. Colossal cliffs of volcanic rock were veined with later intrusions and ribbed like a moulting reptile. He asked, 'Where are you from?'

I said, 'From Wales.'

'In the United Kingdom.'

'Yes.'

'Where do you live?'

'Cardiff.'

'The capital. Is it a big city?'

'One tenth the size of Santiago. A nice size for a city. I live near the centre, I can walk everywhere. Do you go to school here?'

'Yes.'

'Until when?'

'I can stay at school on the island until I am sixteen, then if I want to continue I have to go to Santiago.'

'Have you ever been there?'

'Oh yes, I've been to summer school there. Six weeks.'

'What did you think of it.'

He measured his words. 'It was okay.'

'Do you want to stay on the island when you are grown up, or go to the mainland?'

'Stay here, for sure. I would like to go to visit the States, Wales maybe.' He laughed. 'Come up on top of the cabin.'

We sat in the sun talking. Some children have a maturity most adults never achieve. The trip took no time at all.

Rounding a corner we turned into a sheltered bay with a new steel pier. A slight man in his sixties held out his hand. 'John, I am Reynauld Green, come with me.' Spots of melanoma showed through his short cropped hair. A very beautiful young woman caught my arm. 'Do you have an envelope?'

'No.'

'I am Valeria. You don't have an envelope to bring to me?'

'No.'

'I am expecting a delivery, they said they would give it to a passenger on today's plane and you are the only one.'

'I am sorry.'

Reynauld pulled me away. 'Don't worry, it is common to ask people to bring things over. The hotel is close. Would you like lunch?'

The bungalow was Villa Green. Reynauld's brother, Robinson, carried my bag. It's a common name on the island. The table had once had woodworm. A Pavarotti CD played arias.


*Alexander Selkirk*

Alexander Selkirk was the seventh child and the seventh son of a tanner and shoemaker in the village of Lower Largo in the Kingdom of Fife, Scotland. Seventh sons were lucky and had second sight, and his mother was a dreamer who encouraged the boy to believe he was special.

Selkirk may have been on the 1699 expedition of William Dampier in the *Roebuck*. If so, his first taste of adventure was to limp home from Australia, eventually abandoning the *Roebuck* on Ascension Island, the remote Atlantic rock. Dampier was dogged, took risks, but lacked other skills. As a leader he was a disaster, with a habit of sailing away in ships and coming back without them. By 1703 he was recruiting men for a voyage in the *Cinque Ports* and the *St George* to the South Seas. Selkirk was now experienced enough to be made first mate of the *Cinque Ports* under Captain Pickering. In the press and sweat of the vessel the seventh son dreamed the voyage would fail and the vessel sink.

Selkirk had respected Captain Pickering, but when he died Thomas Stradling took over, a man with a temper to match Selkirk's. When they reached Juan Fernández the crew set about collecting fresh food, fuel and clean water. Captain Stradling fell out with the bulk of the crew, led by Selkirk. The entire crew decamped to the shore, leaving Stradling alone on board with the ship's monkey. Soon a boat came back to the ship.

'Well?' barked Stradling.

'We've come to get the monkey.'

But the crew soon voted to resubmit to discipline and continue the quest for treasure. Stradling cruised north but had to return to Juan Fernández for repairs, anchoring here in Cumberland Bay in October. But as soon as they had taken on fresh food and water, Stradling gave orders to sail. Selkirk exploded, telling him the boat was rotten and if the repairs were not completed it would sink, as it had in his dream. To back his point, Selkirk demanded to be set ashore with his belongings, calling on the rest of the crew to repeat their rebellion. They looked down at their feet and stayed put, while he railed and swore at them. Selkirk's temper turned to stubborn pride and he insisted on being set ashore. Stradling saw his chance to rid the ship of a troublesome ringleader and took the helm of the boat himself as Selkirk was rowed to the beach and his trunk set down on the sand.

They rounded up the last of the men on the island and boarded them, but not Selkirk. The oars swept the last boat out into the buck of the surf. Selkirk lost his stomach for it. Terror took him. He screamed and begged, 'I have changed my mind.' It was the perfect moment for Stradling to teach his crew a lesson on the need for discipline and obedience. 'Well,' the twenty-one-year-old captain replied, 'I have not changed mine. Stay where you are and may you starve.'

He left him begging chest-deep in the warm salt water. Selkirk later said to Steele, 'Resentment against the officer who had ill-used me, made me look forward to this change of life as the more eligible one, till the instant I saw the vessel put off; at which moment my heart yearned within me, and melted at the parting with my comrades and all human society at once.'

Small groups of survivors had to cope with enforced company. The reaction to unwanted society could be extreme. In 1540 Pedro de Serrano was shipwrecked on a bare hot South Pacific island. After three years another sole survivor crawled ashore. Within a month they quarrelled, divided the island in half and lived separately. Two Calibans.

But solitary maroons had to live with themselves. It was the custom to leave such men a pistol, a little powder, and one ball. The next boat often found a skeleton on the beach, the pistol in the small bones of the fingers, and a round hole in the skull. Selkirk was thrown from the crowding and bustle of a small ship into solitariness. He lapsed into depression from which only hunger could rouse him. Sea lions came ashore for the mating season and roared all night. He boxed himself in a small cave until he could build a stone hut.

The journalist Richard Steele, who founded *The Tatler*, interviewed Selkirk several times on his return and, like Woodes Rogers, he found him both an interesting and likeable man. He described how he thought the sea would provide easier food, and he feasted on turtles until his stomach turned against them and he could only boil them and eat the jelly. He read the Bible and studied his navigation book. He grew to love the voices of the seals and sea lions.

There was cress, purslane and cabbage palm. Turnips planted by privateers had flourished; there were goats and ships' cats gone wild. The adult cats were too vicious to train, but he took kittens and tamed them with tit-bits, until he could sleep with a mattress of purring fur, guarding him from the rats which had once eaten his clothes and bitten his naked feet. He taught the cats and young goats to dance, and read them sermons to preserve his power of speech.

One day he caught a goat, above a low cliff hidden from him by bushes. The goat kicked and they both fell. He turned the goat under his body and landed on it saving, just, his own life. By the moon he knew he had lain there three days. He crawled to his hut and nursed himself back to health. From now on, his great fear was of being ill or injured and dying of slow starvation. He caught kids, lamed them a little so they would never run swiftly, then marked them with a cut through the ear.

Selkirk was not the first person who had been marooned there, but his stay would be the longest. On the last day of January 1709 the Bristol adventurer Captain Woodes Rogers, in command of the *Duke* and *Duchess,* completed his log. 'At seven this morning we made the Island of Juan Fernández.' On the *Duke* was an old friend of Rogers, a man getting a bit long in the tooth for privateering. It was William Dampier, hired as a South Sea expert. Rogers said Selkirk was dressed in goatskins and looked 'wilder than the first owners of them'.

Fifty sick sailors tottered ashore or were lowered in canvas slings. Selkirk relished caring for the sick seamen, greeting them with crawfish, fresh water and goat and herb stew. Many could not chew because their teeth were loose with scurvy. They brought a bulldog ashore to help kill goats for the ship. Selkirk was not impressed. Racing off on foot he overtook the dog and got to the goats first. The bulldog caught nothing, and retired to the ship to bark at rats. Selkirk asked the fate of the *Cinque Ports*. It had limped and leaked towards the Bay of Panama but Stradling had been forced to drive it ashore in Colombia before it foundered. Most of its crew drowned, the rest were captured by the Spanish.

Selkirk reached home in the spring of 1714. His share in the privateering voyage came out at £800. If Daniel Defoe ever did meet him to hear his tale first hand, the author, forever chasing prospects and money, was much the poorer man. Just as Coleridge grew to see the Ancient Mariner as his own questing and suffering otherself, a navigator through life's troubles, Defoe would begin to make an allegory of Selkirk to mythologise both their misfortunes.

Defoe was a writer who made the story live, not by reporting the facts, but by manufacturing the fiction. Even his critics admitted he was the master of taking a story and embellishing it until it was passed off as truth. He would have made a perfect travel writer. He may have met Selkirk in King Street in Bristol docks in a pub called the Landugger Trow. But there is no proof. He had obviously read other people's accounts of Selkirk's adventures, but there is little detail in *Crusoe* to prove that he knew more than was in common circulation. Defoe may simply have felt well enough prepared without it; Selkirk's history was just his springboard, and he changed it at will. His setting is still an island, but he moved it to the other side of the continent, in the mouth of the Orinoco River. It has been argued that this proves that the main aim of Defoe, as a good Puritan, was not to write a history but to make a moral allegory. If it was, Selkirk's history included details which Defoe could have turned neatly to his purpose, but didn't. So perhaps he did not trouble to meet the man and hear his story first hand.

His hero and his audience were British, and mostly English. He was not just reaching out to, but helping to create a new reading public, from servants, soldiers, artisans and small businessmen. They were literate but not great readers, and Defoe could please them standing on his head. They were Little Englanders, and Little England is what Crusoe builds, with his hut for a home, his field of corn, his cats and goats. He calls his fortifications his castle. He is self-made and independent. In due course he is rewarded with a servant, Man Friday.

When he got back home to Scotland, Selkirk soon began to spend more time alone. He taught tricks to his brother's two cats, but otherwise could be surprised in tears, when he could be found at all. Behind his father's house he dug a half cave and put up a tent across it. If it was fair, he walked or fished. If foul, he took to his cave and stared at the grey sea and wept for the loss of his island. Selkirk's interview with Steele had concluded: 'I am now worth eight hundred pounds, but shall never be so happy as when I was not worth a farthing.'

*Crusoe's Isle*

A wooden bridge crossed a small stream where a hobbled grey horse strained to get down the bank to the lushest vegetation. At the edge of town, the sea on my right played in round boulders, slippery as soap to walk on. Small crabs with brilliant turquoise sides scuttled in the surf. The cemetery was squeezed into the last triangle of land where the hill behind the town came to the sea in huge vertical cliffs. A black anchor with new plaited rope sat before a little whitewashed obelisk.

On the morning of 14 March 1915 the Great War came to Juan Fernández. The German light cruiser *Dresden* was cornered by the *Kent* and *Glasgow* below these cliffs. She was damaged and needed urgent repairs. She refused to surrender. The British ships poured fire on her. A blaze took hold and in five minutes she sank. It is believed the captain blew up the magazine. Clambering at the foot of the cliffs I found round holes five inches across. At the bottom, lightly corroded, was the back end of a four-inch shell. Seals basked in the waves, washing their faces, and tenting their eyes.

Back in the town Robinson Green hailed me from the bar on the quay. I said 'Coke.' He said 'What's the problem?' I promised it would be a beer at six o'clock. Another beautiful black-headed woman, luscious in a wet suit, stopped to talk, holding a shining blue and white fish with glistening pink gills and sparkling eyes. I looked at it hard so as not to stare at her. At six I returned for the beer and Robinson told me to go to the big party in the social club.

Everyone would be there. I agreed but, tired, went to bed at eleven. At half past one in the morning my bedroom door opened and a voice called out, 'You haven't forgotten the party?' It was Robinson.

'No.' I dressed and went with him. He was wearing white trousers and a Hawaiian shirt. He danced with every girl in the room. Robinson was sixty.

I like dancing, but I come from a generation where dancing was a hands-off, do-your-own-thing activity. This was hands-on Latin stuff and the locals were good. I drank and waited for courage to come. I saw women leaning on the walls and swaying to the music. I saw their husbands and fathers with two-litre bottles of Coke, bottles of pisco, and a sheen of sweat. Every five minutes Robinson asked me if I was having a good time, and urged me to dance. The beautiful woman from the quay came in, mercifully changed out of her wet suit. In desperation Robinson introduced me to his daughter. She nodded and returned to her friends, used to this. I never found the courage. Outside, Orion was upside down and the Milky Way blazed.

In the morning I set out for the ridge behind the town where Selkirk is said to have kept his four-year watch for friendly ships. I began where the path entered a mature forest plantation which tests different species for cultivation. The whisper of eucalyptus trees cut off all outside noise and the medicinal scent of their oil swam up from the drifts of dry leaves. I climbed above them into the native vegetation. A dark green and black hummingbird drank from flowers, another tiny scarlet bird danced through the bushes on the edge of vision.

The slope was lush and humid. The stream was lined with giant rhubarb and cabbage, and the water was spiked with cool arum lilies. The slope grew steeper and a precarious path cut across the face of it in long zigzags, at times little more than a ledge. Tiny-leafed maidenhair ferns grew on the trees. Suddenly I had climbed up out of the wood and was stepping on to the ridge. On each of the higher neighbouring ridges a lone palm feathered the skyline, emblematic, like a palm in a Hockney painting. On the ridge I found a long view opened out over the next valley and the dry arm

269

of the island in rain-shadow to the east, baked in ochres and browns, pottery and clay colours. The ridges are so knife-edged that this is the only safe place to cross without ropes.

I had arrived alone, in the heart of the island I had imagined since childhood, green at my back, desiccation before me. I would not want Selkirk's loneliness, it becomes addictive, but I played the game we all play when we read *Robinson Crusoe* and think of castaways. What would it be like to rule a republic of one? 'Little islands are all large prisons,' observed the explorer Sir Richard Burton. 'One cannot look at the sea without wishing for the wings of a swallow.'

I had many reasons for my trip, the reasons I told my friends, my family and the strangers who quizzed me all along the three-month journey. I gave them the answers I had prepared for myself in advance. I was following my Liverpool ancestors who came here either side of the turn of the nineteenth and twentieth centuries, rounding Cape Horn. I had wanted to go to the place where the golden, twisted torque of civilisation had come full circle and the twentieth century tipped horns with the Stone Age, in the last place man came to and stayed.

I had left all that far to the south. But to be standing on this ridge, with the burnt pottery colours of rainshadow before me, and a lush green skirt at my back, was the apogee of my journey. The first half of my own life had curved round on itself and, for a brief pause, touched up here. Like Magellan I had crossed the earlier path of my imaginary voyages, starting where all journeys begin, in books, in childhood; a circumnavigation through time.

I needed a boat to get to where Crusoe probably lived. His dwelling was an extended shallow cave, and there is only one on this side of the island. Reynauld Green said, 'Go to the harbour and ask for Ilke.'

A woman with cropped blonde hair sat in the stern of the *Galileo*, one of the slender locally made lobster skiffs with an elegant high-swept bow at each end. She and her son were taciturn. They already knew who I was and what I wanted. Ilke motored out past the cemetery and the basking seals. A couple of miles down the coast the cliffs fell back and a verdant dish of valley opened out with a line of cypresses behind the beach at the left hand side. Ilke put the boat in under a rock. We agreed a time for my return. I jumped.

I went ashore where a broad parabola of a valley half a mile wide cut right through the line of the cliffs. The beach was made of small boulders crossed by a stream. Above, a stone tongue ran out from the cliffs, on to the beach, and finished in a tent shape. Under it was a shallow cave just a few yards deep. Here, in all likelihood, lived Alexander Selkirk, building outwards a few yards to extend his property. I stripped off and swam away. A gentle longshore current took me back to his home. Here he killed the seals for the fat to cook the goats. Drinking water ran near his door, and he could run swiftly to the ridge behind to hide, or keep lookout. It was as nice an empire as you might build on any scrap of remote sub-tropical volcano.

He read the Bible to his cats, but when rescued still found great difficulty talking. He was not, like *Treasure Island*'s Ben Gunn, eager for either conversation or cheese. I waited until the last minute to go back to the boat.

## Jamaica Discipline

The island is a strange place to visit because the ridges separating the valleys divide it into pieces, each one isolated. The main street and a few tracks are the only roads. You walk the coast where you can, or take a boat. Shelvocke was shipwrecked here on the north of the island for five and a half months without seeing the south. It was probably off this beach in Cumberland Bay that his *Speedwell* anchored.

This was the end of the voyage where Simon Hatley shot the 'disconsolate black albatross'. Its purpose was a little polite licensed piracy. Shelvocke, a Royal Navy trained officer, was offered command of two ships, the *Success* and the *Speedwell*. He resented the owners' last-minute transfer of command to Captain John

Clipperton, who had been twice to Chile and Peru, and sailed with Dampier, but was no Navy man. Shelvocke was left as captain of the lesser vessel, the *Speedwell*. The owners bought each captain a copy of Woodes Rogers's *A Cruising Voyage Round the World*, published seven years before.

They sailed in 1719. In the first storm Shelvocke lost contact, and made sure he never regained it. Clipperton found his fleet halved, with all the supply of wine and spirits on the missing ship. He knew what Shelvocke was up to because he had pulled this trick himself. This was the same Clipperton who had done a bunk on Dampier off Peru.

Shelvocke then prompted the crew to dispute the articles of agreement under which the booty would be shared among owners and crew. Feigning reluctance he agreed new ones cutting the owners' share. He blamed Hatley, calling him 'bad enough to act any unhandsome part'.

Even without Hatley's pot-shots at albatrosses, the omens were gloomy. On 8 January 1720 'the sea was all day perfectly red, appearing as if vast quantities of blood had been thrown in.' They rounded the Horn and coursed up and down the west coast taking and missing modest prize ships. Primed with drink, Hatley was persuaded by mutinous crewmen to make off in one, and was captured and imprisoned by the Spanish. The *Speedwell* itself got trapped against the shore by a more powerful Spanish ship and was badly shot up before she escaped and headed for Juan Fernández to repair and restock.

Shelvocke moored half a mile out in the bay on the single remaining anchor, while the wind freshened and the swell grew. On 25 May she broke the cable and drove ashore so violently that the rotten shrouds snapped and all three masts shot forward into the sea. One man drowned, the rest made it ashore.

The literary circle binding writers and adventurers was being closed. In the sunken cabin swam the Woodes Rogers account of meeting Selkirk, which led to *Robinson Crusoe*. Fresh in Shelvocke's diary lay the account of the albatross which Coleridge gave to his *Ancient Mariner*. Shelvocke's published memoir would be taken from the wreck of the *Wager,* and read by John Byron, whose account was used by Lord Byron in *Don Juan.*

The next few days showed a pattern similar to the loss of the *Wager.* Men in shock ignored discipline and went about small personal jobs of no urgency while their helpless captain watched the storm complete the destruction of most of the goods, tools and ammunition which were vital to their survival. Despite his problems Shelvocke appreciated the beauty of the place. 'In short, every thing one sees or hears in this place is perfectly romantic. The very structure of the island, in all its parts, has a certain savage, irregular beauty, which is not to be expressed.' The once plump captain lost several stone, and his gout vanished.

But even so the nights could eat into the soul. 'Nothing of the kind can be conceived more dismally solemn than to hear the silence of the still night destroyed by the surf of the sea beating on the shore, together with the violent roaring of the sea-lions, repeated all around by the echoes of deep valleys, the incessant howlings of the seals (who according to their age make a hoarser or a shriller noise) so that in this confused medley a man might imagine that he heard the different tones of all the species of animals upon earth mixed together. Add to these the sudden precipitate rumbling of trees down steep descents; for there is hardly a gust of wind stirring that does not tear up a great many trees by the roots, which have but a slight hold in the earth, especially near the brinks of precipices.' Selkirk had suffered such torment alone.

The new boat they built did not, they all agreed, belong to the owners of the *Speedwell.* The *Recovery* was theirs. The men proposed Jamaica Discipline – the pirates' communist regime where all was shared. Shelvocke got back to South America, and his starved, desperate men with little food or provisions were reduced to firing the clapper of the *Speedwell's* bell as ammunition. After several attempts they took a Spanish vessel and sailed it back to England. Clipperton and others had got home first, and one of the owners had Shelvocke thrown in jail. The captain had enough money to bribe his way out, and the owners never got a penny out of him. He died a well respected man.

*Turning Home*

I went to bed and listened to the night's wind, wondering if the plane would fly. The morning brought rain, which cleared slowly. Robinson and Reynauld walked with me to the fishing boat taking me to the airport. I waited in the boat while two fishermen loaded live lobsters into cardboard boxes, breaking their antennae to make them fit, and winding the boxes round with packing tape. A port official in naval uniform watched as they wrote Sña Romera 17/25, then he stamped them with a circled N and signed his name.

'Santiago?' I asked.

The fisherman nodded. 'They sell for seven thousand pesos here and twenty-five thousand in Santiago.'

In Anson's day the lobsters swarmed in the shallows; now they set pots for them far out to sea. There is a photograph of Cumberland Bay in 1917. A fisherman is holding up a pair of lobsters two to three times the size of the ones I watched being packed. Such shrinkage is a typical symptom of population pressure.

The wind had stayed up and the sea rolled in long coasters fifty yards apart and fifteen feet high. I was in the bow. We steered directly into the wind. A local girl of about fifteen buried her head in her father's jacket. The cliffs looked like a Spielberg film set. Black-browed albatrosses followed us all the way, coming closer than I had ever seen them, just yards from my head. The cove below the airstrip was a cauldron of foam. We had to jump on to timbers on the side of the pier and climb up.

The pilot was the co-pilot from my flight out. He said, 'The plane is full. Would you sit in the cockpit?' I jumped at it. We came down the ski-run and shot away level from the top of the cliff. The first sign of land was the disembodied snow of the Andes, the snowline level, and the peaks ragged, like halved maple leaves.

I went back to the Vegas Hotel. The strike building had a single banner on it: '*La Consultación*' – 'Our Compromise with Chile.' There were no chains on the gates, no letters stuck to the walls. The politicians were back in control. The woman at reception said a deal had been struck; the remaining hunger strikers had gone to hospital in ambulances. All survived.

*The Elusive Mr Daskam 3*

The room cooked. There was a fan, no air-conditioning. To outdo the Bruce Springsteen song 'Fifty-seven channels and there's nothing on', the cable TV had fifty-eight. Some MTV-style programmes were so fragmented that I thought the channel scan was still on, hopping from one programme to another. It is impossible to plan how to watch fifty-eight channels. Reading a TV guide doesn't help; the programmes change as fast as you read. You cannot watch, you can only snack. If you can't find beginnings, only intercept items, you have no context for what you see. When life arrives it has already been put through the shredder and tied in a green bag.

I hid from the heat till six-thirty. In the early evening the pavements were still hot through my shoes, the sun blinded the length of Avenida O'Higgins. I went for a beer in the central square. I felt light-headed, the face in the mirror looked as if it was going down with a cold. Back in the hotel I fell into jagged sleep and dreamt I was still in Juan Fernández, worrying whether my flight back would go.

In the morning I rang Mr Daskam.

'I don't have time.'

'Listen, I have a medical problem.'

'You went to Juan Fernández, right?'

'And you got back?'

'I have no time right now.'

I wandered the hotel. My room was the only place with a picture of Lake Constance. All the corridors and halls were filled with fine old photographs of Twenties and Thirties Santiago, and reproductions of paintings. The paintings were beautiful. They were all by the same artist: Tomas Daskam.

# Coda

*Virginia Choquintel*

A year later, returning again from Antarctica, I found myself back in Ushuaia where demonstrators waved placards about the *hielos intercontinentales,* the world's second biggest ice cap, up to 500 miles long and 50 miles wide, straddling the Andean border. It is white on the map, black and white on the ground, and Chile and Argentina occasionally threaten to go to war over it. Because it also means 'international ices' it took me some time to realise that the demonstrators were not striking ice-cream workers.

I again stayed in the Hotel Alakaluf, where a conker-coloured native head was modelled in resin above the door. Like the cigar-store Indian, culture had become commodity. There was still a couple of days to kill before my flight home. A half-day drive took me through the mountains and on to the toe of the pampa on the eastern side of the island of Tierra del Fuego, to Rio Grande. From here I thought I would visit the Candelaria Mission, a short distance northwards up the coast, where they had tried to protect the last Selk'nam. The travel agency where I hired a car and driver was called Ona Travel. More heritage. Neither hotel nor agency had used the tribe's own name for themselves.

The Candelaria Mission now houses a spanking new museum. A thin student sat at the reception desk, plugged into a Walkman.

276

José Augusto Alazard had a white face, a brittle jawline and a strong southern Argentine accent. *Capilla,* normally pronounced cap-pee-ya, became capeesha. He insisted on showing me around and telling me things I already knew. I read the captions while pretending to listen. We stopped before a picture of two Selk'nam in front of a log wigwam. He began to explain about the house. I not only knew the picture, I knew the people in it. I tried a heavy hint: 'Yes, this is Tininisk the magician and his wife.' He nodded and continued with his prepared talk.

We moved to a picture of a little girl learning knitting from a thin kindly-faced nun with watchmaker's lenses in her round spectacles. 'The last 100 per cent Selk'nam,' he said. I woke up, trembling, to what he was telling me. 'But all the books say the last was Paachek, he died in 1994.'

'That's what they thought. Then they found Virginia Choquintel, she had gone to live in Buenos Aires and been forgotten about.'

'When did she die?'

'Die? She's still alive, living in the north, I think. The travel agent in town will know her address, ask for Dario Romero.'

The books were wrong.

I was flying home the next day, but had to change in Buenos Aires. If she still lived there, I might be able to juggle the time and look for her. I walked to the coast, crossing the road and entering a picket-fenced square overlooking the wind-whipped shore. The Atlantic coast was open and flat, almost like the edge of a great estuary. The cemetery was ill cared for. Stone tombs subsided and tilted, wooden crosses peeled and split, the grain of the wood was raised and ridged through desiccation. Some Spanish-name graves still bore inscriptions and dates; none of the native ones did.

To the north was the brown roller of Cabo Domingo, with its vertical cliffs, the killing cliffs. At the top of the beach lay a Magellanic penguin. It was this year's chick, just into adult plumage, but dead. The tide is very long on the flat shore, and it had swum in a high tide, walked ashore on to the narrow beach, and returned to find the sea had disappeared. It seemed to have died of exhaustion and heat.

A construction rig hammered piles into the shore. They were building a two-kilometre pier to handle the oil drilled in the east of the Magellan Strait. When it is finished, a tide of development will engulf the Candelaria Mission. The bodies of the last Selk'nam will lie in an urban graveyard beneath the flares of a refinery.

In Ona Travel Dario Romero bounced to his feet and shook my hand in his well upholstered paw. A comfortable moustache nestled on his plump face. 'Alive? Yes! – but not in Buenos Aires.'

I sagged.

'No! Here in Rio Grande!'

'Here?' I pointed to the floor to be sure.

He tore a sheet from his notepad. He wrote down the district, Chacra II, frowned, then he remembered the street, Maria Auxiliadora. 'The number, I used to know the number. It's gone, they will know at the museum, ask for Carlos.'

I looked at my watch, ten to five. 'What time does the museum close?'

'Five o'clock.' He shrugged. 'Don't worry about that, our driver will take you.'

We got there as the museum shut, and the uniformed security guard was letting out the office staff. We knocked. Carlos was out, could we come back? I explained I couldn't. They let me in and found an archaeologist in a smart red suit and tiny feet, who knew the street number. 'It's opposite the Quilmes Video Store,' she called after me.

I let the driver go home and gave a taxi-driver the address. Chacra II is a modern development that could be slipped into any urban British council estate. Concrete was used for buildings, paving and walls, and relieved only by asphalt. Any scraps of green landscaping had been kicked into submission. Many ground-floor windows were boarded up. The street numbering had a large gap in the range I was looking in. I knocked at random, and waited. A boy and a girl on bikes did circuits round and round, through the arch. Graffiti: 'Kill 'em all.'

A tiny old woman peered out, then opened the door. 'Ah, the Indian! Over there.' She gestured under an archway to a steel door, painted in anti-rust primer. When I tried to shut her garden gate, she shrieked at me. I looked down. I had picked up a section of loose fence instead.

I knocked. The first woman continued to watch me through her curtains. A thin, high voice asked who it was, and while I was still answering she began to loosen locks and bolts. I stood back and looked at the window. Between the net curtain and the pane was a Christmas stocking, still there in March. The flat went silent. As I thought to speak again, she opened the door.

Perhaps sixty years old, her flat grey hair was swept back and held by an Alice band. Virginia was short with a brandy glass-shaped body. Her broad-cheekboned face was very little darker than my own white skin. She wore a nightdress and a bra, and suddenly seemed to become aware she was not dressed. She pulled on a cardigan.

We sat down at a Formica table which she cleaned by pulling the sleeve of her cardigan across it and catching some of what fell in her palm, and tipping it back on to a plate. Behind her on the wall was a photograph of the King and Queen of Spain, signed by them both. On the sofa a friendly-looking ball of grey hair chewed a lamb chop bone.

She told me she was orphaned. Her father, Napoleon, had seen what the white man was prepared to do at Cabo Domingo, and could no longer bear to suffer on what had been his own land, under his own 'sky'. He went away and died 'on the other side', as Virginia put it, meaning in Chile. He was back where he came from, along the shores of Lago Deseado, Longed-for Lake, just to the north of Lake Fagnano.

There are photographs taken early this century of a group of Selk'nam moving camp along the shore of Lake Fagnano. The women carried the guanaco-skin shelters, the cooking gear, the babies enshawled in fur. Each woman's bundle might weigh two hundred pounds. One picture showed two families walking through the shallows on a sandy beach, all wearing large guanaco fur capes. The definition of the faces was poor, all seemed black, most were lost. They are walking on their toes, their bodies are reflected in the sheen of the wet sand, spelling out their symmetry with the land, dancing on their own souls.

This was how Napoleon would have lived as a child. He might well have been one of those faceless babies. He went back to his own old map and died, but his wife, Marguerita, had the body brought back to Candelaria Mission, and he was buried under one of the little tilted crosses in the cemetery beneath the frozen wave of Cabo San Domingo. He was put back on a Christian map in the shadow of a monument to the ranchers' greed.

Marguerita died soon after, leaving Virginia an orphan, aged twelve. She was sent to the Candelaria Mission. 'The sisters brought me up, everything was lovely, very nice. It was good that I had an education and so on, but I know no traditional crafts. People ask me "Virginia, do you know how to do traditional crafts?" The nuns taught me how to knit, embroider and so on, but traditional crafts? – no.' Virginia calls her people Ona. The last survivors had grown used to other people's names for them; she thought Selk'nam was just for academics.

When she finished school the sisters found her a family further north, off the Selk'nam map in former Tehuelche Indian territory in Chubut Province, at the small town of Comodoro Rivadávia. Later she moved to Buenos Aires and married Antonino, a Sicilian bricklayer. Just six weeks before I arrived, he had died of cancer. She picked up his picture from a dresser, a handsome man in his sixties, with a white moustache and black beret. 'He was a builder,' she said, adding with very physical affection, *'¡Qué hombre!'* She looked up towards the corners of the room. I followed her eyes upwards, to a bare light bulb, a broken fitting, a lake of staining from the flat above. 'I used to live in Buenos Aires, you know, it's lovely up there. Here the wind and cold are terrible, I liked Buenos Aires but here I am afraid of the cold.' She shivered and drew the cardigan closer about her shoulders. 'I lived there so long ago, it seems like a hundred years. I lived there for twenty years, and now I've been in Rio Grande eleven years. I'm fifty-six and I am alone.' She looked a little older, but talked in a little girl's sing-song voice, pitched high and light.

She had been happy in the balmy north where the men drew the maps and deeds that ignored ten thousand years of her race. Antonino and Virginia came back to Tierra del Fuego because the south was booming. Oil triggered construction on a massive scale. Sleepy backwaters like Rio Grande became bustling cities where taxi-drivers complained about the traffic, and tankers and trucks toiled up half-made roads pulverising the dry land up into the wind. There was lots of work for Antonino.

Virginia worked as a cleaner, and they tried for children, without success. She took in puppies and dogs, perhaps in compensation, perhaps also because her father would have hunted with dogs, flushing sea-otters out from under low thickets and chasing guanaco. Although she was brought up in the orphanage, she had heard tales about their former life from Lola Kiepja, and her own godmother Angela Loij, the two main sources of Selk'nam traditions. When the neighbours had had enough of the noise of eight or ten dogs running round a small flat, they called the police. The carabineros took away all but one, the fur-ball Carolina, on the sofa.

When her husband died in a town that was not really home to either of them, she decided to stay. The local authority pays her a pension as one of the last of the indigenous peoples.

'Cancer!' She returned abruptly to Antonino's death. 'He didn't suffer much.' She twisted in her chair to look at a portrait of Christ. 'I believe in Him. I have Him, and I believe. No, it was quick, I'm okay about it, but the wind drives me mad. Would you like a coffee?'

I walked out into the wind. Where the earth ends, and ceaseless winds blow out of the three dreaming skies of the Selk'nam, the static, sufficient world of the natives was destroyed. It passed from life into memory, and the minds which cherished those memories die year by year. The black hair, brown skins and high cheekbones still show through in faces you pass on the street. But they have surnames which are Spanish, Croatian, Irish, Scottish, Welsh, and they live in families which call themselves German, Swiss or Austrian. Peasants, miners, shepherds and barons came here for space, for land, for money, for golden lodestones, and walked on Sundays and holidays through the waves of grass combed over, silver-backed, by the wind's insistent press.

In the emptiness of the land, next to the unbroken curve of the sea, some towns can divide space into pieces small enough to stop you going mad, to stop city people going mad. But the straight roads of Rio Grande's gridiron don't do that. At each intersection on my walk back, four sightlines went on and on, crossing the whole town and revealing, always, the pampa, the emptiness beyond. The Indians had succeeded where the colonisers failed, in forming a sane vision of this enormous space. Little of that vision remains. Only above my head did the Selk'nam maps of Virginia's ancestors survive, disappearing into an infinity of sky, in three directions.

# Acknowledgements

I have been lucky enough to have the support, advice and encouragement of Elaine Brennan, who took on as a partner someone who had already committed his spare time and money, for years ahead, to a book of which not a word had been written. I vanished into the study, evening after evening, weekend after weekend, and to Spanish nightclasses for over five years, then off to the ends of the earth. When she could get to see me I raved about obscure tribes, Aristotle and krill. I eventually gave up my job to make sure this work became a book worthy of her belief. This condensed tribute is some small thanks for all she gave, to me, to the writing, and to the ideas which kept me going.

Special thanks are also due to the following: Mum, Dad, Marion, Jim; José Augusto Alazar, Rocío Perez de Baines, Gillian Beer, staff of the Museum of Mankind, Tony Bianchi, Peter Finch, Nicola Forster, Tommy Goodall, David Jenkins, John Rees Jones, Mandy Kierspel, Robert Headland, Mateo Martinic, Tôpher Mills, Cristina Moroy, Jan Morris, John Murray, Hugh Price, Robin Reeves, Keith Richards, Dario Romero, Oliver Seeler, Brian Shoemaker, Stephen Spittler, Bernard Stonehouse, Ifor Thomas, Christine Turnbull, Roser Gaitano Valls, Rory Wilson. They all know how they helped. Without their generosity, this book would be poorer.

I am grateful to *New Welsh Review* for permission to include in *The Ritz 2* material previously published in Number 40, Spring 1998. I would also like to thank all those authors from whose books I have quoted extracts:

Renato Cárdenas Alvarez, *El Libro de la Mitología* (Atelí, Castro, Chile, 1996)

E. Lucas Bridges, *The Uttermost Part of the Earth* (London 1951, 1987)

Jorge Díaz Bustamente, *Crónicas de Última Esperanza (Last Hope Chronicles)* (Atelí, Punta Arenas, 1994)

Herbert Childs, *El Jimmy, Outlaw of Patagonia* (J. B. Lippincott Company, London, 1936)

Joseph Conrad, *The Mirror of the Sea* (London, 1906)

A. C. Crombie, *Augustine to Galileo* (Heinemann, London, 1959)

Elizabeth Dooley, *Streams in the Wasteland: A portrait of the British in Patagonia* (Imprenta Rasmussen, Punta Arenas, 1993)

Jon Henley, 'Lighthouse at the End of the World' (*Observer*, 14 December 1997)

Stan Hughill, *Sailortown* (Routledge and Kegan, London, 1967)

J. B. Killingbeck, 'The Role of Deception Island in the Development of Antarctic Affairs' (unpublished thesis, Scott Polar Research Institute, 1977)

Basil Lubbock, *The Nitrate Clippers* (Brown, Son & Ferguson, Glasgow, 1966)

Pablo Neruda, *Confieso que he Vivido* (Penguin, Harmondsworth, 1978)

Anthony Pagden, *European Encounters with the New World, From Renaissance to Romanticism* (Yale University Press, New Haven and London, 1993)

Felix Reisenberg, *Cape Horn* (Robert Hale, London, 1950)

R. B. Robertson, *Of Whales and Men* (The Reprint Society, London, 1958)

Ernest Shackleton, *South*, ed. Peter King (Century, London, 1991)

Eric Shipton, *Tierra del Fuego: The Fatal Lodestone*, Readers Union, Newton Abbot, 1974 (first published by Charles Knight)

Dylan Thomas, 'Ballad of the Long-legged Bait', from *Deaths and Entrances* (Dent, London, 1946)

Carlos Pedro Vairo, *Ushuaia* (Zager and Urruty, Ushuaia, 1998)

Carlos Pedro Vairo, *El Presidio de Ushuaia* (Zager and Urruty, Ushuaia, 1997)

## Acknowledgements

Alan Villiers, *The Set of the Sails* (Hodder & Stoughton, London, 1949)

All translations from the Spanish are by the author, except that of Pablo Neruda which is by Hardie St Martin.